THE KHANJAR'S CRUSADE

Z. S. WINTERS

ISBN(eBook): 979-8-9916114-0-4
ISBN(Paperback): 979-8-9916114-1-1
ISBN(Hardcover): 979-8-9916114-2-8
Library of Congress Control Number: 2024920293

Cover by JD Smith

Title Production by The Bookwhisperer.

For my mother and szaty, and my editor

CHAPTER ONE

The streets of Haifa echoed in an eerie silence. The howl of the wind and the whimpering of stray dogs had replaced the once bustling center of traders, merchants, and thieves. Windows that once framed the lively city now stood closed, shutting out the outside world.

Dzintara wrapped the *keffiyeh* around her face for protection from the sun, sand, and the black crosses. Her feet moved carefully and with every step. She crossed her own path to ensure she wasn't followed. She was searching the narrow street for a door. A door with a green mark.

When she found it, she knocked quietly, and the door cracked open. It was dark inside, dust particles escaping into the beam of sunlight, entering through the opened door.

"*Mashallah*, you have made it," whispered a voice from the darkness.

She quickly scanned the narrow alley and pushed into the room, shutting the door behind her. A candle flickered in the young man's hand. His boyish face was patchy with facial hair, and his moist eyes and skin were damp in the candlelight.

"Where is he?" she asked.

"In the back, not doing well, we were—" tears splashed onto the stone floor.

"Akbar, show me where he is now." She reached out and wiped the tears from his face. He led her through the adobe home, his feet slapping against the floor. They crossed the *majlis*. The sitting room floor was covered with scattered rugs embroidered with intricate designs of stars, polygons, diamonds, and calligraphy. Cushions embroidered with vegetal motifs rested gently in the soft light. In the back, next to the wall, stood a large wooden chest.

"Here," Akbar said softly.

He pointed to a tapestry hanging on the wall, its bottom concealed by a chest.

"Help," he gestured and lowered himself to all fours.

His arms strained, and the sinew of his neck tightened as he bore the weight and pushed at the chest. Together, they pushed, and it inched forward little by little.

"He's in there," he whispered.

"What happened?"

"We were on a raid. It was the usual attack: kill the livestock, poison the wells, get out. Then they came. Hundreds of them in their armor and their Allah-cursed crosses...Saladin's men broke and ran."

Dzintara moved the tapestry aside, revealing a small dark opening at the bottom of the wall. Lying flat on her stomach, she pushed her leather satchel through the narrow opening and crawled to the hidden room. Her eyes slowly adjusted to the darkness.

"Light."

Akbar slid through the passageway with the candle.

A bundled body lay on the ground, wrapped in white cloth. Dark splotches marred the surface. A leg moved. Gently, she placed the candle on the cold, smooth floor and cut the cloth open with her khanjar, peeling back the fabric. Her fingers smeared with crimson, she laid bare the raw flesh and tissue. The gash ran from his thigh to his stomach.

He shuddered.

From her satchel, she took a vial and poured the liquid into the gash; garlic, wormwood, helenium, and hollow leek. The dying boy seethed through his teeth in pain. Then she rubbed animal fat on his wound and let it sit to draw out the infection.

She cradled the boy's head and waited awhile. Eventually, the bleeding slowed, and she reapplied the potion.

"Water," she called out to Akbar.

Akbar crawled out, and moments later, an amphora was scuttled through the hole. Dzintara washed her hands and asked Akbar to change the water. He did as she asked. In the clean water, she soaked a piece of linen to cleanse the wound. Her fingers followed the edge of the wound up to his rib.

"Long sword?"

The boy nodded.

"It's a miracle you got away alive."

The boy's eyes went white.

"Stay with me."

She shook his head, and the boy opened his eyes.

"Where am I?"

"You're home."

His eyes shut. She frantically shook his head, but this time, there was no response.

She placed her fingers against his throat, feeling for a pulse. She lay her head on his chest, listening. Nothing. The body was still. She sat there looking at the boy's face. Tears dripped from her eyes as she gently covered the body and his face.

Akbar paced anxiously as she crawled back into the main room. He looked at her, covered in blood.

"What happened?"

"He's dead."

He let out a loud wail and collapsed to the floor, slamming his fist into the geometric decor of the rug.

"You need to leave now. They are probably looking for you as we speak. Go find Saladin's men. They will protect you."

"They left us to die." The boy wept.

"Find them. Ask to join their cause. You have no choice."

She replaced the bloody robe with a new one, then placed the tapestry back. Akbar continued to bawl.

"You need to get out of this city. Listen—" she grabbed his face and forced eye contact. "Listen! Leave!"

He gazed up at her.

"Get up," she grabbed his arm and yanked him to his feet. He stumbled forward, choking on his sobs.

"Your brother is gone," she whispered, one hand to his cheek. "There is nothing you can do about that, but you can still save yourself. Avenge his death."

His wet gaze met her fiery eyes. "Don't let his death count for nothing."

She walked through the majlis, opened the front door, and departed.

The sun was high in the sky. She followed the winding, barren street. The labyrinthine alleyways branched off in serpentine curves. She rounded a corner and came to an abrupt halt. Two armored men in long white robes bearing black crosses pounded on a door. She swiftly pivoted and hastened away.

"Stop! You. Stop!"

She sprinted, her heart pounding in her chest.

She could hear their armor clanking as they came after her.

"Stop, or we'll beat you bloody!" They shouted.

She came to a narrow alleyway, barely wide enough for her to squeeze through. Grunting with effort, she pushed forward. The alley alternately widened and narrowed as she followed its path. At one point, she had to turn sideways and edge along the wall, moving slowly as the sun traveled across the horizon.

She emerged on the outskirts of the city, fortunately near the place she had left her mount. She could spot him at a distance, grazing at the sparse desert foliage. As she neared her mount, she watched the approach of another band of crusaders on horseback, heading towards the front gates of the city.

In one quick motion, she mounted her horse and took off into the vast expanse of the desert. The wind blew sand into her eyes as she galloped towards the horizon. A feeling of fear and loneliness settled over her, reminding her of what she'd felt so long ago in the slave markets of Kyiv.

She thought of her brother, now grown into his manhood. As a boy of her father's bloodline, he'd been molded into strength and fearlessness, ready to lead men and keep the peace among the tribes of the north. From infancy, they taught her that her purpose was to gut herring, bear offspring, and clean and obey. She had to obey the Kur men's demands.

The women in her family had not fared well. Her mother fought against a raiding Semigallian and was killed in battle. Her own people stabbed and dumped her grandmother in the Dvina because they feared her power. Her aunt, ousted from her tribe for her radical ideas, froze to death mid-winter. Dzintara was the only woman in her family who had made it past twenty-five winters. All had fire and purpose beyond tribal life. They were warriors, leaders, and peacemakers. Yet, they'd all died so young.

CHAPTER TWO

It was a day's ride from Haifa. Night had descended by the
time Dzintara arrived back to the refuge. Their sanctuary
nestled beside an oasis in the heart of the ever-shifting desert.
As she approached on horseback, a call echoed through the arid
expanse, reminiscent of a desert dog's yelp. She responded in kind.
Mujahideen warriors materialized like desert phantoms into the
starlight. With a grace born of necessity, they helped her dismount
and led her horse to the life-giving waters of the oasis.

An elongated hexagonal tent fashioned from tightly woven
camel hair stood before her. Weathered wooden stakes driven into
the sands at a deliberate angle secured its sturdy frame.

Inside, earth-toned patterned rugs covered the ground. Dzintara pushed open the flap of the tent, her body aching from the
day's ride. Inside, the air was thick with the scent of burning
incense, and Muhammad paced restlessly near the tawila—a tea
table low to the ground. His eyes locked on hers the moment she
entered. "Where have you been?" Muhammad's voice was sharp,
cutting through the silence. His body, tense with frustration, radi-
ated heat as he stopped mid-step. "You left defying my orders. Do
you not realize how dangerous it is?"

Dzintara ignored his glare, walking to the chest in the corner.

With her back to him, she began carefully placing the vials of medicine into the chest. Her hands moved mechanically, but her mind seethed.

"I don't need your permission," she said, her voice calm, defiant.

Muhammad crossed the room swiftly, his breath coming faster. "Permission? You don't understand how perilous things have become. You leave us exposed with your recklessness. What if you'd been caught? Tortured? And they came for us. That would be the end of our mission."

"Exposed?" She turned her head slightly, not facing him fully, as she placed the last vial inside. "You're afraid of looking weak in front of your men. But you don't understand—every time we lose someone, a brother, a father—it breeds ten more ready to fight back. If we help them, they'll fight for us."

Muhammad stood still, his fists clenched by his sides. He knew her words held truth, but anger continued to rise in his chest. He took a step closer, his voice lowering, his frustration clear.

"This isn't about vengeance, Dzintara. It's about the mission. You think you're saving them, but you're risking everything."

She whirled around to face him, her eyes blazing.

"You just don't see it, do you? They need us, and we need them. Every life we save strengthens us. Vengeance is our weapon," she yelled.

Muhammad's restraint finally snapped. In one swift motion, he grabbed her arm, pulling her towards him, his eyes filled with both fury and desperation. "You can't keep defying my orders. If they see us divided, we fall apart." His voice trembled, and before he could stop himself, a single tear slid down his cheek.

Startled by the intensity of his grip and the sight of his vulnerability, Dzintara reacted instinctively. She grabbed him by the throat, her grip firm.

"Don't ever lay your hands on me again," she warned, her voice low and dangerous.

Muhammad's breathing was ragged, but he didn't let go. "Don't leave without orders again. It's too dangerous."

They were close now, their breath mingling. Both their eyes burned with passion and desire. Without another word, the tension between them shifted. Their defiance morphed into something else. Something deeper. Their lips collided in a passionate kiss, full of pent-up frustration and longing. His hands tore at her clothes, desperate to feel her skin.

Dzintara gasped as he kissed her neck, biting and nipping at her flesh. She retaliated, biting his neck hard enough to make him yelp in surprise. He pulled back for a moment, then with a playful growl, he threw her onto the goat pelt and straw. She landed with a thud, but motioned for him to join her with a sly grin.

Muhammad didn't hesitate. He was on her in a flash, their mouths meeting again in a frenzied kiss. His hands roamed her body, and soon she was on her back, her legs wrapping around him as he entered her. His thrusts were deep and demanding, her nails digging into his back as he kissed her breasts, his lips worshipping her body.

She moaned softly, biting his neck once more, and he groaned in response, losing himself in her completely. His hands moved over her body, his lips trailing kisses down her skin, until with one last thrust, he shuddered, releasing into her.

As they lay together, their bodies intertwined, Muhammad's hand gently caressed her face. He kissed her softly, and they lingered in the afterglow for a few moments. Then, as if remembering the weight of the world outside their sanctuary, Dzintara whispered, "The town is flooded with them...they're hunting us."

Muhammad sighed as he rolled off of her, the tension still lingering, though softened now by the intimacy they had just shared. "We'll face it. Together."

"Akbar's brother is dead," she said.

"Unfortunate, but a sacrifice for the greater cause," he offered in consolation, trying to forget the argument.

"More will die."

But it was not the boy alone whose memory haunted her. She spoke in an anguished whisper, barely audible, "I thought of my brother as the boy died in my arms."

A solitary tear traced a path down her cheek, and he wiped it away for her. Muhammad's eyes glistened in the dim candlelight, his hand reaching out to brush her cheek.

"Dzintara," he rasped, his voice mirroring the arid terrain around them, "your brother loved you—"

But she couldn't bear the thought left unsaid. Her trembling index finger rose, a silent plea for understanding. With a shuddering breath, she continued, "I could have saved him from my father after you freed me, but I didn't. I stayed."

Muhammad's calloused fingers tenderly sifted through her hair, offering comfort as her confession hung heavy in the air. "We must not dwell on the past," he advised.

"All this time, I dealt with it by assuming he was dead," she admitted, her voice barely more than a whisper, "but as that boy died in my arms, I just saw him. The young boy I was torn from long ago, now a man."

"Looking back brings sorrow and suffering. We must look ahead. Keep our eyes on the mission," he said, caressing her face. With a sad smile and wet eyes, she placed her head on his chest. He lifted her chin, and they kissed. "I'm here, and I will never leave you."

She pressed her lips against his, and he caressed her thigh. She laid back on the goat pelt as Muhammad gently spread her legs and laid on top of her. They kissed and gazed into each other's eyes as they made love again.

CHAPTER THREE

S and blasted in her face as the wind intensified. Dust clouds swirled the air under the relentless midday sun. The Kishon River, a blue artery cutting through the ancient, bone-dry terrain, surged towards the distant Mediterranean.

After the ambush, the ghazi dragged the dead bodies and piled them atop each other, creating a grim barrier across the river's narrowest stretch. Amid the blood-soaked sands, they moved with purpose, arranging the fallen to construct a macabre dam. The dead, layered upon each other, transformed the river's flow into a morbid stream tinted with the color of blood.

Astride her horse, Dzintara watched. Urging her mount forward, she approached a man in a white tunic and liṭām. Muhammad's eyes, surrounded by deep lines, focused intently as he directed his men.

"We've halted their advance. We need to track the survivors," she shouted over the gusts.

Muhammad yelled back pointing at the dam of the dead, "That, will stop anyone who follows the river."

Dzintara glanced at the blockade of corpses. "We need to track the survivors who escaped," she said again, "They'll return with reinforcements."

Muhammad's voice carried a grim certainty.

"This river will flow with death. Anyone who drinks from it will be cursed. The kuffar will follow the river, they'll set up camp and draw water from it, consuming death.

His answer was not satisfactory for Dzintara. The ambush had gone according to plan but the Knight Commander escaped. The Crusaders presence was increasing each day and the moment the survivors reached Atlit they would return with an army tenfold strong.

"I will take four men and track them down," she yelled, pulling the reins.

"No. Stay. Attend to the wounded. Our mission is not senseless killing. It's to wear down the intruders," he yelled glaring at her.

"If the Knight Commander reaches Atlit, we're dead. The mission is ruined.

"Then we die together. Go tend to our wounded," Muhammad ordered.

Her earth-colored robe flapped in the desert wind. Defiantly, she shot him an angry look, pulled up her reins, and rode off, ordering four men on horseback to follow.

THE SCORCHING SUN beat down relentlessly, casting long shadows across the desert. Anno trudged through the sand, his lips dried and cracked. His piercing blue eyes scanned the horizon for danger. His black beard, matted with dirt and blood, ran down his white robe marked by a black cross.

After escaping the ambush, Anno ordered his men to discard their armor to move faster; some had shed their robes as well. In any other situation, he would have punished the men for discarding their robes, but this was no ordinary circumstance.

Five survivors followed him with heavy steps, all carrying various wounds from battle. Among them, one man stumbled, clutching a deep wound in his side. Blood seeped through his fingers, leaving a dark trail in the sand.

A knight with a bleeding cut on his face, Roland de Montfort, caught up to Anno.

"He's not going to make it," he said, glancing nervously at the wounded knight. Anno stayed silent, eyes fixed on the shimmering heat waves on the horizon.

"Knight Commander, he's slowing us down, and we can't just leave him behind," Roland pleaded. Anno closed his eyes and listened to the incessant trembling of the cicadas. The wounded man groaned, collapsing to the ground. His breaths grew shallow and labored, his eyes glazing over. They halted, except for Anno.

"We have to bury him," another said.

Anno opened his eyes and faced them.

"Leave him. We have to keep moving. Otherwise, we may as well be dead."

Anno turned and continued his trudge.

"They'll find the body and they'll track us," Roland interjected, and Anno stopped.

"Cover him in sand. Quickly," Anno said without turning.

Roland knelt next to the dying knight, gripping his hand firmly as they had done many times before in battle.

"I'm sorry, brother," he whispered.

"Make it quick..." the dying knight murmured.

Eyes brimming with tears, Roland drew his dagger and slit his brother-in-arms' throat. The knight's life ebbed away in moments. The group hastily piled sand over the body and kicked away the trail of blood. Anno knew the infidels would not let a Knight Commander escape. It was only a matter of time before a death party came riding in their direction. In all his campaigns of subjugating heathens and infidels, he had never been caught off guard like today. His father would have been disappointed. At that moment, he was thankful he wasn't alive. One of the knights slumped on a rock next to the body from exhaustion.

"Move," Anno ordered.

The knight fell over, begging for water. Roland pulled him to his feet, and with arms around him, they pushed forward to Atlit.

THE SUN BEGAN to settle on the horizon, and the survivors reached a rocky valley. In the distance, they could see the Mediterranean—or was it the heat waves on the horizon? Suddenly, Anno halted.

"What is it?" Roland asked.

Anno raised his hand to silence him. He turned full circle, then stopped and stared past the men. There it was, dust clouds riding towards them. Exactly as he predicted. His heart quickened.

"Hide!" he hissed, urging his men to take cover behind a rocky outcrop.

The men mustered what strength they had and climbed with anguish up the mountainside. They lay on their stomachs behind the outcrop, waiting.

"Do you think they found the body?" Roland asked.

Anno put a finger to his lips. They watched in silence as a group of riders approached, the dust billowing around them. The five riders slowed, then stopped.

DZINTARA SCANNED THE ROCKY VALLEY, pulling the reins of her horse, and circling. She dismounted and drew her sword, walking to the foot of the mountain, slowly pacing and looking up at the rocks, sensing they were hiding nearby.

"Dzintara, they're not here," Amir called out.

"They're unarmed and exhausted. Easy catch," Dzintara yelled back.

"What if they're already in Atlit?"

"Impossible," she said.

A large rock outcrop halfway up the mountain caught her eye. It was large enough for six men to hide behind. Dzintara began climbing toward it.

"Dzintara, what are you doing?" Amir called out.

"They could be behind that rock."

"The men we are chasing are either fast on their way to Atlit or dead. By the time you climb up and back, it'll be dark," Amir yelled after her.

She stopped the climb and looked back at Amir.

"Our best chance is to keep going towards Atlit, not waste our time looking behind rocks," he continued and looked at the other ghazi for support.

Although Dzintara agreed they had better chances of finding them on the way to Atlit, something still pulled her. She resisted and climbed back down the mountain toward her horse.

"You're going to get us killed sitting idle out here," Amir said.

Dzintara mounted her horse and shot a look at Amir.

"After you," she gestured.

Amir clicked his tongue, and the five riders rode off towards Atlit.

ANNO LAY with his dagger clenched in his fist. Death was but a stone's throw away. They watched as the riders rode off towards Atlit. As night fell, Anno and his remaining men cautiously resumed their journey. The rocky valley provided some cover, but they knew they had to reach Atlit by dawn.

The full moon lit the desert like a sunny day. In the distance, they saw the moon reflected on the Mediterranean and the profile of Château Pèlerin. Anno breathed a sigh of relief and made the sign of the cross.

"So close," Roland whispered, standing next to Anno.

"We'll be at the gates by sunrise," Anno responded.

Roland stayed silent, staring at their destination. Anno stared at his friend and confidante. He knew his mind was on ale, whores, food, and a bed.

"Tomorrow, we find the infidels who are responsible," Anno said with exhaustion.

Roland glanced at Anno and forced a smile.

"If we make it. They're struggling."

Behind them, the remaining three survivors dragged their feet in the sand, holding on to each other.

Roland looked at Anno with a peculiar stare. "Unless..."

"No, we march together to Atlit," Anno responded and marched ahead.

Just up ahead, a man approached on foot leading seven horses. The survivors stopped and watched as the man approached, the beasts towing one after the other. Besides Anno, none of the others looked like crusaders. He waved to them as he slowly passed.

"Halt," Anno ordered, but the man kept on.

"Ta-waqqaf!" Anno tried again, and the man stopped.

"What are you doing?" Roland whispered.

Anno pulled his dagger.

"We're not a band of thieves, Anno," Roland reasoned.

"No. But why is he walking away from Atlit in the middle of the night with seven horses?"

"Probably a peasant. Let's go," Roland pulled him, but Anno shook his hand off. He nodded to the others and they too pulled their daggers. The passerby raised his hand and was rhythmically reciting something in his tongue. The four of them circled the horses and the man.

"Anno, we're wasting time," Roland pleaded with them.

Anno touched the tip of his blade under the man's eye.

"Where are you headed...fejn sejjer?"

The passerby began to pant heavily. "I...I...," he scooped pockets of air towards his mouth and pointed at the horses.

"I think he wants to say he was going to water the horses," one of the survivors said.

"Atlit must have run out of water."

The three others laughed and the passerby looked around in confusion.

"Infidel? Ghazi?" Anno interrogated.

Tears flowed as he frantically shook his head and shoved air towards his mouth. The horses snorted and shuffled restlessly. All seven horses were saddled and ready for mount. Anno saw this and knew the man lied. If he wasn't a ghazi himself, he was sure as hell helping them.

Anno lowered his dagger and stared into the eyes of the frightened passerby.

"Accept Christ."

Snot bubbles formed around his nose and spit dangled from his mouth as he bawled. Ever so gently, Anno placed his hand on the back of his neck and they touched foreheads. Anno's blue eyes glowed in the full moon.

"Accept Christ," he whispered again.

He broke Anno's eye contact and looked to the ground. Anno pulled him in close by the neck and stabbed him in the stomach repeatedly. The body thumped to the ground, and the men mounted the horses and rode back towards Atlit.

CHAPTER FOUR

Twilight descended as Dzintara arrived back at camp. A soft hiss of wind blew across the sand. Small tents stood in a sunken valley of rocks on the way to Acre from Haifa. A large tent sat in the center of the camp. She walked to it and entered.

Muhammad glanced up at her before returning his attention to the wounded. Blood covered Muhammad's white robe. Many died, but a few were saved. Veiled women moved through the ranks, cleaning wounds and comforting the dying. The air was heavy with iron and decay.

"Word has gotten back to Atlit. More will arrive soon."

Muhammad knelt next to a fallen soldier, opening the young man's robes. The broad cut had sliced open his belly, with his guts shimmering through. Gently, Muhammad tugged the skin open, working the boy's intestines back into place. He took an amphora, pouring water into the wound, washing away the blood and debris.

"Did you hear me?" she asked.

Muhammad motioned to a woman, who quickly brought him a skein of silk and a sharp iron needle.

Muhammad ignored her.

"We needed to know if there were more coming." She replied.

"Look around. Where do you think you were most needed?" He took up thread and needle, preparing to close the boy's wound.

"I made a decision," she said. "If we get caught by surprise, we're dead. All of us."

His hands were stained with blood. He struggled to pull the boy's flesh closed. Then the boy seized, his body going rigid. Finally, he went limp, still. Muhammad placed his palm on the boy's throat, hoping, waiting. Muhammad shook his head and lay down his needle.

He stood, wiping his hands on his white tunic, and faced Dzintara. "A decision that was not yours to make. Insubordination. We are small, and everyone matters. Today was a blessing. But what about tomorrow, the day after? If we aren't united we are weak."

He was furious with her.

"I did what needed to be done! Even if you weren't willing!" she spat back at him.

He slapped her, leaving a trace of blood from his hands across her cheek. The women gasped, the men whispered, and the tent became silent. All eyes were on them.

Her hands trembling and her eyes swelling up. Muhammad regretted the action the moment he committed it. She returned the slap and ran out of the tent. Muhammad looked around and the men looked away, whispering to each other. He pursued her into the night. She ran aimlessly in the desert moonlight.

"Wait!" He called out for her.

But she continued to run, and he caught up to her, grabbed her arm and she turned and slapped him again.

"I'm so sorry!" Muhammad said, tears flowing from his eyes.

"Why would you do that?" she screamed at him, tears flowing.

He cupped her face with his bloodied hands, "Because..."

"You always say it's 'you and me' but it's always your orders and your way. Why?" she cried.

Muhammad searched for the words he had wanted to say to her for a long time.

"Because I'm scared," he said softly, looking into her eyes.

"Scared of losing this goddamn mission? That's all you care about."

"No! Scared of losing you! I would give up this mission tomorrow if it meant saving you. If I lose you, I will die."

Dzintara looked at him and saw him. The fear of losing her flickered in Muhammad's eyes, his face tightening as tears ran unchecked down his cheeks. She wiped the snot from his nose, and they both smiled. In between sobs, Muhammad said, "Every time you go out there, I accept you aren't coming back. When you do, I'm overwhelmed with joy and relief, and so angry at the same time. I cannot lose you."

Dzintara smiled at him. "You won't."

She took his head and kissed his dry lips. His greying beard rubbed against her face.

"We have to leave at dawn tomorrow," he said between kisses.

"What about the wounded, the dead? We can't just leave them," she asked.

"There are greater forces at work. There is a group led by the Saladin who asks for our help. They want to take back Jerusalem. Our reputation as healers and warriors is traveling. He wants our forces to join him," he said.

Muhammad gently touched her face. "With reputation comes responsibility. A blessing and a curse. And we..."

"Must go and help them." She finished his sentence.

He smiled at her. "I was going to wait to give this to you, but tonight Inshallah told me it was the right time." He reached into his tunic, withdrawing something that shone in the moonlight. He placed the object in her hand, the steel cool against her fingers. The embossed blade seemed to give off a faint glow. Dzintara drew a sharp breath. She had no words. She stared at the khanjar, mesmerized. This khanjar was modest compared to some, not decorated with precious materials or made of gold. Even the hilt was dull. But in keeping with tradition, the blade bore intricate designs with writings etched into its steel surface.

This one was humble because its purpose was to protect and avenge. Its only adornment was the color of blood. The thin blade's sharpness compensated for its lack of festive design.

"This khanjar belonged to my grandfather's father. It is now your responsibility. Protect our people and cut down the ones who come against us. In darkness we come, so in light we may prevail."

She sheathed the khanjar and tucked it into her robe, then gently cupped his face and pressed her lips against his. Rising on tiptoes, she embraced him, love and fear intertwined.

CHAPTER FIVE

The next morning, Dzintara stirred, reaching out instinctively for Muhammad, only to find his side of the bed cold and empty. Her heart skipped a beat. The tent was eerily quiet, save for the soft rustle of the wind outside. She bolted upright, a wave of dread crashing over her.

"He's gone," one of the ghazi said quietly from outside the tent flap. "He rode to Atlit to meet a contact of Saladin."

Her chest tightened. Panic set in. *Atlit?* The name alone made her blood run cold. Atlit was crawling with Crusaders, and she had warned him—warned him last night—that they were preparing for retribution.

"What?" Dzintara's voice cracked, and she fumbled to get dressed, her hands shaking. "Why didn't he tell me? Why would he go alone?"

Her mind raced as she hastily strapped on her boots, her heart thudding in her chest. *How could he leave me behind?* She fought the rising anger, but beneath it all was fear—the fear of losing *him.*

She threw on her cloak, grabbed her satchel, and ran out of the tent, her mind spinning. As she mounted her horse, the enormity of the situation hit her. *Atlit was full of crusaders. They're hunting us. If they find him...*

Her fingers gripped the reins tight as she spurred her horse forward. The wind whipped against her face as she rode, thoughts spiraling. Why would Saladin have him meet there, of all places? What was so important that he had to go now, when they were vulnerable? She imagined him, surrounded, outnumbered, Crusader blades drawn.

Her pulse quickened with every stride. The sand and wind blurred together as she charged down the path, every beat of her heart screaming one thing: she had to reach him before it was too late.

He should never have gone alone.

Her mind wouldn't rest as she pushed her horse harder, her breath coming in ragged gasps. The closer she got to Atlit, the more the fear took hold, twisting her gut. She wouldn't lose him. Not like this. Not to them.

The lush green Carmel mountains sloped down into the Mediterranean. Olive groves surrounded her as she rode, and cicadas vibrated their timbals. Plain wood and stone houses were dotted about the landscape.

Above the city skyline, she watched the half-built tower of the Chateau, workers busy atop the scaffolding. She passed a caravan of wagons carrying stone from a quarry nearby. The men's faces were white from the rock dust.

She tied her horse to the gnarly trunk of a fig tree just outside the city walls. The main gate groaned open with a heavy clank, and in the distance, a company of crusaders rode toward Atlit. It was a spectacle for bystanders: horses in golden armor adorned with scenes from the struggle of Christ and men in white robes with black crosses, their shining steel armor gleaming.

"I'll be back," she said to her horse, fixing his reins and allowing him to graze.

She crossed over to a dry well next to the city wall that was once a watering station for horses. Dzintara looked to make sure no one was watching, then whistled three times into the well and waited.

No response.

She repeated the signal with no success. Dzintara retrieved a rope from her horse's saddlebag and tied it to the base of the broken shadoof — once used to lift water from the well, with no bucket and no counterweight. To test its strength, she pulled on it. She slid over the stone edge of the well and lowered herself into the dark.

Reaching the bottom, she took a candle from her bag and struck flint and steel together until sparks lit the wick. Rats scrambled at the sight of light. She crawled through a small opening in the wall of the well and followed the tight man-made cavern until reaching a dead end. She reached up and rubbed her hands along the walls until she felt a wooden stake peeking out from behind a rock. She placed her foot on the first and felt up the wall to the next and then the next. When she reached the top, she poked her head up through the lavatory opening and found herself in a dilapidated outhouse. She pulled herself through the lavatory and pressed her eyes to the cracks between the wall planks.

The silence unnerved her. The wind howled through the narrow streets, kicking up the sand, but the stillness was suffocating. Dzintara cautiously stepped into the desolate alley, her footsteps muffled by the dust-covered cobblestones. Market stalls lay abandoned, their baskets overturned, crates left scattered as if the entire city had fled in haste. Her heart quickened. Something was wrong.

A faint cry carried on the wind, followed by the low rumble of an angry crowd. It vibrated through the air, a distant yet unmistakable roar. She followed it, weaving through the maze of narrow alleyways. The deeper she went, the more suffocating the tension became. The city square loomed ahead, and the closer she got, the more oppressive the energy felt, like the city itself was holding its breath.

The roar grew louder, a mix of shouts and cries that reverberated off the walls. Dzintara strained to see over the crowd that poured into the square. Frustrated, she ducked back into the shadowed alleys, the noise rattling her nerves. And then, a voice cut through the chaos—a voice that sent a chill down her spine.

"The infidels will know the true meaning of fear. I am the bringer of retribution, and I will leave a trail of blood for any who dare oppose the Holy Mother Church!"

Her stomach clenched. The voice was deep, commanding, laced with a violent promise. She pressed herself against the wall, heart pounding, and moved with urgency. Skirting the crowd, she found an opening between two buildings and began to climb. Her hands gripped the rough stone walls as she scaled upward.

Reaching the rooftop, Dzintara lay flat, her body blending into the shadows. She crawled to the edge and peered over, her breath catching in her throat.

Below the square was a sea of chaos. Crusaders stood in front of the frenzied crowd, their white robes spattered with dirt and blood. Her gaze drifted across the square—and then she saw it.

Akbar.

His lifeless body lay sprawled in the dirt, his head severed, the pool of blood soaking into the sand. Her breath caught in her throat, and for a moment, the world seemed to tilt on its axis. *Akbar...the boy who fought for her cause. The boy whose brother died for the same mission.* And now, his life had been brutally snuffed out, his body desecrated in front of the masses.

Tears welled in her eyes, but she blinked them away, her hands trembling against the cold stone. Her pulse pounded in her ears. Rage mixed with helplessness twisted inside her. *How could she let this happen?*

Anno stood tall before the blood-soaked ground, his voice booming as he riled up the crowd. He raised his arms high, a preacher of death and violence.

Beside the Knight Commander knelt a man, bound and hooded.

"We demand the surrender of the infidels who ambushed and attacked our caravan," yelled the Knight Commander.

He pointed his sword at one after another of the gathered crowd, who each cowered back in fear.

"Was it you? Or you? Perhaps it was you!"

Anno ripped the hood off the kneeling prisoner and pulled him to his feet by his hair.

"He is one of those responsible," Anno yelled. "Point out who is with you!"

Dzintara felt her breath sucked from her diaphragm. Time stopped. Muhammad's eyes were black with blood from a severe beating. She couldn't move or breathe. She held her mouth to keep herself from screaming.

ANNO HELD Muhammad by the bounds with his sword pointed at the crowd. "Point to those who are with you, and you will be spared," he said to Muhammad. But Muhammad said nothing.

"This man, this surgeon, treated one of the infidels yesterday. His brother." Anno pointed at the beheaded body lying on the sand.

"That makes him an enemy of the one true God," he continued.

Anno looked at the other knights, who all drew their swords. A rock flew from the crowd and landed next to Anno.

"Let the physician go!" someone yelled from the crowd.

"*Mal'unin!*" others in the crowd began chanting.

The flow of the crowd pushed forward, and the knights stepped to block Anno and the prisoner. Their swords were held with two hands aimed at the crowd.

"Don't you want to save yourself?" Anno asked. "You and I are not so different," Muhammad wheezed.

Surprised at the response, Anno grabbed Muhammad's neck and pulled in close. "I'm no infidel."

"You are to us. You came uninvited. So we kill each other until one of us surrenders...except we don't kill the innocent," Muhammad said, looking down at Akbar.

Anno kicked the back of Muhammad's knee, and he knelt with a grunt. More rocks fell next to Anno as he raised his sword. The crowd was yelling *Barbar* in unison. Muhammad looked up at him and smiled. "With every death, the mission strengthens, and your mission becomes weaker."

He hesitated and looked at his men.

"Do it! Before this turns on us," Roland urged.

But he just stood there with the sword raised above his head. At that moment, all the lives he claimed flashed before his eyes. Images of faces flashing one after another. The sword dropped from his hand.

"What in God's name are you doing?" Roland screamed, but Anno just stood there, frozen.

Roland stepped into Anno's place and raised his sword. "You can kill an innocent man for his horses but can't execute an infidel?"

Anno snapped back, and, with a swift motion, Muhammad's head fell from his body.

On the rooftop, Dzintara pressed her knuckles to her mouth, biting down hard to keep the scream from escaping as hot tears streaked down her face. Below, the crowd roared—anger, grief, disbelief—all blending together into a cacophony of despair. Her vision blurred, but she couldn't tear her eyes away as Muhammad's lifeless body crumpled into the sand, his blood staining the earth beneath him.

Her chest tightened, making every breath a battle. She gasped, desperate for air, her body trembling uncontrollably. *This is a dream.* The world felt distant, muffled, as though she were underwater, drowning in her own helplessness. She wanted to scream— to leap from the rooftop and rip the world apart, to kill every Crusader with her bare hands.

But she couldn't move. She was frozen, paralyzed by the

horror before her. Her fingers dug into the rough stone beneath her, nails splintering and breaking as they scraped against the surface, leaving bloody streaks in their wake. Her whole body shook, a silent scream caught in her throat, suffocating her.

Her heart pounded violently in her chest, each beat a reminder that she was still alive while he was not. *Muhammad.* The name echoed in her mind, a hollow sound that only deepened the emptiness inside her. She stared at his body, the man she loved, broken and discarded like he meant nothing.

But to her, he was everything.

"Any harm that comes to any of us is punishable by death," Roland shouted to the assembled crowd. Anno stood there frozen with his sword bloody as rocks rained down, striking their helmets.

Without hesitation, the knight brothers turned on the crowd, slaughtering indiscriminately. Anno and Roland rushed towards an alleyway for escape. Dzintara stood and jumped onto the roof of a market stand and climbed down a post. She pushed into the sea of the crowd. She unsheathed her khanjar.

She forced her way toward Anno. A knight was holding a woman against the wall, preparing to violate her.

Dzintara came up from behind and pulled the rapist's head back, slicing into his jugular. His body hit the ground, and she breathed in the surrounding chaos. Another crusader was holding an old man to the ground, ready to cut his throat. Rocks and stones continued to rain down. Dzintara stepped forward and sliced the attacker across his gut. His intestines spilled onto the sand. She took his sword and handed it to a younger man in the crowd, who began to hack away at the invader's head. The crowd surged, and the remaining Crusaders became suddenly aware that they were outnumbered. Dzintara spotted the Knight Commander rushing away, disappearing into the alleyways.

Dzintara tried to give chase, but the flow of the crowd was too thick. The remaining knights were trapped in the square. Suddenly, a hand grabbed her shoulder and threw her to the ground. Two knights stood over her, swords ready. She rolled, jumped, and ran, escaping the way she had come. When she glanced back, the two black crosses were following, but their heavy armor was no match for her agility. She dodged around corners and jumped over piles of refuse until she. She came upon the outhouse. She quickly ducked inside, holding her breath, listening for the sound of the armor.

She let out a sigh of relief. Tears flowed, and she collapsed to her knees, covering her mouth to stifle her sobs. The thought of *him* gone so instantly was unbearable. She climbed back down through the lavatory and into the cave. As she emerged, she found her horse waiting patiently, tossing its tail at the sight of her. She quickly swung herself onto her mount. The beast beneath snorted and stomped its hooves against the sand. They raced through the olive orchard.

When she arrived at their refuge, it was too late. Tents were burned, and the ghazi executed. All that was left was the blackened ash and soot of their home. Her men were decapitated.

There, in the rubble, a body rose from the sand. It was Amir. She rushed over to him and pulled him up on horseback. Amir told her how the Crusaders came out of nowhere as if they knew exactly where the refuge was.

The full weight bowed her. Her home of the past ten years was gone, Muhammad was executed, and their mission was now in rubble. Disbelief turned into pain. And the pain molded into vengeance. There, in the decay, she vowed vengeance on the man who killed *him*.

CHAPTER SIX

The heavy oak door to the hall burst open with a loud crash, startling everyone present. Guards dragged in a bloodied, barely conscious man, his clothes torn and face a mask of bruises and cuts. They placed him in the hall's center, visible to all the gathered men. The hall shone with the hearth's light, creating long shadows in the stone room. Atop the hearth stood four proud coats of arms, symbols of power and influence in the city of Riga.

"Speak!" commanded Albert, a behemoth of a man draped in a flowing cloak of black and purple. His black mitre cast a dark halo as he leaned forward, his eyes fixed on the dying man. "Tell us what happened."

The man coughed, blood splattering his lips. His voice was weak but determined. "The Curonians...they struck our ships coming up the Dvina. We...we were ambushed. The ships, the crew, the cargo...all lost."

Silence filled the room, the weight of news pressing on the men. The man in the yellow tunic, Hendricks, stood slowly, his face a mask of controlled fury. "Naught remains but silence in this hall?" he demanded, scanning each of the faces of the seven men seated around the table.

Albert sipped his wine and sucked air through his teeth. "Anno, what is the meaning of this? The Brotherhood is paid to protect the route up the Dvina and the great reputation of this city," he challenged, clenching the stem of his chalice. "Since your return from the Holy Land, you have not been the same."

Next to Albert, a small, bald monk meticulously scribbled the proceedings of the meeting. Anno sat tall, his broad shoulders draped in a rough-spun cloak of indigo. His long beard, a river of midnight spilling down his chest, and his eyes, dark and piercing, looked straight through Albert. Despite his humble appearance, he exuded regality, authority, and purpose. The symbol of the red cross, embroidered in a thread upon his breast, was a testament to his unwavering devotion to the cause and teachings of St. Bernard of Clairvaux.

Anno stayed calm, black beady eyes shifting between Hendricks and Albert. He gave a gentle tug at his beard as if he was pondering. "Resources," Anno finally spoke firmly. "Recruits are hard to come by. Those recruits need to eat. They need weapons. Armor. Cogs. Horses. Are you starting to see the picture, Albert?" he said, turning to the head of the table.

"I gave you one-third of all the land you subjugated. What do you mean you lack resources?" Albert yelled and leaned in towards him.

Anno ignored the outburst and looked back at Hendricks. "Hendricks, the levies on merchants are simply not enough for us to protect your cargo along the upriver journey."

Hendricks sank in his seat as the others whispered in each other's ears at this news. "Anno, are you implying that Albert should raise levies even more?" Hendricks asked.

"No. I simply mean we can't protect your cargo," Anno said.

"Then what are we paying for?" Hendricks shot at Albert. The hall fell silent. The monk scratched quill against parchment, recording the meeting. Guards dragged the dying man out of the hall.

Anno gazed unyieldingly at Albert. "From the levies, Albert takes two-thirds. We are left with practically nothing. You expect us to protect your cargo upriver, conquer new subjects, and defend the city. Our coffers are dwindling. The land he generously allows us to keep is barren," Anno spoke softly but sternly.

"Nonsense! The agreement was for you to subjugate and defend," yelled Albert.

"The land is not fertile. We are forced to collect land rent in the summer—for you," Anno pointed at Albert. "And in the winter, we cannot break new ground. It's too dangerous, and we don't have the recruits. We are living to survive at this point. Not to protect and expand," Anno said.

Albert waved him off angrily. "Albert, Anno has a point," Hendricks said, a quiet diplomacy at work in his voice. "Protection and expansion need an excess of resources, and so does defense. An infusion of gold and silver with the understanding that returns won't be for a long time. Perhaps only your children's kin will see those returns," he looked at Baron Wilhelm for support. "If we can't rely on the Brotherhood, then we have to arm ourselves, which costs gold and silver."

"What exactly are you saying, Hendricks?" Albert tilted his head in a challenging way.

"If we must bear the burden of our own protection, then what purpose does our pact serve?" Hendricks stood, and his chair clanked against the stone floor as it fell back. "The levy? I speak not only for myself but for the Germanic Merchant Guild. Let it be known that if the passage up the Dvina remains unsound, the news will spread like wildfire, and trade with our neighbors shall wane. Our vessels will cower in our ports, afraid to set sail. Secure passage must be secured, or all is lost."

"May I recommend a solution?" A thin, old man, stooped and gaunt, with skin stretched tight across his bones and a long, thinning beard of coiled silver, spoke up. Stone dust had seeped into his skin, leaving it powdered white.

"What could the Mason's Guild possibly offer as a solution?" Hendricks mocked.

"Let the guilds hold sway and impose the will of the freemen," Kristoff declared, his voice a low rumble. "They shall adhere to the teachings of Christ. They shall pay their tithes. But let the guilds rule and enforce."

Albert tapped his finger as the quill scratched against the parchment. He leaned over and briefly read the writing. "Du musst dies reparieren und diese Händler schützen," Albert said, looking at Anno.

"We must reevaluate our agreement. Allocating two-thirds of the land to the Sword-Brothers and one-third to the church would provide sufficient resources to attract new recruits and conquer new territories," Anno responded diplomatically.

"Absolut nicht!" Albert's voice boomed through the hall.

"There is also the issue of the freemen," said Baron Wilhelm, sitting beside Hendricks. His face was aglow with warmth, his dark hair slicked back, and his features softened by a friendly and diplomatic demeanor.

"What of them, Baron Wilhelm?" Albert asked.

"They refuse to tithe or attend mass. They continue to hold their heathen festivals. Most importantly," he raised a finger and took a beat of silence, "they refuse to trade with us. They have set up their own trade posts along the coast of the sea. They trade with one tribe with another. Convert to convert. Bypassing our levies."

A thin-faced bishop interrupted. "They refuse to pay the mortuary fee and—"

"Then hang the naked body above the cathedral doors," Albert interjected.

The thin-faced bishop looked down and scanned the faces. "We have done that. They come at night and remove the body and burn it in their own traditions."

Baron Wilhelm raised his thick hands, motioning for the bishop to stop talking. "The fees for the dead are but a paltry offering compared to the trade with merchants that are evaded," Wilhelm said softly to Albert.

Albert pinched the bridge of his nose between his thumb and forefinger, then closed his eyes in frustration. "Albert, we can take the burden of governing off your hands and still generate the levies and tithes you seek," Kristoff said.

Albert opened his eyes and sighed. He sat back in his chair, slouched, and poured himself wine from a silver jug into his silver chalice. He drank.

"Have you considered, my friend, that perhaps governance may not be your greatest strength? Though we all acknowledge the significance of your achievements—bringing the knights and subjugating the heathens, taking this city from a mere outpost for the church to what it is today—sometimes the talents required for enduring success are distinct." Hendricks stood over them, eyes piercing at Albert's, his dark silver beard shining in the flame light. Albert scoffed and drank another.

"So the heathens are restless. We are running short on resources, and you," he pointed at Hendricks, Kristoff, and Baron Wilhelm, "you want to be here," he pointed at his seat.

No one breathed. He placed his hands palms down on the rough-hewn table, splaying his fingers and tapping rhythmically as he spoke. "Here is what will happen. Anno and his men will punish the Curonians and put an end to this intertribal trading. Then you will get new recruits. Then you will get your heathens to obey. In the meantime, levies stay. And more importantly," he pointed to himself, "I stay here. Don't forget I built this. You're all here because of me."

"I regret to hear your decision, Albert," Baron Wilhelm stood and wobbled to the door and left.

"Wilhelm is right. Fix this, or we take matters into our own hands." Hendricks followed, stepping around the chair and shutting the door loudly behind him.

"Anno," Albert growled, his voice filled with authority, "this falls on you. Rectify the situation or else. I asked for you to come back because of your reputation. You need to put an end to this Curonian nonsense."

Anno stood, his eyes dark and intense. "Mark my words, Albert," he growled, "the winds of change are blowing, and they'll sweep you away if you're not careful. You'd be wise to heed their call."

Albert smiled mockingly, dismissing Anno. The old mason sat tapping the tip of his fingers together.

"May I suggest—" Kristoff started.

"What are you still doing here? Get out!" Albert barked at Kristoff.

"Anno speaks the truth. The ebbs and flows of change move with the sun and the moon. The tide is coming in," Kristoff pushed himself up with the palm of his hands and scurried out of the hall.

"Masons Guild. A joke. Hans—" Albert said, looking at the bishop sitting next to him.

"They built your Cathedral."

Albert scoffed and dismissed the comment. "You need to go to Rome," Hans said, dropping the quill.

Albert shook his head and refilled his wine. "Leave," he demanded of the remaining bishop, who complained of the mortuary fees.

The room cleared. Albert and Hans sat alone in the large hall, silent. The fire crackled.

"Mortuary fees. What a tall tale," Albert finally said, shaking his head and sipping his wine. "What did you write down?" he asked Hans.

"Not everything. I am selective about what gets submitted to the Holy records."

"Good," Albert said.

"We will not survive without their support. Coffers are almost empty," Hans forced a smile as he spoke.

"Every winter, they complain, and every spring, they forget," Albert said.

"Yarn around the Blackheads is you've fallen out of favor with the Pope. That you're unfit to govern. In fact, merchants are muttering that the Brotherhood may be a better choice over you."

Albert furrowed his brows and stared at Hans. "What is a bishop doing at the House of the Blackheads?"

"Informer," Hans smiled and tapped his temple.

"I'm not going to Rome. It's—"

Hans raised his finger as if to warn Albert of his next words, but he continued, "I'm finishing what my uncle started. No one, and I mean no one, will get in the way of that," Albert sighed.

"Reputation and perception matter the most. The rest is chicken shit," Hans said, lowering his finger. "Remember, I am here at the request of His Holiness to aid in your cause."

"Don't remind me," Albert said.

"I am a trusted advisor to help you navigate these predicaments."

"Did your informer tell you there is news of the lost gold and silver? That I have information regarding it? I have confirmed that he hid the gold. He knows where it is."

"Information or yarn?" the monk said, more a statement than a question. "Going against the shipwright will worsen your position with the guilds."

Albert threw the chalice to the ground. It echoed through the empty hall.

"Albert."

"Hmm."

"There is one more thing."

"What?"

"I've received word from Venice that there is some type of curse heading north."

Albert walked to the hearth and grabbed the fire poker hanging on the stone wall. He poked at a log engulfed in flames without any real purpose. "A curse?"

"Yes. There is no other word for it. Punishment of God. We can say what we want to the subjects."

"What is this curse?"

"It wipes out villages overnight. Cities in days."

"This is a godforsaken land. Even a curse will turn around before coming all this way."

Embers spewed upwards towards the ceiling as the poked log fell to the hearth floor. Hans stood next to him and watched.

"Kristoff you can dismiss, but Hendricks and Wilhelm will find a way to get what they want. His son, Friedrich, also has an appetite to rule."

The wooden Christ hanging above the mantle stared down at them.

"Have you looked at the levy catalogs lately?" Albert asked.

"Yes."

"What are Hendricks and his son trading these days?"

"Amber," Hans said.

"Amber?" Albert looked puzzled.

"Yes, thick substance from tree bark, sold as jewelry and also used for some type of medicine."

Albert cocked his head and looked at the monk.

"Quite lucrative, I might add. For imports, they come back with wax, wine, beer, and pelts," Hans continued.

"Maybe we levy amber leaving Riga. Castrate him some while keeping other merchants at ease. Curb that fool Hendricks' ambition."

"Perhaps, or Hendricks will turn you in the open," Hans looked at him and searched for the words. "They have asked me to rally on their behalf to build another shipyard. Friedrich wants to build cogs to compete with Ako."

Albert snickered and shook his head as if this was one big mockery of him and his city. "One who controls the river and the seas governs," Albert spoke to the fire. "We let them have the ship-yard. It's a matter of time before that family turns on us. Ako is indebted to us. He's ours. I know his secret."

The sound of iron hitting the stone floor echoed through the hall as Albert dropped the poker and turned back to the table to refill his chalice. "Gather up all abled, fighting men and have them meet me in the courtyard of the cathedral. Offer them handsome rewards."

"Are we engaged in a war I don't know of?" asked the monk.

"No, we are going to find out if certain information is true."

CHAPTER SEVEN

The sun bore down upon the jagged cliffs of Al-Harara. The sound of cicadas reverberated. Dzintara laid low in the rocky terrains and watched the valley below. It had been two years since his death. Refuge destroyed, she and Amir hid, moving towards Damascus. Slowly but with determination, she and Amir rebuilt the forces to continue the mission Muhammad had put into motion. They were fifty-strong, and sometimes they hired mercenaries when needed. For her, it wasn't so much about the mission anymore. It was about finding the executor — the Knight Commander who had taken everything away from her. She already lost everything once as a child, and then to lose everything again changed something in her. Her demeanor was calloused and merciless. The blade of the khanjar was the answer to everything for her. As she lay there, she glanced over at Amir, his face weathered by the elements and the battles fought.

"Are you ready?" Amir asked, catching her stare.

She nodded.

"Spread out," she whispered.

Al-Harara — the village below in the valley— appeared abandoned. A serene breeze ruffled the tattered banners that adorned
its narrow streets. It was a deceptive calm. One of the ghazi looked
at her with a questioning gesture.

"They'll come. They will."

She clenched onto her khanjar. The minutes lingered, and the
men grew restless. Suddenly, a dust cloud rose in the distance.

The men gasped and whispered among themselves.

"Steady. Wait for my command"

The Crusaders rode into the town and dismounted next to
the well. Their shining armor glittered in the merciless sun.
Swords drawn, the Crusaders advanced into the deserted streets.

The ghazi's fingers tensed around their weapons, waiting for
the signal. Dzintara shook her head. "Not yet. Wait until they are
all by the well."

The soldiers combed through the vacant homes, all appearing
hastily abandoned.

Dzintara watched, sensing the Crusaders' unease. After their
cursory sweep, they motioned their wagons into the square. A
company of thirty knights, along with the caravaners, crowded
around the well, drinking fresh water and enjoying the moment of
relief from the sweltering heat.

Dzintara looked at Amir and gave a slow nod. He made a
small fire and lit the arrowhead. Amir pulled the bowstring taut.
It creaked as it stretched. Then, letting go, the arrow flew and
implanted itself into a barrel near the well with a loud thud,
igniting a hidden cache of oil.

A knight glanced at the burning arrow, but before he
reacted, the ground shook with a loud roar. Flames and black
smoke erupted into the sky. The explosions rocked the town,
sending plumes of fire and debris into the air. Crusaders
screamed as they were engulfed by the fire, their steel armor
cooking them alive.

Dzintara leapt over the rocks, sprinting to where the horses
were hidden. The ghazi followed close behind. They mounted

their horses in one swift motion and charged down the rugged slopes, racing towards the flames of Al-Harara.

The village square lay in ruins. Stone houses were reduced to rubble, and the surviving knights fought to extinguish the fires that threatened to consume them.

"The Knight Commander is mine! Otherwise, we take no prisoners," Dzintara shouted as they closed in on the square.

The few crusaders left standing struggled to regroup. Swords clashed, arrows whistled through the air, and the acrid scent of blood mixed with smoke.

As the smoke and dust began to settle, she and the ghazi readied to seize the caravans filled with food and weapons. Dzintara jumped from her mare and made her way toward the caravan. Out of the smoke, a knight came charging forward, wielding his long sword. Dzintara rolled to the ground, blocking the blows with her khanjar. As she swiftly dodged, she unraveled her keffiyeh from her head and deftly ensnared the blade with the fabric. With a sharp yank, she pulled the weapon from his hands. A slice against the jugular, and he fell knee first.

She stood, waiting for more challengers, but none came. Dzintara couldn't shake the feeling that something was amiss. This had been too easy; the company of crusaders was too small.

She ripped a wagon flap open, and her heart sank. The caravans were empty.

"No! It's a trap! Fall back!" she screamed.

But it was too late. The ground began to shake as an army of knights rode toward them. Amir took aim, rapidly firing his arrows into the oncoming knights as they began to surround the outskirts of the village. There was no escape.

"Find shelter and escape if you can!" The fifty-some-odd ghazi scattered.

She, Amir, and the other wounded found safety in one of the unburned abandoned houses. They pushed all the furniture against the door, a makeshift fort. Then, they sat in silence and waited.

"We're dead." Amir shuddered.

The wounded ghazi breathed heavily as he bled from his thigh.

"What happened?" Amir asked with a whisper.

"One of them pretending to be dead stabbed me in the thigh."

"Shhh. Quiet," Dzintara warned.

"What's the plan?" Amir asked.

"Shut your mouth, and if they come through that door, kill them."

The ground stopped shaking when the horses stopped. There were some inaudible murmurs and orders given. Outside, the clanking of armor signaled the arrival of the knights. They made their way through the abandoned village. Suddenly, the sound of steel clashing pierced the air, followed by several screams. Dzintara knew it was her men. She looked down at the ground. "Shit."

They listened to the knights, going door to door. The rhythmic clank of steel echoed closer, then a slow-growing rumble. Their makeshift fortress began to jitter and shake.

"What is that?" asked Amir.

"Maybe more of them," she guessed.

Amir peeked through the window shutter.

"What's happening?"

"More horses...looks like from Damascus," Amir said.

"That doesn't make sense. They don't have Damascus," she said, more to herself than him.

Pounding knocks hit the shutter, and he quickly dropped into the darkness. Moments later, screams and confusion erupted outside. The knights engaged in battle against an unknown force.

"We need to escape while there is confusion," Amir said.

Dzintara looked at the wounded man. his face pale white. "We can't leave him."

The wounded fighter motioned to her, and she knelt and took his hand. "Dzintara, your heart is filled with vengeance, but nothing is more important than the survival of our kind. Rid your heart of the anger and vengeance, and only then will you save us. Vengeance only brings blood and doom."

She cupped his face, and they touched foreheads.

"Go, I'll hold them off," he said, struggling to his feet and reaching for his sword.

Dzintara stood, and they pushed aside the furniture blocking the door. Amir peeked through the door. The street was empty.

"We make for the mountains. Go!" she ordered.

They sprinted towards the edge of town. She knew that once they reached the mountains, pursuing them would be nearly impossible. The cave systems provided the ghazi a ghostly escape. With the clamor of the battle echoing behind them, they sprinted desperately toward the town's outskirts. They were close. But as they approached the outskirts, seven ghazi on horseback materialized before them. In a heart-pounding instant, their path was abruptly sealed off, and the riders brandished gleaming swords. The two skidded to an abrupt halt. Their leader, riding a large brown courser, approached. He looked down and said: "In darkness we come, so in light we may prevail."

CHAPTER EIGHT

Anno's breath formed a mist in the cold hall. The towering ceiling reached the height of five or six men. Small, square openings were carved into the walls for light and air, now slick with condensed ice. A crackling fire burned in the hearth behind them. In the center of the hall stood a vast pine table long enough to seat thirty men, with stiff wooden benches beneath. The sole chair was positioned at the table's head. In one corner stood an altar with a wooden cross and a modest prie-dieu before it.

Wrapped in a pelt, Anno leaned back in his chair and sighed. He stared at the scrolls unrolled in front of him. Next to him sat a man wearing a dark brown robe with cold blue eyes and a closely trimmed black beard. The fire cast a warm glow in the hall as the winter darkness outside settled. Anno picked at the corner of the scroll.

"Brother Anno, I cannot guarantee of what request."

Anno pushed a sealed scroll towards him.

"Deliver this letter to Hochmeister Salza," Anno said.

Taking the scroll, he observed the insignia—a cross stamped onto red wax.

"Brother Markus, you have always advocated on our behalf in

Marienburg. Tell the Hochmeister this will benefit the order and expand the order's influence in these lands. Whatever you have to tell him, but the Livonian Brotherhood of the Sword and the Teutonic Knights must unite."

Brother Markus gazed past at Anno.

"The Teutonic Order recognizes the Brotherhood and your leadership..."

"Then why the resistance to joining of forces?Anno stood, walked to the altar, and gazed at the cross. The door opened, and a boy entered with two wooden cups and a sack. He placed cups on the table and poured wine into them, then left.

"The efforts in the Holy Land have gone awry. We've moved our headquarters from Acre to Marienburg. The infidels have gained much ground. There are rumors of brothers who are living unholy, hedonistic lives. Those rumors have reached the Vatican. These scandals have been brought before His Holiness. One brother testified that our knights raped more women than the infidels. The list goes on," Markus said.

"A life by the sword brings out the darkness in a man. But that doesn't mean the cause and his will are unholy and unjust," Anno replied, tracing the mensa with his finger.

"It's just not the right time, Brother Anno. His Holiness wants to see some progress."

"Call for a Crusade in these lands and make me Provincial Master. I will see to it that we are victorious."

"Word is that the Pope's coffers are empty. Bernard of Clairvaux is struggling to raise an army to take back the Holy Land. The pope will not risk his reputation supporting a lost cause in these lands. It's a recipe for failure, Anno. The order's focus is diplomacy; to gain the favor of the Pope equal to that of the Templars. That will open many doors."

"When my men and I came here with Albert, it was just us. That's it. What we have built here speaks for itself. Consider the converts, this great city, the merchant trade, and all the land yet to be taken east, north, and south of here."

"Your will is impressive."

"Don't patronize me, Markus," Anno's words echoed across the hall.

Anno walked back to his chair and sighed as he sat. He looked Markus in the eye.

"Markus, my childhood friend, our survival through the winter hinges upon your support. The guilds have been relentless, demanding that we safeguard their cargo. Our lands yield little, and our coffers are dusty. It is gold and silver that I require. If you're truly grateful, now is the time to show it. Call for a crusade in these lands, make me Provincial Master, and I will see to it that the Teutonic Knights are victorious. It'll be my last call to battle. Then I will govern this land."

Markus leaned back on the bench and placed his hand firmly on Anno's.

"Not yet. The time is not right."

Anno pulled his hand away.

"But why? Why is it not the right time? Do you wish to see this order wiped from this land? Is that what you wish, Markus?"

"No."

"Then why will you not plead our case? The Hochmeister listens to you."

"Anno, the situation is delicate. We lost the Holy Land."

"I was there!"

"The Pope's holy office is beset by one outrage after another. Now is not a time for rash action in the Northlands."

"Now is the time for action." Anno insisted, enraged.

Markus' patience snapped, "Do you truly desire to know why, Anno?"

"Yes."

"It's you, good Brother."

"Me?"

"Yes." Markus spat, his eyes blazing. "You. Your men. The reputation that surrounds you threatens my ascension to Grand Commander. I'm so close. I have the recommendations from all

the elders. It has taken me a lifetime to get here. I won't risk it by
endorsing you and your band of—"

"Markus, you had better choose your words wisely."

"Do you know what you're called in Marienburg?"

Anno drew his sword and slammed it on the hall table. "Tell
me. What?"

"The Butchers of Livonia," Markus said. "Your men's bloodlust is known far and wide."

"Don't blame the hammer because you dislike the result. We
are a necessary tool for your—for the Pope's ambitions."

"It's only a matter of time before your reputation reaches the
Vatican. I would be ruined. Do you understand? Ruined. I'll be
blamed for it all. Just like when we were children."

Anno scoffed. "Even as children, you were a coward."

"Choose your next words wisely, Anno."

"You chose the life of a brother-monk. You wished to insert
yourself into the order as a man of cloth and governance. The
enlarging of Christian lands doesn't happen from behind a desk
in a room full of comforts, Markus. It requires those men," he
pointed out towards the courtyard, "the ones you call butchers. It
requires sending a message that even the most stubborn heathen
understands. Not from a snake's tongue in a bathhouse."

"Scurvy Saracen! After all I have done to protect the reputation of your family. Your father was nothing more than a drunken
gambler slurring orders from the back of the line."

Anno leapt forward and grabbed his face. "Do not talk about
him."

Terror filled Markus's eyes as Anno pressed his forehead
against his, gripping his jaw tightly. Markus shook his head frantically until Anno released him, gently touching his bearded face
and smiling, "I want to show you something, brother. My dedica-
tion to the order."

His robe dropped to the cold stone floor. Anno unstrapped
his vest and removed his linen shirt, revealing a landscape of scars
across his back, chest, and limbs. He turned with arms

outstretched, palms facing upward. The fiery glow of the hearth behind him cast a warm light on his pale skin, highlighting the deep shadows within his scars. Markus shuddered and sat down.

"I've bled for Christ, and for his Holiness, twenty times over. Each time, I rose again, stronger." Anno growled, "My sacrifice. This is as close as you'll ever come to serving the divine will of Christ. Markus, I will spill blood one last time, then I wish to govern. No more bloodshed," he finished, simply.

"I can't help you," Markus said. "If it's resources you need, then go back to Albert and renegotiate your share. I have too much to lose."

Anno let out a bitter laugh. Markus turned and walked towards the door. Hand on the door, he glanced at childhood friend.

"Anno—"

"Your horse is waiting, Brother Markus."

"Anno, I respect our friendship—"

Anno raised his hand.

"No need. Your horse. It's waiting."

"I hope you will grow to understand."

The wind howled as Markus opened the door, leaving. Anno picked up his sword from the table and slammed it tip-first into the bench, the future of his Brotherhood weighing on him. The souls of those he killed lurking in his mind.

CHAPTER NINE

The patient lay on a rug covered in vibrant reds and greens, adorned with intricate geometric patterns. They made the man piss into a clay pot before gently turning him onto his back. Naked, the man lay there with sweat beading on his brow, hovering in the liminal space between consciousness and oblivion. The mud-brick room was dark, and the candles gave it an eerie atmosphere reminiscent of an occult ritual.

Muhammad took the clay pot and swirled the liquid, sniffing as he scrutinized the urine's dark orange hue. "Scent of iron."

"Now, we must check the eyes. Some will look at the stars to determine a man's sickness. You must always look at two things first —urine and eyes."

He pulled the patient's eyelids open with his fingers. They were glassy and unresponsive, the pupils rolling upwards. He turned and examined the glass bottles next to the patient, choosing one with his long, skinny fingers. Muhammad's thin, angular face was serene, accentuated by the soft curve of his lips that peeked through his dark, well-groomed beard.

"Here, smell this." He uncorked the bottle. Dzintara took a deep sniff and began to cough violently.

"Camphor. Made from bark. We try this first," he said.

Muhammad waved the bottle under the patient's nose. He did not stir. Next, he took another bottle and poured a couple of drops into the first. "Vinegar. Many do not recommend it, but it makes the smell stronger."

He offered the vial to Dzintara to sniff, but she declined. His teeth flashed as he smiled and let out a gentle laugh.

"You do it." He pushed the bottle towards her. She hesitated. Muhammad took her hands in his own and wrapped her fingers around the bottle. "Here."

She took the bottle and wafted it under the patient's nose. A sudden gasp and a convulsive cough followed, nearly knocking the bottle out of her hands. The man sprang upright, eyes flying open.

Muhammad patted him on the back, helping him to catch his breath. Once the patient was breathing calmly, Muhammad lay the man back down and then reached for another large glass amphora. Muhammad uncorked the container and carefully retrieved a shiny black creature, placing it gently on the patient's temple. The creature latched on instantly.

"Leeches. Good for infection. They clean the blood. Here. Put this one on his ankle."

With a quivering hand and a steadying breath, she mustered the courage to grasp the repulsive bloodsucker and place it on the patient's ankle. But the leech wouldn't lock.

"Like this." He put his hand over Dzintara's and drifted the leech up a finger length. As he guided her hand, the leech locked on and began to suck. Dzintara let out a gentle laugh. In the soft light, she caught the reflection of her beautiful, unscarred face.

Dzintara awoke to a scream in a nearby cell. She closed her eyes and wished to go back there with him. It has been a torment-filled week in the dimly lit confines of the hot dungeon. The anguished cries of captured crusaders, her grim companions.

On the seventh day, they came for her, and she was shown to her newfound quarters within the fortress. A humble room, with just a bed, wooden table, and solitary candle.

What puzzled Dzintara most was the small gold cross resting

atop the table. With a furrowed brow, she picked up the golden cross from it and studied it, tracing the delicate contours.

In the quiet room, the creaking door broke the silence as it gently opened. A bearded man, his face reflecting a life filled with both hardships and victories, walked in. Dressed in simple linen, he moved with a grace that contrasted with his humble clad.

The room dimmed when the door shut. He regarded Dzintara with a calm intensity.

"Do not be afraid. We are on the same side," he said.

"Where is my khanjar?"

He crossed his hands in front of him and smiled. "We needed to ensure you weren't with them."

"My men?"

"Come. Let's go for a walk."

She shook her head. "No."

She backed as he approached.

"Where am I, and where are my men?" she pressed.

"I will take you to them," he said, opening the door and motioning her to follow.

Navigating the labyrinthine corridors, he moved quickly. Dzintara quickened her pace, struggling to keep up with her guide.

Holding back the question she truly wanted to ask, afraid of the answer, she instead asked: "What is this place?"

"The Citadel," he responded without slowing or turning.

"Damascus?" she asked.

But there was no response. The figure continued to move forward.

Then she asked: "Who are you?"

He halted, his lips curving upward as he pivoted to face her. "I am Saladin."

As they resumed their brisk walk, Dzintara's face betrayed a mix of shock and apprehension at the revelation. After all, it was Saladin who sent for Muhammad. It was he and his men who cowardly fled, leaving Akbar and his brother to the Crusaders. Did he know who she was? Why had he spared her?

Their path led them to a courtyard where massive gates loomed overhead. Villagers lined up for rations, and statesmen came and went on official business. Dzintara stopped, watching Saladin's people distribute food to the crowd.

"How did you know where we were?" she asked.

His gaze fixed upon her. "Nothing occurs in these mountains without my knowledge."

He paused for a moment.

"I also wished to meet you, Dzintara. Your reputation has reached far and wide."

Dzintara looked perplexed. He chuckled and moved purposefully through the courtyard, villagers blessing and praising Saladin as he passed.

Then he stopped and pointed. "There."

She looked and saw her remaining ghazi mingling with Saladin's army, gathered around the fire and sharing food.

Dzintara smiled, relieved to see Amir among them.

"How many survived?"

"My men counted eighteen, but one passed last night. His flesh turned black."

"You should have called me," she said, angrily.

"I needed to know whether you are with us or with them?" He pointed to a body dangling on a rope clad in a white robe embroidered with a black cross.

"What makes you certain of my identity?" Dzintara challenged.

Saladin glanced downward, hands clasped behind his back. "Muhammad. He was the greatest physician in the land."

"Time's passed. It's been many seasons since his death," she said, pushing the pain down.

"And you have managed to continue his work," Saladin praised.

"It's what he would have wanted. More than half my men died in that ambush."

Saladin stared at the sand beneath him as if silently saying a prayer for the fallen.

"Not all is lost, Dzintara. Times are changing."

She watched as an elderly man took his rations in wrapped linen and kneeled to praise his saviors as if they were gods.

"Why is there a cross in my chamber?" she asked.

"You'll find out soon," Saladin said, glancing at her before his gaze returned to the sand.

Dzintara scoffed, "It's an insult. Since the day of his death, I've spent every day looking for the man responsible. Eradicating them one by one."

She awaited his response, but there was none. They stood in silence, side by side, observing their men laughing and joking with one another.

"Thank you for the hospitality, but our mission isn't done." Dzintara whistled, and Amir waved to her and ran over.

He bowed in front of Saladin, took Dzintara's hand, and put it to his forehead. "Inshallah, you are alive and well."

"We leave now," she ordered.

Amir obeyed and relayed the order to the remaining ghazi. They left to retrieve the horses.

She extended her hand, palms facing up like she wanted something. "Where is it?"

"It's in a safe place," he gazed at her.

"It belonged to Muhammad and was passed on to me."

"I don't intend on keeping it," he said.

"A khanjar must be returned to its rightful owner," she demanded.

"Join us," Saladin asked.

Her men came from the stables already lined up on horseback, ready for leave, with an extra mare waiting for her.

"Stay," Saladin said.

"I will be back for my khanjar. I may not be so polite next time," with a swift motion, she mounted the mare.

Saladin waved with his right arm, and his ghazi rushed to block the gate and stood, ready to draw their weapons.

"Stay as my guests. I insist," Saladin said.

CHAPTER TEN

Steel clashed against steel. Blocking blow after blow, her men tried to advance on her. She dodged, blocked, and returned blows with the sword in one hand and a dagger in the other. Men grew tired and gave up quickly.

Dzintara wiped the sweat from her brow and scanned the parapets where Saladin's guards strolled, weapons in hand. The sun hung low on the horizon, casting long shadows across the training grounds.

Amir stepped forward and drew his sword. They faced off against each other, and Amir charged at her. Dzintara moved with precision, her blade a deadly extension of herself.

Amir thrust his blade at her, but she deflected.

"Dzintara," he said between breaths, "I'm starting to feel more like a captive than a guest."

Dzintara paused for a moment, her dagger held at the ready.

"I've been feeling the same," she admitted.

The sparring continued. Amir faked left, then hit her right. She leaned left, and he missed.

"What does he want from us?" Amir asked between strikes.

"I don't know."

"I've heard rumors from his men. He is a friend of the Hospitallers. Dzintara, he is not to be trusted," he said, shifting into a high guard, deflecting Dzintara's blow. She delivered a well-placed shin into his chest, sending him to the ground. Laughter erupted from above. Amir coughed and gathered himself.

"Stick to bow and arrow." She smiled at him, extended a helping hand.

Amir accepted and returned to his feet. They walked to the well while others sparred on the training ground.

"He wants something from you, Dzintara. We shouldn't stick around to find out what that is."

The call to prayer sounded, and the men walked off the training grounds to perform their acts of worship.

Dzintara watched outside the mosque as the men's foreheads touched the ground. The hypnotic guide of the Imam reading from the Quran echoed throughout the Mosque. Saladin was nowhere to be seen.

Dzintara walked the halls of the fort until she came to his door. She gently pushed it open. Candlelight flickered on his face as he gazed up at the visitor.

"Enter," he motioned to her. His desk was filled with parchments of maps, scrolls, and stacks of messages.

"I didn't see you at prayer," she said.

He smiled at her and leaned back in his chair. "There are more pressing matters at hand. I'm sure I will be forgiven." He kissed his fingers and raised them to the ceiling.

Silence fell between the two of them.

"Thank you for your hospitality," she said, breaking the silence. He nodded in response.

"I believe it is time for us to leave. Continue Muhammad's mission of medicine."

He contemplated this and gazed at Dzintara as he thought about his answer.

"You asked me about the golden cross in your room," Saladin said.

"I was curious."

Saladin chuckled, "Curious no more?"

Dzintara shrugged, and he motioned for her to sit.

"I prefer to stand."

"The cross represents more than just a symbol of their faith. It's a reminder of our goal: coexistence. True coexistence isn't about annihilating those who are different. It's about finding a way to live together despite our differences. In times like these, defending ourselves with the blade becomes a necessary evil."

"Hm. So you'd rather surrender? That doesn't fit your reputation."

Saladin smiled at this. "It's not that simple. If we were to lay down our arms and let them conquer us, we'd be forced into hiding and persecuted for our beliefs, just as they were during Roman times. By standing our ground and showing strength, we aim to make them see that bloodshed is futile and that peace is the only lasting solution. The cross serves as a reminder of this end goal—a future where we can coexist, even if it seems far off now."

Dzintara was unimpressed and unconvinced. Saladin let out a sigh of submission, "You are guests and free to leave at your will. But I have a business I must attend to, and I need your help. The Franks have increased their patrols since your ambush, and they are more vigilant now than ever. I must ask that you and your men escort me to Haifa, and then you may go where you please."

"And if I refuse?," she asked.

Saladin rose and strode to the wooden cabinet in the corner. He opened a drawer, retrieved an item, and placed her khanjar on the table. "Go on. You're the rightful owner."

She lifted her khanjar from the table and tucked it in her girdle.

"We are both wanted men— well, you a woman, but they don't know that. With you and your men at our side, we stand a better chance against any ambushes or Crusaders. It's mutually beneficial."

Dzintara nodded as she pondered the offer. Her encounters

with Saladin's influence had always ended grimly. How could she know if this time would be different?

"I have always put my mission first, even if it meant leaving allies on the battlefield to die. But when we ride together, we will need each other, as we are a small force," Saladin said, as if reading her mind.

"I'll consider it."

"After, you'll be free to go as you please."

"So, it's an order?" she asked.

The aging warrior smiled at her. "A firm request."

Dzintara turned and made for the door.

"Dzintara, a vessel, is set to depart north from Haifa's port. After the escort, I strongly recommend you board it," he suggested.

"We're not finished," she said, holding the door handle without turning it.

"The tides are changing. The dawn of diplomacy is upon us. Soon, bloodshed will be a thing of the past. Your mission —"

"We'll escort you to Haifa," she said, turning to face him. "After that, we're both free to pursue our own missions."

"Bloodshed breeds bloodshed. There are more effective ways."

"When do we leave?"

Saladin sighed. "At dawn, in three days."

They exchanged a long, silent gaze, and then Dzintara left Saladin's chancery.

AT DAWN on the third day, Dzintara and the remaining seventeen ghazi sat poised on horseback. Saladin and twenty of his men joined them in the courtyard. The gate opened, and they rode out into the awakening desert.

"You and your men take the front," Saladin ordered. Saladin, riding on his white stallion, hunched over, tired-looking. He was old, nothing like the fierce warrior he was once rumored to be.

Dzintara took the lead, riding at a steady pace. Haifa was a four-day ride, weather permitting. They followed Via Maris for three days, camping off the route at night to avoid drawing attention. Saladin's men seemed tireless, patrolling vigilantly and never removing their hands from their sword hilts. She barely slept, often watching Amir, who feigned sleep. Doubts crept in—had she made a mistake dragging him into her mission? Vengeance was hers alone, not his. The thought of her homeland made her shiver. A brother she once knew, and a father who deserved the blade of her khanjar.

For years, she had nightmares about a snow-covered cog on fire. Barrels and trunks of gold, hauled away and hidden in a cave. As dawn approached, she steeled herself, ready to face the last day of their journey.

Mid-day, they passed a long line of caravans heading in the opposite direction. Bedouin raiders and the warriors gazed at each other suspiciously as they passed. Saladin, covering his face behind a headscarf, caught up to Dzintara.

"It will be safer if we take the mountain pass."

Dzintara gazed at the blazing sun and the distant mountains.

"There are forty of us. No matter where we go, people will notice," she replied.

"Via Maris is too dangerous. We're getting close to Haifa, and too many souls have seen us. We are both fugitives. Should word get out, we will not make it."

Without looking at Saladin, she pulled the reins and headed for the mountain pass. Amir caught up to Dzintara, riding next to her. "What are you doing? The mountains are a death trap."

"This is what he wants."

"Dzintara, he's planning something. Let's just break away and ride out."

"We are outnumbered, Amir. Do you think it's a coincidence he brought twenty of his best men?"

"Then what do we do?" Amir asked.

"The mountains will slow us down. We wait for darkness and make our move. Spread the word."

Amir glanced at Saladin and his soldiers.

"It looks like they are slowing down."

"Good, it will make it easier to outride them," she said.

"They are falling back. I don't like this."

As darkness descended, Dzintara and her ghazi readied their weapons, their horses keeping a steady pace. Glancing back, she saw Saladin's party, once a distant shadow, now steadily gaining ground.

As they rounded a bend, the silhouettes of mounted men appeared, shrouded in darkness on the ridgeline ahead. Dzintara raised her hand, and the group halted.

An arrow whizzed past Dzintara's head, embedding itself in the throat of a ghazi behind her.

"Take cover!" she shouted over the sound of men galloping toward them. Beside her, a man on horseback suddenly pitched forward as an arrow struck his back. Dzintara turned to see Saladin's men drawing bows, their arrows cutting through the darkness toward them. It was a trap. Men on horseback were closing in ahead.

Her men frantically scrambled, some dismounting and taking cover in the rocks, others staying by her side. Amir fired arrows into the dark direction of the chargers.

"Charge at those swine!" she ordered, pointing at Saladin and his men. Seven charged at the traitors. "If we die, we die fighting!"

Then she saw it. The shining glimmer of the armor and white robes flowed ahead in the moonlight. At that moment, she realized Saladin's coexistence meant giving up those who fought against the Christians. Coward. Pointing her sword at the crusading knights, she let out a war cry.

"Don't," Amir shouted to her between arrow fire, "Go after him. The traitor."

She spurred her horse higher, looking down to see seven of her warriors colliding with Saladin's forces, slaughtering the traitors despite Saladin's numerical advantage.

Amidst the maelstrom, the white stallion darted up the mountainside. Dzintara guided her mount up a steep incline, around massive boulders, and ascended narrow trails, hoping to cut him off.

Suddenly, a cascade of rubble echoed through the stillness, followed by the shriek of a horse. She watched as the stallion tumbled down the mountain and into the valley. She made it over the mountain top. Oddly, she didn't see Saladin in the tumble. Dzintara scanned the valley, looking for signs of life. A movement at the bottom of the mountainside caught the corner of her eye. Dzintara wasted no time. She followed, riding her way down the rugged terrain. She found the beast crumpled at the base of the mountain. She pulled her horse around in a circle, looking for Saladin. She saw nothing but the outline of rocks and boulders in the dark valley.

Slowly, she dismounted and unsheathed her khanjar.

"Saladin!" she called out into the black.

Nearby, she heard the sound of rocks crunching gravel. Without warning, a blow landed on the side of her head. She blocked the following blow with her khanjar, her eyes adjusting in the starlight. Saladin wore a golden claw over his fist.

He swung at her, and the golden claw left three deep gashes across her face. Another strike followed, and another, but Dzintara dodged each blow. Clang! Her khanjar locked with the claw. She yanked while Saladin struggled to break free. She delivered a powerful kick to the back of his knee, sending him crashing to the ground. His golden claw stuck fast in her khanjar. With a swift twist, she dislodged it, breaking Saladin's arm.

Dzintara jumped on top of him, unleashing a flurry of punches. The sound of bones cracking beneath her assault.

"Please, spare me!" Saladin begged, blood staining his lips. "I have information you seek."

"You have nothing I need," Dzintara replied, pressing her blade against his throat.

"I know where to find the Knight Commander who killed Muhammad."

"Liar!"

"I swear it."

"Then tell me," she said, pressing the blade further into his throat.

"Let me up, and I'll tell you."

"I will not hesitate to kill you, Saladin."

She stood, khanjar pointed at the aging warrior struggling to stand. His broken arm fell by his side.

"Ah," he wiped at his face with his good arm as he stumbled and looked at his hand, "Stupid girl. You won't stop until we're all wiped out. You still don't understand. Muhammad's death should have been a warning."

"Where?"

He spat blood and reached into his garment, pulling out a rolled parchment the size of a finger, which he then tossed to her. "Here."

The note fell in front of her feet.

Saladin looked her in the eye and pointed to a rock. "Mind if I sit?"

She gave a quick nod, and Saladin limped over, grunting as he sat.

"That note," he said, pointing at her feet, "your brother sent that with one of my messengers. He was looking for you."

Silence fell between them.

"You're lying."

"Read it," he said, pointing.

"When?"

"Some time ago...just after Muhammad was..." Saladin ran his hand across his throat.

She felt her heart pounding like a war drum.

"What does it say?"

Saladin shrugged and smiled. His teeth were stained black.

Dzintara stepped to Saladin and sliced his face. "Enough with the games, old man."

He screamed, holding onto his face. "Your brother marches north in your homeland."

"What does that have to do with the Knight Commander who killed... him?" She demanded.

"The man you seek, Anno the Conqueror of Livonia, he's in your native land. Summoned by the church to convert the tribes. Your brother marches with them. It's all right there," he pointed at the note.

"What else? Now."

"He's been trying to find you. He's said something about... 'He found it'."

Dzintara walked to the note and picked it up with one hand, putting it inside her tunic. Heading towards her horse, she left Saladin in the darkness of the desert night.

"They'll kill you!" Saladin yelled after her in the darkness, "You stupid girl, you should have left our land."

She rode back across the mountain, looking for her men. Those not dead had vanished. Amir was not among the dead. Amir was a survivor — she hoped.

She found the Via Maris and rode into Haifa. At the ports, she asked around for a ship heading to Northumbria. The captain informed her that the ship would make several stops and wouldn't go further into the North Sea. She paid her fare and set sail for home.

CHAPTER ELEVEN

The wooden gates clanked and creaked as they lifted on their chains, and Anno, along with two others, rode out towards the Guaja River. Above the arch window in the north wall, a red cross was carved in stone. The fog thickened as they arrived at the Guaja, riding north along the shoreline. The river rushed past in the white, cloudy darkness. They found a narrowing and crossed with their horses. The beasts neighed and snorted as they pressed through the freezing water.

On the other side, they climbed the steep hill of the Guaja Valley. Anno rode in silence, staring off into the distance. Muhammad's face was etched in his mind, and the words "...your soul will grow weak" echoed through his thoughts.

"Knight Commander, everything all right?" Artur rode up next to him. A tall, slender man with light hair and whiskers for a beard.

Anno looked at him and said, "Yes, all is well."

"You looked as though you were somewhere else," Artur said.

The horses' hooves crunched the snow beneath. Anno remained silent for a moment, then spoke, his voice heavy but distant, "Do you know what they call us in Marienburg?"

"Hm."

"Butchers of Livonia," Anno said.

Artur furrowed his brow. "Convert or defeat by any means."

"Do you ever think about them?"

"Who?"

"The defeated."

"They come in dreams sometimes," Artur said. "Do you, Knight Commander?"

"More so lately than before."

"When they come at night, I remember my reward in paradise that awaits me," Artur said and looked at Anno.

Anno kicked the side of his horse and rode ahead.

Sometime later, heavy snow began to fall, and the wind picked up. The moon slid out from the heavy clouds, silhouetting in the distance a tower.

They came upon the winding dirt road now covered in white, a landmark entry to Turaida Castle. Low-slung barns, farmhouses, and workshops leaned against each other next to the road. Silence surrounded the riders lest the crunch of the snow under the horses' hooves. When they arrived at the gate tower, a guard looked down and called out to them.

"Who goes there at this time of night?"

"It is I, Anno, the Master of the Sword Brotherhood of Livonia, Protector of Cargo for the Merchant's Guild, subjugator of Heathens for his holiness Albert Von Buxtheoven."

"What is your business?"

"To discuss the affairs of expansion."

The profile of the guard disappeared, and the three waited in silence. The snow fell harder. The wind blew stronger.

Eventually, the gate lifted, and Anno and his men entered the castle.

The riders dismounted in the courtyard. A stableboy promptly took their horses to the barn. Left, a stone house in the castle walls housed bishops and servants. They approached a four-story section on the south side, its entrance marked by a heavy iron door with a large circular ring. As the door opened, Hans greeted them and led them inside.

"*Êwir Heiligkeit, ich præsentiere êuch diu Livländischen Brüder von dem Swert,*" he turned and faced the knights and then proclaimed, "Archbishop von dem Riga, Albert von Buxtheoven."

Hans exited the room, leaving them in the presence of a grand stove that soared to the stone house's fourth-floor ceiling. Intricately adorned with multicolored tiles, each one featuring the image of a saint, pope, or bishop—holy men whose unyielding gaze seemed to watch over the room. A lavish dining table took center stage, laden with an assortment of meats, fish, and wine, while a chandelier of flickering candles cast a warm glow from above. Albert sat at the head of the table in his woolen night robe, each shoulder embellished with a golden cross.

The three riders took their hoods off.

"Anno, what brings you out of your castle this cold night," Albert licked his fingers and kept looking at the meat in front of him as he spoke. He crushed and tore a chicken wing and sucked the meat off the bones.

Anno's black hair was thicker on the right. He had a lined face with a groomed beard and mustache that curled at the end. His eyes were deep and dark.

"Albert, we are about to unite with the great order. I will be Provincial Master of the Livonian chapter."

"How wonderful. I didn't prepare a gift for you," Albert mocked.

"I came to discuss our agreement."

Albert looked up and dropped the meat in his hands onto the wooden plate in front of him. The room fell silent, and Albert leaned back, his eyes fixed on Anno.

"Hm, our agreement," Albert grunted.

Anno retrieved a rolled-up parchment from his robe, sealed with oval red wax, the insignia of a sword surrounded by vines and a cross, and around the edges of the seal, a cursive script: *MAGISTRI ETFRM MILICIE CRI DE LIVONIA.*

"Official. Really, nicely done," Albert mocked again.

He tore the seal and read in silence. Anno watched as Albert's eyes squinted in the light, then widened and then narrowed. His mouth transformed into a frown while his eyebrows moved down and together as he read.

When he was done, Albert threw the parchment on top of the food and leaned back.

"Two-thirds," Alberts stabbed himself in the chest with his index finger. "One-third," pointing at Anno and his brothers.

"My men will not fight for you anymore," Anno said. "They won't protect the cargo. Your debt is due. Your levies from the merchants have not made it to my coffers in many moons."

Unfazed, Albert smiled, and Anno retrieved another parchment.

"If there is no renegotiation, then consider this visit a collection visit."

He walked toward Albert and placed it down in front of him. The Archbishop glanced over it briefly.

"Right here, I have a detailed account of all the levies that were supposed to reach the Brotherhood." Anno pointed at the parchment, which contained scribbled line items of levies.

"The discrepancies are at the bottom, Albert."

"What is your intention if I refuse? Kill me?" Albert laughed, glancing at the two brothers who remained hooded by the door.

"Albert, the Holy See is losing in the east. Jerusalem is a lost cause. An embarrassment at best. The church's coffers are empty. The only one that can fund the crusades here in the north is the Teutonic order. It's only a matter of time before the Teutonic order merges with the Templars. A unification of great resources able to wage any war. Are you seeing the picture, Albert?" Anno asked.

"Hm," Albert wiped his lips and returned to tearing away at the chicken in front of him.

"I've heard that to prevent further disgrace, our esteemed Pope will entrust the mission of converting the heathens in these territories to the most capable hands. In this context, 'most capable' invariably refers to those with the fullest coffers." Anno pointed to himself, and Albert slowly refilled his wine goblet.

"I would offer you and your men some wine, but I have a strict rule about being hospitable to swine traitors."

"Albert—"

Albert put up his finger to disrupt Anno. "Shh. Excellency. It's Your Excellency."

He rose, approached the stove, and examined the painted faces on the tiles. He ran his fingers across them.

"The artwork is exquisite. Surprisingly, it was crafted by a herring eater, a convert nonetheless. When we arrived with twenty-three cogs and two hundred of you," he pointed at Anno and his brothers, "this land was barren except for a small ecclesia in the upper Dvina, settled by my uncle, and another in the lower Dvina, also his doing. Despite their backward ways, the herring eaters were surprisingly advanced, with their own currency and intricate trade routes. Nevertheless, we subjugated them, converting the resistant by the sword."

Albert cleared his throat, turned from the stove, and looked back at Anno.

"You—" Albert pointed at Anno "—and your mercenaries," he looked over at the other two by the door, "killers, all receive one-third of the land we subjugated. I, the visionary who saw the opportunity, the one who saw what this could be for the Holy Mother Church, receive two-thirds. That's the order of things. Do you want to know why?"

Silence. The painted eyes of the saints on the stove tiles seemed to blink.

He motioned for Anno to entertain his mockery by answering the question, but Anno stood stoic.

"I'll tell you. You are replaceable. You die in battle, and another one sprouts like a bad weed in a garden. Men like me, however, are God's eyes in the world. We see things that aren't there but ought to be. If I die, it will be another hundred years for someone like me to come along. That's why two-thirds and one-third. Scarcity."

Albert walked over to the table and picked up the parchment. With a big smile, he looked at it, and then he coughed violently and repeatedly until the phlegm was to his satisfaction. He spit on it, rolled it up, and handed it back to Anno.

"That's my answer," Albert said with a grin.

Anno refused to take the bait, and Albert dropped the parchment to the floor in front of him.

"Keep it. Times are changing, Albert."

Anno circled his finger, and the brothers went to the courtyard.

At the threshold, Anno stopped and turned around.

"I know you arrested the shipwright."

"So?"

Anno lowered his chin and looked at Albert.

"That gold and silver you're after is a myth. What's not a myth are the vessels we could use—to protect merchant transports up river."

Albert sucked his teeth and took another bite out of a chicken thigh.

"Let the man go and let him get back to work," Anno said from the darkened doorway.

"The herring eater is in a good, hospitable place. No need to waste your mind worrying about him."

Anno pushed the iron door open, and the cold winter wind howled. The Brothers waited, shivering, as the stableboy retrieved the horses.

"Prepare the men for battle when we get back, Artur," Anno ordered.

"We're coming back?" Artur asked.

"No, we need to survive winter. We're going to collect from the Curonians."

"That would be doing Albert a favor and giving him gold and silver when he is dry," Artur said.

"No. We have lived under Albert's thumb long enough. From this day forward, we conquer lands for the Brotherhood of the Sword of Livonia. No one else."

The stableboy brought back the horse, and the riders left into the winter night across the Guaja.

CHAPTER TWELVE

"God's Blood!" shouted a merchant from his wagon as Dzintara leaped out of the way. Disguised as a man, she wandered Billingsgate Wharf, seeking a ship for her journey home. Clad in plain clothes, she covered herself with a pelt to protect herself from the cold. She used a keffiyeh to wrap her head and conceal her feminine facial features.

The smell of fish filled her nostrils. Fishing boats and ships dotted the wharf, with fishermen hauling their catch onto solid ground. The shouting and cursing of men bargaining rented the air. Wagons pulled by beasts rolled up and down the wharf, carrying barrels, fish, and other cargo.

In the distance, a tapestry of colors filled the horizon as cogs bobbed on the river's surface. These were Single-masted vessels with high forecastles, capable of carrying large amounts of cargo. Flags representing diverse kingdoms, guilds, and leagues fluttered in the breeze. Seagulls squawked and swooped overhead, swooping down and stealing breakfast from unsuspecting traders.

An old man stood scaling and gutting fish on a wooden block.

With precise movements, he made three cuts in each fish, emptied the guts, and tossed the cleaned fish aside.

Dzintara approached, "My good man, any word on the ship sailing to Riga?" she asked in a practiced, masculine voice.

The old man didn't look up from his work. "Nay, she's not on this wharf. Look to Queenhithe Wharf," he said. "She'll be flying the archbishop's colors—red 'n white with a pointed hat and a stick."

She walked towards Queenhithe Wharf, looking past the port reeve collecting wharfage and the cargo-filled wagons rolling by, searching. There it was — a red and white pennant embroidered with a mitre and crosier dancing in the wind.

As she neared, she could make out more of the details. A cog that size could fit two hundred hogsheads of cargo and a crew of thirty. A saint carving served as the ship's figurehead. She spotted a young boy hanging from the mast, patching a damaged sail. Large oars for navigating the harbor slanted down the side into the murky bay water.

On the way, she rehearsed her request, pitching her voice low. "I'm Krists. I'm a physician, and I can be of help to you on your journey."

With each step, she honed her tone until she was within earshot. Dockhands and porters were busy stacking the barrels and crates waiting to be loaded. A disheveled-looking and disorganized crew stumbled down the gangplank.

Scribbling quill to parchment, a red-haired man in a grey wool cloak recorded the cargo, pointing and waving at the deckhands.

"No, no, no. That goes in first," he ordered. Two crew members looked at him and scratched their heads.

"First, barrels. Then the wool," he dictated.

Two men began rolling a barrel onto the gangplank.

"Ah, just a moment," with his chicken-bone fingers, he signaled them to halt. He counted out loud, then sent them on their way. The crew and cargo disappeared into the belly of the ship. Another set of sailors returned empty-handed, and he pointed them to the next load.

Dzintara stood, staring at and studying the men who would get her home. A large, brutish man plowed his way down the gangplank, yelling orders at the crew. He paced back and forth, clenching the pommel of his Carolingian sword. A Rus, or perhaps a Viking, Dzintara thought. The girth of the Rus' wrists was as thick as a woman's thighs. His neck matched the breadth of his head, which shifted like a massive rock. A rather impressive dark beard growing down to his waist obscured his face.

Squaring her shoulders, Dzintara approached the two men. One of them, which one was uncertain, was in charge.

"My good men, I am Krists, a skilled physician. I seek passage to Riga. My skills may come in handy during the voyage. I have experience treating many illnesses and am equipped with ointments and ails."

The Rus eyed her keffiyeh with disgust. "The ship's full," he spat.

The keffiyeh marked her as an outsider. She made sure to expose her face, the scars left by Saladin's blade helping disguise her identity as a woman.

"I'm Varkelins, Ship Master, representing the Archbishop of Riga, Albert Von Buxtheoven," the scribbler interjected, executing a modest bow with one hand secured behind his back.

"We could use a physician on this voyage. The North Sea can be treacherous," Varkelins continued.

"Ship Master, we have no room. The men are already in tight quarters," Gorm argued, rubbing his right eye.

A cut across his face had split his nose in half and left his right eye always open, causing it to dry out.

"The first mate here seems to have forgotten who the vessel belongs to," Varkelins chuckled. With this, the Rus glared, storming off to yell at the crew.

"That man is called Gorm," Varkelins said. "He gathered the

crew to get us back to Riga. He does as I say, and so does the crew. My ship, my rules."

"New crew?" Dzintara asked, concerned.

"Worry not. All will be all right. The ship is protected by the Merchants Guild and the Archbishop,"

Varkelins scrutinized her, his eyes narrowing as he took in every detail.

"Where do you travel from?"

"East. I'm a physician who lived in the Holy Land."

That seemed to please the Ship Master.

"You must have treated many brave souls fighting the infidels," Varkelins said.

"I went where I was needed," Dzintara said, avoiding the subject.

Varkelins waved Gorm over. "Very well, you may join us on our voyage. I indict you as part of the Archbishop's Medicus to aid us on our long journey should any harm befall us. Gorm, this man is now one of us."

Gorm clenched his jaw, his lips pressed together. After a tense silence, he rested a hand on his sword. "Aye, captain," and then turned his back on them.

"Wait. I can help," she blurted.

The Rus turned, glaring at her.

"Your eye. I can help." She reached into her leather sack, retrieving a small bottle. "This should ease the itch. Just two drops," she instructed.

He grabbed her arm, yanking the vial from her hand. As she stumbled forward, he burst into laughter.

"You have the strength of a woman! Let the woman aboard. She poses no threat," Gorm guffawed, ascending the gangplank. On deck, he continued to bellow at the crew.

Varkelins waved him off. "He's strong like an ox, yet as witless as a sack of oats. I've been scouting for a crew to sail us to Riga for some time. He was the only one capable of assembling a crew in these turbulent times."

"Turbulent?"

"We'll just have to make do, no matter how intolerable he is," Varkelins said, avoiding the question.

She mustered a forced smile. "A passage home is a passage home."

Varkelins made his way up the gangplank, his cloak waving back and forth as he walked.

"You'll have to sleep below deck with the crew."

"I don't mind," she said, following closely behind.

They reached the deck and boarded the ship. In the corner, Gorm stood talking to a small crew, his voice inaudible, their expressions tinged with suspicion.

"That cabin is mine," Varkelins nodded toward the stern castle. Swiftly, he pivoted on his heel to look at a dark hole in the deck. "And you are there."

She looked at the dark abyss descending and then gazed past Varkelins at Gorm and his men.

"It's all we have," he said.

Dzintara stared on, ignoring Varkelins. He followed her gaze, "Oh them like I said, needn't you worry about them. Dumb as oats."

She nodded. "Payment?"

"We are running with a light crew, so you may be asked to help out beyond just your physician duties."

"I'm no stranger to the sea," she said.

"Good. We'll settle payment in Riga."

Varkelins smiled and strode off. Gorm and his men watched as he passed them.

The sky turned blood orange, with light gray clouds stretching across the horizon. Dzintara looked out at the wharf stretching along the Thames. She retrieved the note from her pocket and looked at it.

"I'm coming," she said softly to herself.

"Prepare to cast off!" Varkelins shouted from the middle of the deck. Two sturdy deckhands strained in unison to heave the heavy wooden gangplank aboard. They lifted and stowed it on the deck, locking it in place to ensure it wouldn't shift or slide in the rolling seas. Once in place, they bolted the entryway, double-checking the fastenings. One of them gave a final, forceful tug.

Gorm and his men stood in the corner, watching the others' work.

"Well," Varkelins turned to them, "did you not hear the order? Tend to your stations."

They looked at Gorm, and he nodded. His men scattered and joined the others, preparing for sail.

Meanwhile, onshore, a team of riggers inspected the mooring lines. Surveying each rope for signs of wear or weakness. Satisfied with their condition, they began releasing them in a orchestrated sequence, mindful of the cog's balance and the harbor's current.

Back on the cog, the crewmen, lined along the gunwale, deftly caught the slackened lines tossed from shore. They worked with swift efficiency, coiling the heavy ropes. The last mooring line slipped from its dock cleat, signaling departure. The oars splashed as the ship slowly drifted away from the wharf.

Dusk settled in as they sailed downriver. The crew roamed about on deck, tending to their duties. With a deep breath, Dzintara looked down into the dark hole and began her descent.

An off-tune shanty, the clatter of knucklebones on wood, and mixed cheers and gasps from winners and losers alike rented the air.

When she reached the bottom of the stairs, the singing stopped, the fist shaking the knucklebones froze, and they stared. Her stomach fell into knots.

Barrels stacked in columns and tied down. Smell of wet wood, livestock, and piss. Sacks of grains stacked. Casks of salt bound by metal hoops. Makeshift beds of canvas hammocks hung between the columns of cargo. Little nooks and crannies that served as living quarters for the crew. Others who couldn't find enough space slept on deck or one level below with a few animals.

After the silence passed, the men returned to their activities.

She shifted the satchel on her shoulder and walked with her head held high. An heir of confidence in each step. The khanjar at her calf served as her only comfort.

"Saracen...infidel...Christ-killer...crucifier." The whispers followed her like shadows.

A man with a half-smile scar gave her a neutral nod from across the table, where he sat with a young boy. They were sharing a meal, but his eyes lingered on her. He looked up slowly as she approached.

"Wulfric," he said, extending his hand. She hesitated, her gaze shifting to the boy. Ignoring Wulfric's hand, she nodded cautiously in return.

"Dat's Vlad," Wulfric said, tearing off a piece of bread and shoving it in his mouth. The boy looked up at her while slurping a spoonful of soup. She moved forward, seeking a place to rest.

As she passed by other crewmen, they responded to her presence with either a curt "No more room here" or a dismissive spit. Giving up, she walked back to the animal hold, making up a straw bed below a ventilation hatch. Occasionally, the sea mist would spray through the opening.

A nanny goat and kid gnawed at the straw. A couple of chickens roamed aimlessly, looking for bugs. The nanny goat's rectangular eyes stared dumbly as Dzintara hid her satchel and lay her head down.

She heard Gorm coming into the hold. The men greeted him and took him to drink. They sang loudly and gambled. Dzintara closed her eyes and covered herself with hay, hoping that she was invisible, her uneasiness keeping her from sleeping.

From her pocket, she retrieved a small vial filled with a thick, clear liquid, twirling the bottle between her fingers in contemplation. The bottle popped as she uncorked it. Carefully, she placed two drops on her tongue and pocketed the bottle. Within moments, her body became numb, and a warm, blissful warmth enveloped her like rising warm water. She let out a sigh of relief, and her lips quivered with pleasure. Soon after, she fell into a deep sleep.

CHAPTER THIRTEEN

Sea mist sprayed the deck, wetting Ako's weathered face as his creation cut through the waves. Its towering double masts, adorned with vivid sails, stood proudly against the sea's challenge.

Ako, his bronzed face and white beard marking years of seafaring, stood beside the captain and, with a confident hand, directed the course. The captain hollered commands, prompting the crew to swiftly arrange themselves on deck. Together, they navigated the ship into a graceful lean as it turned. This move surprised the nobles on board, dressed in their Riga finery. Clinging to the sides, they admired the ship's agility and responded with applause.

Dressed simply in a brown tunic and goatskin cloak, Ako contrasted with the nobles' colorful attire and fur-lined cloaks. He preferred letting the ship's workmanship shine, choosing not to compete with the wealth displayed by the nobles.

Lamekins joined Ako at his side. Once a freeman warrior and Ako's oldest friend, Lamekins now served as Ako's advisor. His face bore the marks of past battles, and a bald patch on his head circled the spot where he had suffered a head injury years ago.

They watched as a younger man on deck drew a small crowd. Some in the audience listened intently, while others dismissed him. His eyes flicked toward Ako and Lamekins, a silent challenge in his gaze and a menacing smile on his lips.

"Looks like competition is on board," Lamekins remarked.

"I invited him," Ako said without looking at Lamekins.

"What about his father, Hendricks? Was he not available?" Lamekins asked with disdain.

"No, I specifically invited Friedrich."

"Friedrich would gut you and feed ya to the sea if he could," Lamekins warned. "another shipyard would mean competition."

"I hear the yarn Lamekins."

"Then why invite him?"

"Know thy enemies," Ako looked at him and smiled.

"Just give me the word, and I'll throw him overboard."

They both laughed, and Ako patted Lamekins on the back.

"What do you think, Lamekins? Are the nobles of Riga ready?" Ako asked, looking out at Riga's finest strolling on deck and admiring his creation.

"About as ready as baited fish," Lamekins joked with a chuckle.

Ako stood, motioning everyone to gather around. The old shipwright cleared his throat and raised his arms to the sky.

"Two masts instead of one," he spoke confidently, pointing to the additional mast on the deck. "Double the sail area means it can capture more wind and move faster than the traditional single mast. Improved balance and control. Fast enough to make two trips to Novgorod in a week, doubling trade in the summer."

They nodded in agreement as the cog cut through waves.

"This cog, my friends," he said, "is the first of its kind. Faster and larger than any other sailing to or from Riga. This is a new dawn. We can carry three times the cargo of any other vessel. The profits made from these ships will elevate you to the status of kings."

The cog pitched sharply, its bow soaring upwards before plummeting into the trough of the waves. The nobles let out a collective wail, clutching desperately for balance, while Ako stood unfazed.

"This cog will diversify trade, taking us to uncharted lands with exotic cargo and unknown luxuries," Ako proclaimed. "It's a godsend, and the natural world follows the same laws, regardless of human beliefs. Gold recognizes no deity but itself."

His voice carried across the deck and resonated in their minds. Ako paused, allowing the significance of his words to sink in. With a smug grin, he gestured for them to follow as he made his way below deck. A feast waited for them below with the finest ale and wine.

They found their seats at the trestle top. A servant added a log to the stove, ensuring a steady warmth spread through the cargo hold where the feast took place. Ako stood at the head of the table, inhaling the earthy, wood scent of the ship's timbers.

"I love that smell," Ako exclaimed, and his audience let out a loud laughter.

The nobles raised their cups, clinking them, and drank.

"Now, we have three cogs of this kind available, with fifteen more coming in spring. You can reserve yours now with an advance, but it must be a minimum of two cogs," Ako said. "Let's enjoy the feast. When we return to Riga, my accountant will take your orders."

Two musicians in the corner played a lively tune. One plucked the strings of a gittern while the other handled the rebec, creating a joyful melody that filled the ship. They devoured the roasted pig, its mouth stuffed with vegetables, its skin crisped by the fire. Their appetites were impressive.

Ako moved around the table, engaging in conversation. Ako returned to the head of the table as the meal ended and the singing started.

"All right, all right! Quiet down, you bunch of Wends," Ako said jokingly.

They let out a loud laugh.

"Truth is, as you grow older, years slip away like greased eel.

You know me as the shipwright, and if I were to pass, it wouldn't mean much more than that. I don't recall ever inviting any of you to my home. Sunrise, I was at the shipyard, and sundown, I was still at the shipyard," Ako spoke, drawing a light chuckle from the table.

"To truly know someone, you must know their story, and you deserve to know mine," he continued, taking a small sip of ale. "So that we may truly call each other friends."

"My story begins in Lower Saxony. My father was a dry-land merchant, a caravaner. He was so afraid of water that he refused to even drink it," he paused for the expected laughter.

"My mother's origins were a mystery. I spent my youth traveling and trading with my father, from one town to the next, forming connections across Harz. By the time I turned thirteen, I knew everyone who bought and sold in those places. I always thought traveling on foot was too slow and limited in profit. At fourteen, I left my father's house and sailed with a trade crew on the North Sea. That's where I fell in love with cogs. I studied cogs meticulously, their hulls, the wood, creating intricate drawings. One day, in Emden, I met a man who owned a shipyard and needed an apprentice. I filled that role for him. Over the years, he became like a father to me. I kept saving, and he passed away in my twentieth year. I tried to buy his shipyard, but it ended up with his debtors. He was a talented ship-maker, but he was also a drinker and gambler. That's why I rarely indulge in such vices," Ako glanced at the wooden cup and the foamy ale inside.

"I arrived here during the great migration of Saxons. The great Archbishop himself granted me permission for my shipyard. From that day forward, I worked every day to get to create the vessel that you are now aboard. This is my life's work."

He raised his palms, arms outstretched to signal the end of his story. The audience applauded, and Ako bowed. Afterward, he excused himself and went back up to the deck.

Ako walked around the ship, inspecting it with a practiced

eye, his hands tracing the timeworn wood. Soon, Lamekins joined the old man.

"I know that pacing," Lamekins said, in a jolly tone. "We haven't won their gold over yet."

Ako tugged on the ratline. "What is the word down below?"

Lamekins tone turned serious. "Friedrich told them your story is a lie." He waited for Ako to respond, but the old shipwright just kept tugging at the line. "He told all of them you are a freeman passing as a burgher shipwright and that you sold your daughter off to the markets in Kyiv."

"Oh, that makes for quite an interesting feast conversation," Ako said.

"Aye, he is quite drunk and— lucky for us, the nobles are waving him off as an ass."

"That was the plan." Ako winked, and Lamekins couldn't help but laugh. "I knew he couldn't handle his ale."

With their laughter fading, a comfortable silence settled between Ako and Lamekins.

Lamekins finally spoke. "It was foolish to invite him, Ako. What if the rumor gets out? And people find out who you are?"

Ako ran his hands along the gunwale. "Let it. Only Albert knows the truth, and he knows better than to reveal it."

"They will hang you in front of Blackheads, Ako. Letting Friedrich poison the minds of your patrons is dangerous," Lamekins pressed.

"Albert depends on me to keep his coffers full. That, my friend, is a dependable relationship. If Friedrich makes an ass out of himself, no one will take him seriously."

Lamekins scratched his head and followed Ako to the helm, where Ako took control of the rudder.

"Friedrich and Hendricks will continue to tarnish your name until they get what they want."

"My work is one of a kind. It cannot be so easily replaced. Especially by those two," Ako said.

Lamekins let out a sigh. "I'll follow you until the ravens call our names to the beyond, but I hope you know what you're doing."

ALBERT PACED in front of a small army of thirty raggedy, flea-ridden men dressed in the tattered garb of peasants. Among them, some brandished short swords, dull as stone, while others carried long swords far beyond their rightful possession. A few wielded clubs as crude weapons, but most clutched rocks or whatever tools they could lay their hands on. A handful wore whatever makeshift armor they could cobble together.

Albert cast a disgusted gaze upon the disheveled rabble, and fixed his gaze on Hans. "This is the best you could do?"

"This is what we have," Hans replied.

Albert lowered his voice, lest the men hear his words. "This is pathetic...they're all pathetic."

"Send for Anno and his men. They are much more suited," Hans said.

"You fool. Anno would just as quickly turn on us."

Albert stopped pacing and stood in front of the men.

"God has brought us here today. He has brought you here because he has work for you to do. Our task today is to arrest the shipwright and bring him in front of God for justice."

One mercenary shouted out. "Hah! Quite the flowery speech, ain't it? But words won't fill our bellies, mate. What about payment?"

Albert looked at the man. He slowly approached, and the flea-ridden gang parted like the Red Sea. Albert stopped a hair-breadth from the man, looking him up and down. Dirt covered the man's face, and his teeth were yellow and decayed. A frost-covered steel chest plate covered his upper body, which was one of the few with armor. His hands were thick, and he wore shoes made of goatskin. Albert noticed a marking on the right side of his ear.

"You're a heathen," Albert accused.

"A freeman. And a fucking tither."

Albert scanned the other men.

"In fact, most of us here are," their leader said.

Albert shook his head in disbelief. Hans shrugged. "I found men who were willing to fight."

"God bless me," Albert cried, burying his face in his hands.

"Why don't you cut the fancy talk and get to the point," their leader spit on the ground.

"This is a mission from God—"

"The God we all serve comes from the ground. Gold and silver. So, tell us how much."

Albert edged his face close to the man's. They could hear the whistle of each other's breath.

"Five pieces of gold per man for bringing him in. Alive. Nothing if he dies."

"Wasn't so hard now, was it? Save all of us a bit of time and breath."

"If you betray me, you and your families will die of starvation this winter," Albert said.

Men laughed, while Albert scanned room, confused.

"Why are they laughing?" Albert asked.

"These men and their families haven't eaten in weeks. They're reduced to hunting rats and rodents. They have nothing to lose."

"Good," said Albert.

He scanned the men again, hoping for a transformation. Realizing there was none, he resigned with a dull sigh before trudging towards the cathedral door. Hans made his way toward their leader and handed him a rolled parchment sealed with the archbishop's seal.

CHAPTER FOURTEEN

Sandy beaches dotted the shoreline at the river's mouth, interspersed with stony outcrops and a low stretch of cliffs. The cold, brackish water mixed with the river's freshwater with the salty sea. Thin sheets of ice shone in the sun atop the water.

The massive two-mast cog was a strange sight among the untouched barren birch and green pine. The Dvina was wide and meandering. Frozen-over bogs rested just inland from the shore. Slowly, the wind dragged them up the river.

"Steady. Keep an eye out," Ako ordered.

A longboat emerged from the distant haze, Ako, and the captain watched its approach. The karve, floating high on the water, glided past them, its gunwale smeared with red. The small boat appeared abandoned.

"Curonians?" asked the nervous captain.

"Hm. As long as the wind is with us, we will be fine," Ako replied.

Up ahead, the river bent out of sight. They drifted slowly upriver around the bend, the deck quiet except for the occasional groan of the masts. Desolate, snow-topped marshland stretched along either shore. The wind whipped through the tall grass, sending ghostly whispers of snow flurries into the air. Their breaths smoked in the cold. The captain squeezed the rudder while Ako fixated on the flapping sails as the wind softened. The stillness of the land and its icy beauty haunted Ako.

As the last light of day faded, the city emerged in the distance. The water bustled with activity as fishermen pulled their filled karves to shore, the oars of bateaux slicing through the icy waters in perfect rhythm. The small vessels bobbed and weaved, dwarfed by the massive two-mast cog.

The eroding stone walls and towers of Riga loomed ahead, a bulwark against the dangers of the land. The city gate buzzed with activity as merchants bustled in and out, their carts and wagons loaded with goods. As the cog approached the port, a sea of sails obscured the skyline. Seamen shouted as they hoisted their cargo.

The shipyard stood next to the bustling port outside the city walls. Three docks held two-masted cogs in various stages of construction. Ako's skilled builders moved with purpose, astride scaffolding and planks, putting the final touches on one of the two-masted cogs. Workers stood on the deck, holding tight to the thick rope as they raised the mast and secured it into place.

Another worker, his face glistening with sweat, was meticulously carrying buckets of linseed oil from a large cauldron simmering over an open fire. He stepped cautiously, carefully carrying the buckets of linseed oil to the hull to ensure none of the precious oil was wasted. With a practiced hand, he dipped a wide-bristled brush into the bucket and applied the oil to the hull. The brush strokes were smooth and even, coating the wood in a protective layer. On the second berth, men labored, carrying lumber to frame the next cog, still in its infancy.

The nobles, wiping sleep from their eyes, ascended half-drunk from the belly of the ship and turned to watch Riga approach.

Suddenly, chaos erupted. Men in plain clothes and some in armor, brandishing weapons, stormed the dock of the shipyard. The air reverberated with a fierce war cry. The nobles hurried to the gunwale, calling to each other in surprise.

The small army attacked the builders on the berth, causing them to fall to the ground or be cast into the freezing river. Panic spread as the violence escalated.

"The shipyard is under attack," Ako screamed at Lamekins, grabbing him. "Ensure that none of the nobles are harmed."

"Including the bastard?"

"Including Friedrich," Ako nodded.

"Who is attacking our shipyard?" Lamekins asked.

"Hendricks." Ako stood watching the bloody scene unfold.

The skeleton of the cog under construction suddenly went up in flames. Builders jumped into the freezing river to escape the fire.

"Ako, your cogs!" Lamekins called out.

Ako pointed to a berth near the city gates. "Get these men to safety!"

The oars dropped into the murky water, and the ship began to drift towards the berth.

The gangplank hit the ground with a thud, and the nobles disembarked from the ship, eyes fixed on the unfolding attack further down the river at the shipyard.

Ako gathered the crew, including Lamekins, and they moved toward the battle. As they approached the shipyard's entrance, the leader of the unruly group marched toward them with fervor. "Ako, the shipwright, you are under arrest!"

"What in hell is the meaning of this destruction?" Ako demanded.

The man squared up, coming inches from Ako's face. He hawked and spat to the side before retrieving a parchment scroll from his person. In response, Lamekins unsheathed his Carolingian. Ako recognized the weathered, faded markings on the leader's face, a sign of his tribe.

"Read it for yourself." He shoved the parchment at Ako, who threw it to the ground.

"Do you know who I am, you fool? I am under the protection of the archbishop. You will hang for this."

"You must have forgot to pay him 'cause he be the one who sent us."

Suddenly, an explosion rocked the docks. The group jolted in shock, instinctively taking cover. Melted tar splattered across the victims. They screamed in agony, some leaping into the river.

In a decisive moment, their leader seized the opportunity and grabbed Ako firmly by the arm. Suddenly, a resounding crash echoed as scaffolding crumbled into the water. The workers, enraged by the destruction of their year-long labor, surged towards the aggressors in a fierce retaliation. They wielded their hammers with deadly intent, bones cracking under the brutal force of their blows. Others frantically doused the spreading flames with buckets of water.

Dragging Ako away from the unfolding chaos, the leader seemed oblivious to the pandemonium behind them. Ako's tear-filled eyes remained locked on his burning masterpieces, witnessing the destruction of his life's work. A spray of blood splattered across Ako's face. Lamekins severed the arm of the man, pulling Ako away. Then he delivered a second blow, cleaving the man's torso open. The leader fell to the ground, lifeless.

With their leader dead, the remaining attackers redirected their fury towards Lamekins. They advanced with their dull swords and battered clubs, ready to fight for their prize.

Ako seized the opportunity and bolted. Glancing back, he watched as a blade pierced Lamekins' side. The old seafarer heard his oldest friend's war cry for the last time.

Ako paused for a fleeting moment to catch his breath. Dead and wounded bodies littered the berths, and flames painted the dusk with a mix of black smoke and the blood-orange glow of the descending sun. As he started to run again, he plowed into two fighters locked in a struggle.

His foreman and an attacker faced off, exchanging punches. They grappled and tumbled to the ground, locked in a brawl. Ako fought his way out and crawled away from the chaotic tangle.

The foreman, now on top, grabbed a nearby beetle and struck

his attacker in the head, continuing to strike until the man's head cracked open.

Ako watched, witnessing all his hard work going up in flame. Time slowed, movements halted, and screams became distant echoes.

"Come with me," the foreman shouted, reaching for his hand.

Ako grabbed the foreman's hand. Together, they sprinted toward the workshop. The foreman took a sword strike to his side, but his leather tunic absorbed most of the impact. He stayed behind to fend off the attacker while Ako continued his desperate escape.

Ako pushed the door to the workshop open and stood there in the darkness, his heart pounding. He crawled beneath one of the cog skeletons and lay on his back. Overhead, the tall windows emitted a soft orange glow. Nearby, coals and embers from the smelter dimmed, filling the workshop with a fading, reddish light.

He found solace in the world of cogs that surrounded him. For a moment, he forgot about the turmoil beyond the workshop walls. As he closed his eyes, he could almost hear his builders at work, the rhythmic pounding of mallets against wood, and the craftsmen shaping timber into vessels. Tears flowed from his eyes once again.

Hans' voice echoed through the workshop. "Find it!"

Ako watched from his hiding place as men ransacked his scriptorium.

"Where is it?" Hans yelled.

"We've looked everywhere," a guard responded.

"It has to be here. This is the place Ako would keep it."

Hans scurried out of the building while the men kept searching. Ako waited and waited. Soon, he drifted off to sleep.

CHAPTER FIFTEEN

Igh-pitched shrieks and shouting roused Dzintara from her elixir-induced sleep. As she sat up, the kid goat chewed on her bed. Their eyes met, and a soft bleat followed.

She grunted, scratching the kid's head right between its emerging horns.

"Ahoy, friend."

Threats and screams continued from above. She fixed her keffiyeh.

"Don't eat my bed," she playfully instructed the kid.

She received a mocking bleat in response, then walked out of the animal hold. Passing sleeping crew members, she heard Gorm's snores amidst the cargo and continued up to the main deck.

The rigid North Sea wind ripped through her pelt as she hit the main deck. The morning light revealed a gruesome scene. The young boy, Vlad, if she recalled correctly, was pinned over a dingy, his backside raw and exposed. His tormentor, a lanky, bearded man, was whipping the boy with all his strength. Among the crew, a clear divide had formed. One group of men was laughing and cheering. The other group was shouting for the punishment to stop.

"I'm in charge when Gorm is gone. What I say goes!" the second mate shouted, his voice cutting through the morning air.

"Release him. He's had enough," Wulfric demanded. His voice held a veiled threat. "One more lash and you'll regret it."

"Where is the Ship Master? Where's Grom?" another crew member yelled.

"Dare you challenge my authority?" The second mate shouted, delivering another brutal stroke with the salt-stiffened rope of the cat-o'-nine-tails. The whip stained a bloody red and left the boy's arse covered in welts and small, claw-like cuts.

Wulfric sprang into action, pulling a knife from his girdle, pointing it directly at the second mate, and rushing forward. Three other men tackled Wulfric to the ground, sending his blade skittering across the deck.

The entire crew swiftly drew their own knives, turning on each other and sizing each other up. Silence fell as the two factions waited for the other to make a move. Only the rhythmic crash of waves against the hull dared to break the tense hush.

Dzintara eyed the mate carefully. Wispy strands of blonde hair littered his face while a compact sword hung at his side.

The whip connected with the naked ass, again drawing more blood.

The boy screamed weakly.

"Stop this right now. You're going to kill that child," she interjected before the crew slit each other's throats.

"He fell asleep on watch," the mate scourged the ass again.

"Enough," Varkelins ordered from the entrance of his cabin.

The mate spit in his direction, and the wind carried it at an impressive distance. His eyes looked directly at Varkelins as his whip came down in defiance.

"Olaf, I said enough. Let the boy up. That's an order." Varkelins marched forward.

"Ship master, when Gorm sleeps, I am in charge," he stated, pointing the whip at Varkelins.

Varkelins halted and raised his hands. He took a couple of careful steps toward Olaf. "Stop, Olaf." His voice quivered. "My ship. My command."

Olaf delivered another heavy blow.

"Take another step closer, and you may find yourself overboard," Olaf threatened.

Dzintara bent down and calmly touched her leg where the khanjar was.

Olaf raised the stiffened rope again, and an idiotic smile appeared on his toothless mouth.

"Don't," Varkelins made one last attempt. Olaf's faction turned to Varkelins in unison, their eyes feral, knives in their hands. Varkelins backed away, retreating to his chamber.

The mast creaked gently as waves rocked the boat. The two factions now faced each other, awaiting Olaf's next move.

"Olaf, what in the hell is going on? I'm trying to sleep." Gorm emerged from below, rubbing the sleep from his eyes.

"The boy fell asleep on watch."

"Water," Gorm ordered.

One of Olaf's crew ran and retrieved a tankard filled with water. The crew lowered their knives, and some sheathed them.

"Where is the Ship Master?" Gorm asked.

Olaf pointed to the stern castle.

Gorm tilted the tankard back and chugged the water, spilling it down the side of his face. He let out a loud, satisfied belch, followed by a morning shiver.

Gorm marched to Olaf and took the whip. "Gimme that."

As Olaf watched, a dumb grimace on his face, Gorm drew his arm back, delivering a blow to the boy's already bleeding backside. The boy barely moved and did not make a sound. He cocked his arm for another blow as Dzintara grabbed his forearm, preventing his swing.

"Enough. You've made your point," she said, holding his arm

with both hands. "Enough. He's past reason. He won't even feel it."

Gorm looked down at the child, noting that his arse had nearly been skinned. He nodded as if satisfied and dropped the scourge.

"Get him up," Gorm ordered.

Two crew members rushed forward, shoving Olaf out of the way. Gently, they pulled the boy to his feet as a third pulled up the boy's bloodied leggings and tied them. Then they took the boy below, casting dirty looks back on Olaf.

"All of you, back to your duty at once," Gorm said to the crew.

"The boy..." Wulfric said. "He needs tending."

Gorm slapped his palm with the flogger. "You want to be next?"

Wulfric and the crew dispersed to attend to their duties, pulling the ropes on the sail, washing the head from shit and piss, and keeping a lookout. They murmured and whispered amongst themselves.

All was not well.

BLOOD SOAKED the back of his drawers. Moving painfully, Vlad slashed and stabbed the sack of oats with his small blade. The kid goat stared at him, chewing his hay. Vlad squared up with the kid, nubs of horn barely visible on its head.

"I'll kill you," he threatened, deepening his voice.

The kid just chewed, looking at the boy. He pointed the tip of the knife at the kid as if to intimidate it. The young goat responded with a bleat.

In a fit of rage, he limped back towards the sacks of oats, his movements neither precise nor methodical, stabbing the sacks in a fit of fury. The nanny goat, alerted by the commotion, ambled in front of her kid, displaying her long horns.

"Let me look at your bruises," Dzintara interrupted the standoff.

Vlad hid the blade and looked at her.

"It's ok. I want to help you." She walked by the goat and kid, retrieved her leather sack from the straws of her bedding, and showed him the contents.

"I have medicants that will take the pain away and help it heal."

Dzintara took in the wounded sacks and the spilled oats.

"He's shit," she said.

"They both are," the boy replied.

"Come here. Let me help."

She stepped towards him, and he pulled his blade, head cocked.

"It's ok. Look."

She removed her keffiyeh, her hair disheveled, the scars on her cheeks visible.

"Some bad people did this to me. I had someone help me heal. Otherwise, it would have been much worse."

The boy lowered his blade.

"Vlad, right?" she asked.

He gave a nod of confirmation.

"I'm Krists."

With pudgy little hands, he clumsily sheathed his blade into a shoddy scabbard that bore the unmistakable marks of his childish craftsmanship. Glass bottles clinked as Dzintara retrieved a couple of them, along with a rectangular object swathed in leather.

"I need you to drop your drawers."

The boy turned and peeled his pants off, tearing away at the crust of dried blood clinging to his skin. She left and returned with a wooden bowl filled with water. With a gentle, motherly touch, she washed his wounds and carefully patted him dry with a separate cloth. Satisfied, she unwrapped the leather package. A blob of animal fat glistened. She took a chunk of the fat, rubbing it on his bottom as he hissed and exhaled loudly.

"How did you get in with this crew?"

"I ran away. But this," he pointed up to the deck, "It's not forever. Soon, I will make my own gold and answer to no one," he said, attempting to sound brave and tough. "What about you?"

"I'm headed back home."

"Why?" Vlad asked, turning to catch her eyes.

"My brother is in trouble," she said.

"Are you gonna save him?"

"I will try."

"Why did you leave home?" He grimaced in pain and then nodded for her to continue. "Did you run away or something?"

"Not exactly. When I was a young...boy, like yourself, I was given away by my father."

"Me too," he said, with a slight tone of pride in his voice, as if the discarded ones belonged together.

She popped one of the glass bottles open. A warm, earthy, and bitter scent, with hints of ginger and pepper, masked the smells of unwashed men and animal dung.

"That smells good."

She handed him the bottle, and he sniffed it over and over, holding onto it with two hands.

"It'll keep the wound from getting sour."

She made him turn around again and rubbed the unguent into his scored flesh. Then, she retrieved a roll of cloth from her leather bag.

"I need you to turn with me so we can wrap this cloth around you."

The boy turned with his trousers at his legs. His boyhood was half mutilated.

"What faith are you?"

He looked down, and his face turned red and covered his mangled penis with his hands.

"That's not what you think," he said, deepening his voice.

She worked in silence, skillfully wrapping the cloth around his thigh, using it as an anchor for support. The boy's eyes remained fixed on her face, observing her every move. With newfound courage, he straightened his posture and dropped his hands as if the mutilation he bore was a badge of courage for the discarded ones like him. Like her.

"I killed the man who did this to me."

"You look tough. Strong."

"I am. That's why Gorm chose me."

He slowly rotated as she wrapped him.

"The dead man bought me in the Kyiv market. He was afraid I would get older and sleep with his women. One night, he held his knife in the fire and came for me. He got the first cut in but didn't finish. I took a flaming log and beat him. When he dropped the knife, I stabbed him in the face until he had none."

Vlad mimicked his actions as he turned.

"You made it out without getting caught, then?" Dzintara asked.

"Aye."

He rotated one last time, and his ass was wrapped in cloth. Dzintara packed up her things as Vlad pulled up his drawers and tied them with a piece of old rope.

"It doesn't hurt quite as much anymore," he said in boyish relief and then caught himself. He straightened and pushed his chest out. "Thank you. Wait here."

Vlad disappeared into the crowd of oat bags and salt barrels. Crouching, Dzintara wrapped her headscarf around her head and watched as the nanny goat chewed along with her kid. The boy returned.

"Here." In his extended hand he held a blade with a wooden handle. "I made this. Take it."

"I can't take that. That's yours."

"We're men of the sea. We return good deeds and punish bad ones."

He forced his hand towards hers, and she took the blade. The wooden handle had a snake carved into it, its mouth open and tongue flickering.

"What about you?"

"I still have one." He reached down and pulled his own dagger from the shoddy scabbard.

"I carved that," he said, pointing at the knife in her hand. "Look at mine."

He opened his small hands. His palms were covered in scars, and his nails were black with dirt. A lion was carved into the handle of his blade, face forward and mouth open, teeth bared.

"I have the lion, and you have the serpent. This makes us brothers."

"Brothers," she whispered, thinking sadly about her own brother. He'd been about the same age as Vlad. Dzintara swallowed hard and turned her face for a moment lest Vlad see her tears.

Vlad put his knife into his breeches and extended his small hand. She smiled and accepted.

CHAPTER SIXTEEN

Vlad's urgent shaking roused Dzintara from her deep slumber. Groggily, she blinked, her mind shrouded in the haze of sleep. Vlad's boyish face hovered over her, his expression worried. Beside her bed lay the small vial.

"What?" she asked, her confusion evident.

He pointed at her stomach, his mumbles forming into words. "You're bleeding."

"What?" she asked again, bewildered, then glanced down between her legs. Dark blotches of blood seeped through her trousers.

"Shit!" She jolted awake. "Get me some water."

Vlad hurried off, and while he was gone, she retrieved a piece of cloth from her satchel and grabbed a handful of straw. She wrapped the straw with the linen and placed the makeshift pad between her legs to absorb the blood. When he returned, she was adjusting the straw rag between her legs.

"Here," he said, handing her a leather sack.

She poured water on her trousers, rubbing aggressively where the blood had seeped through. "Vlad, you can't say anything to anyone."

"Brothers' code."

She stopped rubbing and locked eyes with him. "Not even Wulfric."

Vlad nodded slowly, and she resumed rubbing.

"Did someone cut you?"

"No. It just happens sometimes."

"When that bastard cut me, I bled sometimes, too," he said solemnly. "I won't tell anyone. It's our secret."

"Thank you," she said.

"Where the fuck are you, Vlad?" Olaf's screech echoed from somewhere in the ship's belly.

"Aye, coming," Vlad answered, then hurriedly left the animal hold.

From her satchel, she retrieved another pair of trousers, pulling them on as an additional layer. Next, she grabbed a thick woolen cloak and draped it over her shoulders, cinching it at the midsection. With a cautious glance downwards, she checked for any signs of blood but found none.

Dzintara emerged onto the main deck, where she saw the crew scattered about, some resting, others toiling under the sun's relentless gaze. Their breaths steaming from the cold. She swept her eyes across the endless stretch of deep blue sea, noting the clear sky peppered with wispy clouds. The sun blazed above, showering everything with a fierce, golden light that reflected sharply off the water's surface and warmed her face in the icy weather.

Across the deck, two men worked together, pulling on ropes to adjust the sail's position, while another tested the durability of a pulley with repeated strikes of a beetle. Aloft in the mast, a lookout scanned the horizon for any signs of danger.

Vlad first distributed wooden bowls to each crew member, ensuring everyone had their own before he began to serve. With a large pot of thin fish soup in hand, he ladled the steaming broth into the waiting bowls, each sailor holding theirs steady as he made his rounds. Once the pot was empty, Vlad returned below deck to fetch another batch, ensuring all were fed.

"Piss off," Olaf said, "don't make me get the flogger again."

He laughed and waved an invisible scourge at the boy. The others joined in, waving the invisible whip. Vlad bent down and picked up the bowls.

"Go on and get the man's food," Olaf ordered, and Vlad disappeared, returning a moment later with more bowls of stew.

Some of the crew were shooting glares in her direction. Vlad's eyes drilled into hers with a silent message as he tapped his waist.

She looked up and caught the watch-keep's gaze. He resumed scanning the open sea. Varkelins' cabin door was shut. The huddled glares grew more frequent. Quick bursts of laughter escaped Olaf and the men. A glare. A whisper. Then one stood, his body made of stone and jaw cut like marble.

His eyes locked on her. He advanced, each step measured and unhurried. Clad in her worn trousers, she felt the weight of her khanjar nestled against her calf. As he drew nearer, his smile stretched wide, revealing gleaming blackened gums. A scar wrapped around his neck. His hand rested on the nub of his short sword.

She looked around for Gorm, but he was nowhere to be seen. Marble-jaw stopped in front of her and looked down, smiling. From the corner of her eye, she saw Vlad quietly pull his knife. Olaf watched from a distance, grinning. The curtains in Varkelins' window split open.

One chance. That's all she had. Once they saw the khanjar, the element of surprise would be gone. To her left, a few seafarers had gathered. No iron or steel, just their fists.

She blew her warm breath into her hands. If their blades faltered in the biting cold, she would have a moment of opportunity. Yet if their steel was slick with fat, the advantage would belong to them.

"Top of the morning," said Marble-jaw.

Her keffiyeh flapped in the wind. Her eyes connected with his. Predator to prey. The question was, which was which?

"Nice day, ainnit?" he said.

"Indeed," she paused, "I hope it stays that way."

"Me and some mates over there were just chatting."

"Probably none of my affair," she said.

"Oh, but it is. For starters you haven't paid your keep."

"My business is with that man," she pointed towards Varkelins' cabin, seeing him peeking through the window curtains." Not with you."

"Fuck all, you're on Gorm's vessel," Marble-jaw said.

Varkelins shut the curtains at that moment. Just as she feared, the mutiny had begun. Gorm and his crew were not sailors but pirates. She knew it was only a matter of time before they would kill her. There was nowhere to run and nowhere to hide. Her homeland was a few days away.

"There was a dog where I come from. Every day, this dog barked at everyone behind the fence. It was big with a deep, loud bark. One day, a pack of roaming dogs walked by, and it barked like always. Except, this specific day the owner left the gate open. The pack of roaming dogs tore it apart. To pieces," she said. The crew was hanging on her every word.

"So what?"

"You remind me of that dog."

Blood rushed to his face as the silence broke and the deck with laughter. He tried to unsheathe his sword, but it stuck in the cold.

"Pork lard's a blessing. Let me show you," she said.

With a swift motion, she pulled her khanjar and unsheathed it, and the blade tasted a prick of blood at his throat. Marble-jaw raised his hands from his steel. Gorm stumbled out from below deck and watched.

"What do I owe you?," she spat, looking at Gorm.

"For Christians, ten gold pieces to Riga," Gorm said.

"I mean to speak to the Ship Master, Varkelins."

"I speak for both."

"Is this a mutiny?"

Some of the crew looked confused, so she thought perhaps not all of them were in on it.

Gorm drew forth his Norse blade, its design favoring the slash and cut over the thrust, a testament to the lethal elegance of its purpose. Down the center, the blood groove ran the length of the steel, a subtle concession to weight and grace, marrying strength and suppleness in a deadly union. Gorm admired it, lifting it to the morning sun.

"But that's not the price for you. For Saracens, there's an additional fee: fifteen pieces of gold. It's a protection fee. That's so you don't get accidentally thrown overboard."

Olaf cackled, tilting his head back and forth like a chicken.

Then, silence fell on the deck. Sails shuddered and snapped above them all.

"I must go below for the payment," she said into the wind, "but he comes with me." She pivoted her wrist, severing Marble-jaw's baldric. His sword clattered to the ground, accompanied by the graceless fall of his trousers pooling about his ankles. The crew roared.

"Enough!" thundered Gorm, brandishing his sword. At once, silence fell. He turned his sword towards Dzintara. "Take off your mask. Show me your face."

At that moment, she decided Gorm would die by her khanjar. "I seek no trouble with you. My tribe comes from a different place. My purpose is to get home."

Gorm moved forward, his sword aimed at Dzintara, who had her khanjar at Marble-jaw's throat.

"Gorm, this was not our agreement," Varkelins said, pleading from the safety of his cabin door.

"Take one more step, and I'll cut his throat." Dzintara pressed her blade against Marble-jaw's jugular.

Gorm stopped.

"Enough! That man has business with me, not you." Varkelins said desperately.

Ignoring Varkelins, Gorm kept his eyes on Dzintara.

"Let him go. You and I settle your debt. Like men," Gorm said, slapping his sword against his chest.

Dzintara sent the severed baldric skittering with a swift kick, casting it down into the yawning maw. Trousers around his ankles, Marble-jaw shuffled toward the refuge of Olaf.

"Let's settle it then," she said, accepting the challenge.

A hush fell over the crew as they awaited the opening gambit, each eye fixed intently on their adversary.

In that instant, a sharp blare pierced the air. The crew turned as one to regard the watchman.

"Wends! Starboard!" the watchman yelled and blew the horn again.

Their necks swiveled starboard; a smudge of darkness materialized on the far-flung blue horizon. Steadily, it grew, looming ever closer, a shadow that seemed to defy the very limits of distance and time.

CHAPTER SEVENTEEN

"Prepare for battle!" Gorm shouted.

Olaf's crew scrambled, retrieving Gorm's armor from below, and strapped him into it. Dzintara, meanwhile, looked out at sea, watching as the black dot on the horizon grew larger.

"We must head toward land," Dzintara shouted to the men, trying to reason with them. They ignored her.

Gorm pivoted toward the oncoming vessel, still a smudge in the distance. He smiled and took a deep breath. It was a breath of pleasure as if he could already taste the carnage. "Helm to starboard."

The bow of the cog swung in the waves, aligning with the dark stain, its prow pointed straight ahead as the crew watched with bated breath.

Gorm looked at the crew. "Don't stand there gawking. Prepare yourselves for battle!"

Varkelins emerged from his cabin. "Are you mad? We head for the shore!"

"Any man that stops working will be put to death," Gorm said, glaring at Varkelins.

"No," Varkelins said. "I demand you cease and head for the shore"

"Olaf split the men port and starboard."

Dzintara saw fear mixed with excitement and imagined victory in the crew's eyes. They reminded her of the young men raiding crusader convoys.

"Listen to me! Sail inland. You cannot do this. This is insanity. The Wends skin people alive." Varkelins insisted.

Gorm looked at Varkelins, sneering. "They no longer heed your commands."

"We are outnumbered! Look at these men. They are not trained for battle. They have beetles and hammers for swords. For God's sake, that's a boy, not even a man," Varkelins said, pointing at Vlad.

Gorm ignored him. He took control of the rudder, skillfully adjusting it to capture the wind. The sails billowed, propelling the cog through the waters. The crisp air of the strait between the North Sea and Kattegat soured, tainted by the stench of sweat and vomit as tensions mounted.

In a desperate bid, Varkelins raised his voice, "Gorm, I'll pay double!"

"Glory cannot be bought." Then Gorm let out a war cry, drawing his Norse sword from its scabbard. The watchman sounded the ship's horn in a long, drawn-out melody.

"I will pay three times the original price and one-tenth of revenue from the cargo!"

Gorm peered at Varkelins with disdain, as if regarding a loathsome, wriggling creature.

Varkelins was begging, tears in his eyes. "You can't do this."

"Pathetic." Gorm pulled the rudder right and gave the order to disengage. The crew swung the sails, and within moments, the smudge was stern side.

Varkelins looked up at Gorm. "Thank you."

Gorm spit in Varkelins' face. "I take command from here on out."

Dzintara scanned the crew, watching Olaf and Gorm. She walked over to the mast and climbed the rope to the top. She shimmied past the watchmen and looked out towards the smudge. Squinting, she realized the smudge wasn't a ship. She locked eyes with watchmen who smiled and winked. As she climbed back down in silence, she knew it was a matter of time before Gorm killed Varkelins and her, seizing full control of the ship.

CHAPTER EIGHTEEN

Lamekins lay dying, bathed in the fading glow of the fires. Gently touching his side, he moaned. His fingers were sticky and wet.

"Lamekins, tu vecais muļķi, you old fool." He laughed softly to himself.

He closed his eyes to greet death. But death wouldn't come.

In the distance, the attackers scavenged through the corpses with the ruthless greed of vultures, finishing the wounded.

With an annoyed grunt, Lamekins gave up trying to die and opened his eyes. He found the foreman's soot-covered face staring into his own.

The foreman signaled for silence, then gestured towards the brigands. He pulled Lamekins to a stack of pine planks for cover.

"I thought you were dead," the foreman whispered. Blood covered his face, and his ear was missing.

"Your ear," Lamekins said lamely.

"Aye, forget the ear! We must haste to the woodland. Word was sent to the Curonians."

"I'm meant to die here," Lamekins rebutted.

"Clearly not, you had your chance. Now let's go."

"They won't help us," Lamekins whined.

"Ah, you pathetic shit, you ain't dying here."

The foreman grabbed Lamekins's hands and started dragging him. Lamekins rolled over and struggled to stand. He put his arm around the foreman, and they made their way past the dead.

It was the coldest hour of the night. The two men huddled under a tree in the forest near the road to Riga. Out of the darkness, three men appeared. The foreman started from his half-sleep. They were Curonians. Lamekins squinted and watched the foreman approach them. He was half unconscious or half asleep; he wasn't sure. The cold had slowed his bleeding. Then everything went black.

When he awoke, the first rays of light were reaching across the land, like split arrows darting through the trees.

"The Curonians will help us," the foreman said, wiping his nose.

Lamekins moved his lips, but no words came. The foreman shook his head in confusion.

"I said the Curonians will help us! They will take us by karves in three moons. They'll come back for us. You just have to stay alive."

Lamekins moved his mouth as if he were speaking, but no words came.

"What?" the foreman rubbed his missing ear. "I must be deaf."

Lamekins laughed, and the foreman hit him in the ribs.

"You bastard."

"Never too broken for a good laugh," Lamekins said, chuckling.

"We have to get to warmth and a place where I can wash your wounds."

"Only place is the shipyard. Any other place is too dangerous," Lamekins said.

"Lamekins, you're dumber than this rock. We can't go back there."

"What is your suggestion?" Lamekins said, holding on to his

side. "The estate is too far. We can't go into the city. The shipyard is burned to the ground. No one will be guarding a pile of rubble."

"True," the foreman admitted.

Sneaking through the forest, they made their way back and staying off the main road.

CHAPTER NINETEEN

Since the mutiny, Dzintara had done her best to steer clear of Gorm. Whenever he caught sight of her, there was murder in his eyes. Wulfric had made it his duty to watch her back, setting up his hammock near her straw bed.

For days, she had forgone her elixir, doing her best to sleep with one eye open. Her body ached from fatigue, her muscles stiff with exhaustion, but she fought it, listening to the creak of the ship, to Wulfric's steady breathing nearby.

But tonight, the exhaustion was relentless. Her eyelids grew heavier with each breath, her mind slipping into a haze. A muffled sound—footsteps?—reached her ears, but her body refused to stir. The darkness closed in.

A sudden weight pressed against her chest.

Her eyes snapped open.

Gorm's face loomed inches from hers, his filthy beard swinging over her, his fat fingers digging into her throat. "You swine," he yelled as spit flew from rotting yellow teeth.

She gagged and struggled for air as his grip tightened. She grabbed his wrists, pulling them, struggling to breathe. She heard Olaf's high screech of laughter and saw Varkelins, a sword to his back.

"Saracen scum!" Gorm's thumbs pushed into her throat.

Her vision swam as she fumbled for the khanjar Just as her fingers wrapped around the hilt, something hot and wet sprayed her face, Gorm's grip loosened, and his eyes widened, a blade with a lion's handle sticking out of his throat. Blood pulsed from the wound. She gasped for air as Gorm collapsed.

She sat up and saw Vlad lying on the hay, Olaf pulling the tip of his sword from the boy's stomach. Turning, Olaf faced Wulfric, who pointed a knife in his direction in a failed attempt to save Vlad. Wulfric's knife was no match for Olaf's sword.

"You're next," Olaf said as he walked toward Wulfric.

The crew, whose feet seemed nailed to the deck boards, gazed at the boy's body. Before anyone else moved, Dzintara pulled her khanjar and leaped at Olaf. The decorated blade went through Olaf's neck like a knife through fat. She twisted and pulled. The steel crunched and ripped at the cartilage. He gagged some nonsense, and then blood bubbled from his lips. He fell over, dead.

She freed the khanjar from Olaf's neck and knelt next to Vlad. Muhammad's procedure was carved into her brain. She ripped his shirt open. "Clean the wound."

Her hands trembled as she looked around for water but found nothing. "You, get me water now," she ordered.

Her hands wrapped around the boy's neck softly, feeling for life. His heartbeat was faint. "Tie off the wound to stop the bleeding."

She reached under her straw bed for the satchel and rummaged through it, retrieving her silken thread and a needle. Wulfric bent down next to Dzintara and held a lantern over the boy. "You have to save him."

Water arrived, and she cleaned the cut. She pulled the wound open with her fingers, searching for the cut artery. When she found it, she pinched it with her fingers, but it slipped.

"Fuck."

She pinched it again, wrapping the thread around it to slow the bleeding.

"The wound. It's too deep and wide. It needs to be cauterized. Someone get me steel or wood that's blue hot."

She heard footsteps rushing to obey. "Don't go," she whispered to Vlad, taking his small, soot-covered hand in hers.

When she pulled his eyelids open, she saw they were white, and his pupils were rolled to the back of his head. She checked for life again. There was none. Her head dropped, and from the darkness, a red iron tip was handed to her, but she waved it off.

"Farewell, brother," she whispered. Her chest tightened as she kissed his forehead, the taste of salt and blood on her lips.

Wulfric shook as he bent over Vlad, sobbing.

Dzintara rose slowly, staring at the crew. Her keffiyeh lay amidst the straw, her scars shining in the flickering light. At that moment, a legend was born, tales to be whispered on the windswept seas of years to come. With her ascent, the crew recoiled as if sensing a seismic shift in the fabric of their world. She stepped forward regarding these pirates, making sure they took her full measure.

"Wulfric, your name means the ruler of wolves."

"Aye," he sniffed as he wiped his eyes.

"I take command of this ship," she said, her voice steady. She pointed to Wulfric, "he is now my second."

The crew murmured and whispered among themselves. Dzintara's eyes swept over them, her breath steady now, her fingers lightly gripping the handle of the khanjar. She could see their fear, their doubt—one wrong move, and she'd lose the ship to chaos.

"We sail forth to Riga. Every man works double watch from now until we reach the mouth of the Dvina. Any talk of mutiny or uprising is punishable by death."

"Who the fuck decided to make you ship-master?" Marble-jaw yelled from the shadows.

Dzintara didn't flinch, her gaze locking onto the figure stepping forward—Marble-jaw, sword already drawn.

"You."

"You don't get to bark orders at my men. The cog is mine," he snarled.

The end of the iron rod had started to cool when she seized it and swung, striking his mouth and scattering the remnants of his teeth across the hay. His sword dropped from his hand as he hit the deck hard.

"Anyone else?" she asked.

From the corner of her eye, she glimpsed Varkelins lurking near the shadows. His gaze was steady, unreadable. She would deal with him soon enough.

"King of wolves."

"Yes, Cap'n?" Wulfric responded.

"Can you watch over a pack of dogs?"

"Yes, Cap'n. I can manage."

"This one speaks again, kill him," she said, pointing at Marble-jaw.

"Yes, Cap'n."

She dropped the rod and cleaned her khanjar in the hay. She gathered her things, tucking them back into her satchel.

"Back to your duties," Wulfric commanded, and the crew dispersed, murmuring to themselves.

"Wulfric," Dzintara said as she gathered her things.

"Yes, Cap'n."

"Dispose of the dead," she looked at Vlad's motionless body.

"Aye."

"Give Vlad a proper farewell," she said.

He nodded and wiped his eyes.

The floor planks and the hay were soaked with blood. She looked around for her keffiyeh, wrapped her head, and stood.

"The boy. Do you know if he has any family? Anywhere?"

"Nay. Poor lad."

She headed to the deck and noticed the light in Varkelins' cabin. Moving back down to the animal hold, she instructed the crew to arrange barrels, crates, and sacks into a makeshift private cabin for herself, alongside the nanny goat, her kid, and the wary chickens.

Once finished, she stated, "This is my lodging from now on. No one is allowed in here." The crew nodded in agreement. Some headed up to the deck for watch while the rest retreated to their own nooks and crannies for sleep. It was quiet below deck.

She laid back on the moist straw bed and put Olaf's short sword to the side. She listened to the muffled sounds of the crew working above. Her fingers shook as she unwrapped her keffiyeh. The lion's head on her knife caught the dim light, and suddenly, she felt the tears slipping down her cheeks, falling onto the blade. She hadn't cried for years—not since...well, what did it matter now? She took a swig from the vial, its bitter taste familiar, grounding. Slowly, the ache in her chest dulled. But the memory of Vlad's lifeless eyes lingered.

CHAPTER TWENTY

Ako opened his eyes. It was dark, except for the flickering torchlight against the slick stone walls. As his eyes adjusted, the pure darkness transformed into shapes then outlines, and finally, the clear definition of iron bars. Beside him, a puddle reflected a gray, inky haze. Droplets fell from the ceiling in a steady rhythm, creating ripples in the small pool. Ako grabbed his head and screamed, "Stop!"

He slammed his fist into the puddle, but the drips persisted. He remembered being at the shipyard, lying beneath the vessel's skeleton, before it all blurred.

Letting out a loud groan, he sat up. He touched the back of his head, sticky with half-dried blood.

He crawled until he felt the wall, and he lay against it.

"Ako. Ako...Ako," Albert said, his voice deep and angry.

The shipwright spat and clenched his jaw at the sound of that voice.

"Please don't let the accommodations reflect my sentiment toward you. It's merely a doctrinal technicality."

"You burnt my ships," Ako cried.

"That wasn't the plan," Albert replied, almost compassionate.

"We had an agreement."

A long silence followed.

"You've destroyed years of innovation. My legacy...my name!" Ako's cry echoed through the prison.

"You know what I want, Ako," Albert said.

Ako pulled himself to standing, refusing to answer.

"Ako, you've always been a fool."

"Why am I here?"

Another set of footsteps joined Albert.

"We had you arrested under the orders of his excellency for suspicions of heresy," Hans said.

"Heresy?" Ako asked.

Albert retrieved a shiny object from about his person and held it up between his fingers.

"Know what this is, Ako?"

"Gold."

"Yes, but the mint Ako."

"Out with it," Ako said, both heartbroken and furious.

"Honorius the Third, the man who supported my plans to make this city a church stronghold in the north. This coin was meant to fund our crusade, but it never arrived."

"What has that got to do with me, Albert—"

"Your Excellency," Hans growled, correcting Ako.

"The man who handed me this coin claimed he received it from a pagan. He named you. He told me that you were the one who stole these funds. Murdered for them, in fact," Albert said.

"These coins are common. He could have gotten it from anyone!"

Albert chuckled. "I've never come across one in these lands. You Hans?"

"I have not, Your Excellency."

"You stole from me. From the church," Albert whispered, pressing his face against the iron bars. "Confess and reveal where you hid the gold."

"There is no gold. It's a lie, you damn fool!"

"We'll see about that," Albert said.

Albert and Hans left the dungeon. The old man backed against the wall and slid to the floor. He whimpered as he thought about his life's work. The thought of it all slipping away drove at his heart like a dagger.

THERE IT WAS. The mouth of the Dvina spilled into the sea. Tall pines blanketed the coast. The bow pointed at the delta, and Dzintara smiled. As the mouth sprawled open, merchant ships lined up to make their way up the river toward the thriving port of Riga.

"Prepare to tack!" Dzintara commanded from the helm.

The sail trimmers positioned themselves near the sheets, and other crew members grabbed and held onto the bowlines, awaiting the maneuver. Others secured loose equipment.

"Helm to starboard," she shouted, and turned the rudder right. "Trim the sails."

The crew pulled on the sheets as the cog turned, filling it with wind from a different angle.

"Hold the course."

The sun was setting when they crossed the delta threshold and floated into the main artery. They slowed as the wind died, and then they worked against the current. They dropped the anchor, joining the other lingering ships. Wulfric ran to her.

"We need the beasts!"

Dzintara turned and scanned the horizon of anchored cogs, waiting for their luck to turn. Her breath was like smoke in the cold dusk.

"Wulfric, go and make arrangements."

Wulfric nodded and hastened down to the deck. Together, he, Marble Jaw, and a few others lifted a small paddle boat over the side. Wulfric and Marble Jaw dropped two parallel ropes made of twine and hemp and lowered themselves into the skiff.

The crew above hoisted a thick rope from below and lowered

it to the waiting skiff. Wulfric pushed the dinghy away from the cog.

Dzintara watched as the men drifted towards shore. As darkness descended, the skiff reached the bank. The two men secured a thick rope to a tree and vanished into the forest.

DZINTARA AWOKE to the sound of the crew shouting. She donned her clothes and ran to the deck.

"Steady!" Wulfric yelled from the rudder.

They raised the dinghy and tied a thick rope to the mast. An old peasant drove four oxen onshore, towing the ship upriver. The crew cheered as the ship moved.

Varkelins stood at the helm with folded hands behind his back. At the sight of Dzintara, Wulfric offered up the rudder, and she took it.

"It pulls to the left," he said and then joined the rest of the crew at the bow.

Mid-day, the ship entered the Dvina estuary, heading towards Riga's harbor.

"Drop the rope," she ordered.

The crew dashed to the mast, quickly working to untie the rope. The oxen continued their forward march, eyes fixed ahead. The rope grew taut, making it impossible to loosen. As the old man whipped and shouted, the beasts lost their footing and plunged onto the cracking ice on the shoreline. The beasts lowed, panicked, desperately reaching for the frozen mud at the river's edge. Finally, the rope slackened, and the crew freed it, sending it splashing into the water.

"Now, Drop the sails"

The crew grabbed the bowlines, let the sails out, and the sheets caught the wind, pulling them upriver.

With the setting sun, they arrived at the river's last curve, revealing the city. Docked cogs were dotted across the harbor, set out at anchor. Small skiffs zigzagged along the river, and barges laden with goods floated to their final destination Dzintara gasped at the sight of the city, awed by how much it had changed since she'd left.

Slowly, they drifted past the shipyard. Dzintara and Varkelins observed the charred skeletal frames of cogs, blackened by ash and soaked from the rain. The smell of burnt wood lingered in the air. The berth lay empty, with tools and weapons scattered about.

"I saved your life," Dzintara fixed Varkelins with a glare.

"A fair price for getting you home," Varkelins joked, clasping his hands behind his back.

"Where does Anno the Conqueror lay his head?"

Varkelins' face drooped, and he looked away from her.

"I don't know what you want with him, but he'll kill you."

"Just point me in the direction. It'll never come back to you."

Varkelins raised his eyebrows, about to say something snide. Then he shrugged. "Two days north, in the Guaja Valley. You'll find their fortress there. And God help you when you do."

As they drifted into the port, Wulfric pointed to an opening at the north berth, and the crew directed the cog towards it with their oars.

She turned to leave, but Varkelins grabbed her arm.

"Krists, I never thanked you for saving my life."

"You just did," She jerked her arm free.

"The ship is now under your command," she said, descending into the cargo hold as they docked.

Varkelins looked out into the distance. A sailor's tailor high in a basket sewed patches of skin onto sheet canvas. A dockhand in a dinghy smashed at the ice with a long wooden pick axe. Albert's grand cathedral broke the rooflines of the city.

"Gather all hands!" Varkelins yelled at the crew. Seagulls screamed and circled the harbor.

"Wulfric, assign men below. Prepare the windlass for the cargo lift. What we can't haul, we carry."

"Aye."

The gangplank pounded against the berth.

"Solid ground!" Varkelins cried out.

Below decks, Dzintara stuffed her belongings into a satchel. When she finished, she made her way up to the deck. The crew was busy preparing to unload. With Wulfric and Varkelins out of sight, she swiftly dashed down the gangplank, with no one noticing, and then swiftly walked towards the city gates. Before she disappeared into the crowd of merchants, sailors, and nobles, she unwrapped her keffiyeh and tossed it into the river. Home, at last, to exact vengeance on Anno the Conqueror.

DZINTARA APPROACHED the shipyard entrance just beyond the city walls. She could smell the strong scent of damp smoke and charred wood. Two guards roamed about aimlessly at the entrance gate to the shipyard. They were armed and clad in plain attire, their breath visible in the chilly air. One shuddered from the cold, and the other coughed.

Dzintara picked up a hefty stone and made her way to the riverbank. With a powerful throw, the stone cracked the icy surface and skidded away. She gripped the berth's edge and lowered herself onto the ice.

The ice moaned and creaked beneath her. With a sharp crack, the ice gave way and Dzintara plunged waist-deep into freezing water. A thousand knives stabbed at her leg. Panic surged through her as she laid flat face down and dug her fingernails into the ice. Scraping and clawing, she inched her body forward, slowly pulling her legs back out of the frigid water.

Suddenly, a lantern swung in the distance, and she spotted a guard marching toward her. Quietly, she slid across the ice on her stomach towards the shadows beneath the quay. The guard scanned the frozen river, waving the lantern in front of him. Seeing nothing, he turned away, disappearing into the night.

Her teeth chattered as she crawled face-down across the frozen river, inching forward until she reached the dock of the shipyard. A burnt mast, leaning against the dock, served as her ladder to solid ground. Shivering, she rubbed her legs for warmth, feeling the blood slowly returning.

Surveying her surroundings, she noted the scattered tools illuminated by the moonlight. Half-burnt cogs stood covered in soot and ash. The massive workshop doors had been left ajar. She approached the workshop and peered inside.

Moonlight shone through the workshop windows, revealing the skeletal frames of cogs stripped bare like gutted fish. She stepped through the open door and unsheathed her khanjar. Beyond the abandoned half-built ships was the chancery. Moving around the scattered and abandoned tools, she made her way there, quietly shutting the door behind her.

Scrolls cluttered the table and floor. Nearby, shelves stood askew, one broken and lying on its side next to the desk. Dzintara sheathed her khanjar and felt around the desk, gently tapping the wood, listening for hollow sounds or indications of a hidden opening. She found nothing. Running her hands along the chancery walls and shelves, she searched for any telltale carvings that might reveal a secret.

Iron scraped against the stone floor, followed by hushed whispers. Dzintara held her breath. She cautiously approached the door, peering into the darkness.

She could see someone was moving through the workshop.

Dropping to her knees, she unsheathed her khanjar and silently crawled across the floor. In the moonlight, she watched as the man stumbled and fell, dragging another man.

As the man struggled to stand once more, Dzintara rose to her feet and lunged forward, pressing the blade to his neck from behind.

"Don't scream. It's sharp enough to slice through."

He raised his hands to signal that he was unarmed. A wounded man lay on the ground, bleeding from his side. He groaned loudly in the darkness.

"Tell him to keep quiet," she said in a low voice.

"He's badly wounded. I need to get him to the river."

"Who are you?" she asked.

"We are both freemen. We tithe to the Archbishop Albert and follow the ways of the Christians."

"Who burned the cogs?"

"We know not." The tip of her blade pierced his skin. "I'll tell you. Just don't hurt me. We think 'twas on the orders of the archbishop."

"Where is the shipwright?"

"He was taken in shackles."

Dzintara lowered her blade. A droplet of blood ran down into his tunic. He turned towards her, but she stepped back into the darkness, and from the darkness, she spoke.

"Go on."

"A band of men showed up...freemen," he spat in disgust, "they demanded Ako go with them. When he refused, they killed our workers and burned our handiwork."

Another groan came from the wounded man.

"I need to get him to a healer, or he will die."

"Who are you?" she asked.

"The foreman."

"I'm looking for something"

"I can't help you," he replied, expecting her question.

"You must know this place better than anyone. There is a map. Where is it?"

"I know of no such thing."

"The map carved on wood or marked on parchment?"

The foreman stayed silent. The khanjar emerged from darkness, its blade gleaming in moonlight.

"I swear I know nothing about maps and scrolls," the foreman dropped to his knees.

"Where are the hiding places in the chancery?"

"You and everyone else," the wounded man rumbled.

Straining her eyes, Dzintara tried to distinguish the bearded face concealed in the sack, but she couldn't make him out.

"Come out of the darkness and show your face, coward," he said, with a wet, gurgling cough.

Moments of silence passed.

"Turn me toward the voice so I can get a better look," he ordered the foreman.

The foreman took a step toward him when Dzintara interjected, "Stay where you are."

The foreman straightened with palms next to his head.

"Don't worry. Lucky for you, lad, I'm tied up here," said the wounded man, holding onto his side. That voice sounded familiar to her. But she couldn't quite place it.

The wounded man stirred restlessly. Then, the moon illuminated his features, bringing them into stark relief.

She caught her breath at the sight of the long beard, the weathered countenance, and the scar marring his head where hair struggled to grow.

"Lamek—" she began, her voice trailing off as she retreated into the safety of the shadows. There, she found refuge, a barrier from the world. The voice, so familiar, beckoned like a siren's call, tempting her into the moonlight. Yet she understood the danger for those who yielded to such temptation. She still couldn't believe what she saw. It was Lamekins. Her father's childhood friend. The man who long ago taught her to hunt and ride, and anchored her joyful childhood memories.

"Coward. Step forward and show yourself!" he growled.

"Quiet, they'll hear us," the foreman said, whispering.

Her feet planted stiffly to the ground as if roots wrapped around her ankles while the siren's haunting melody hypnotized her.

"Foe or friend?" Lamekins, changing his strategy, asked with a struggling, gentle voice. His voice was a warm reminder of his kindness.

Stepping into the moonlight, her face bore scars on the right side, like palm lifelines revealing hidden destiny. Both the foreman and Lamekins recoiled, gasping as the sight of her filled the silence.

"My virgin mother. Dzintara! You're home."

A DENSE FOG settled over the once lively port of Riga, shrouding the wooden docks and cobbled streets. The air was heavy with the scent of saltwater and damp earth. Only the muffled waves and occasional seagull cry broke the silence.

Varkelins oversaw the final stages of unloading. Wulfric stood nearby, his brow furrowed in concern as he scanned the fog-shrouded city.

Varkelins spoke to Wulfric, his voice piercing the still night. "The physician?"

"No one has seen him. We searched the entire ship." Wulfric cast a worried look at Marble Jaw and the crew gathered around him.

Varkelins threw a glance in the direction of Marble Jaw and paced down the dock, looking into the murky waters. Wulfric caught up with him.

"You think...revenge?" Wulfric asked.

"He can't be that big of a fool. To kill a man on solid ground"

"Old man, are we ready?" Varkelins shouted to the carter of the loaded wagon.

"Aye." Varkelins turned to Wulfric, handing him a bag. "Wait here. I'll be back in a few days time. There is enough gold and silver here to pay the docking levy."

"What about Marble Jaw?" Wulfric asked. "He has the numbers. With Krists gone, he may make a move."

"Even fools know when not to be foolish."

Varkelins saw his words did not put Wulfric at ease. "Everything will be fine."

Wulfric watched as Varkelins disappeared into the swirling mist with the carter and the cargo.

Left alone on the quiet dock, Wulfric stood there for a few moments, holding the leather bag Varkelins gave him.

"Psst, Wulfric," called one of his mates, standing at the edge of the dock.

Wulfric approached, and his mate pointed towards the water, where patches of ice were beginning to form. A keffiyeh, caught in the current, danced and snagged on the ice. Wulfric's mouth fell open in shock.

"Krists!" he gasped, then turned his gaze back to the ship, where Marble Jaw and his mates were laughing.

"Marble Jaw," he growled.

"No," his mate interjected, grabbing his arm and pointing towards Varkelins.

"What?" Wulfric demanded.

"Krists became the new captain after Gorm after the mutiny. That means Varkelins would have had to pay the share promised to Gorm to Krists." his mate explained. Then it dawned on Wulfric: it was Varkelins who killed Krists.

He stared at the keffiyeh, fluttering in the icy water. "Varkelins."

His mate nodded slowly. "Be careful with him. Once he returns with payment, we find another ship to sail out of this icy hell."

With a silent nod, Wulfric agreed, and they proceeded towards the ship.

"All right, men, we are in for the night. We dock here for a few days until the Ship Master returns with new cargo," Wulfric said, making his way up the gangplank.

Wulfric's boots thudded on the deck. Marble Jaw's fist smashed into his face, sending Wulfric tumbling over the gunwale into the freezing river.

"Cut the moor lines!" Marble Jaw's voice echoed as Wulfric sank. The icy water snatched his breath away, gold and silver coins spiraling down with him. Moments later, Wulfric's mate crashed into the water, lifeless. Flailing, desperate for air, Wulfric finally broke the surface and gasped. He had drifted downriver with the current.

In the distance, he saw the remaining crew moving swiftly, freeing the moor lines from head to stern in unison. Oars hit the water, pushing the ship from the dock. Wulfric swam with the current, spotting a place on the coast where he could climb out of the river.

DZINTARA STOOD IN THE DARKNESS, stunned by the sight of Lamekins. The fog had settled outside, and heavy snow had begun to fall. The inside of the workshop became darker as the glow of the moon disappeared behind the wall of white descending.

"It can't be," Lamekins grunted from the sack.

Dzintara could feel Lamekins smiling in the dark, and she took half a step forward to see his face in the dying moonlight. She fought the urge to embrace him, and the tears wanted to flow, but she fought them too.

"Where is my father?" Her voice quivered.

"Albert's dungeon," Lamekins said.

"Where is the map?"

"It's a myth," said the foremen.

"There is no map. It's a tall tale," Lamekins added.

Lamekins coughed and spat blood. Her desire to help him clashed with memories of his indifference when her father gave her to that merchant long ago. These thoughts battled in her mind. She pulled the note from her satchel and held it out for them to see.

"My brother marches north. Is this true?" She shoved the note forward with her free arm. In silence, Lamekins and the foreman exchanged a heavy glance filled with unspoken sorrow.

"She has a right to know," the foreman said.

"Where is my brother, Lamekins?"

"He died in the Battle of Ice."

"You old fool," Lamekins shouted.

She slipped the note back into her satchel and retreated into the shadows, enveloped in sadness. Each step was heavy with the weight of the unexpected news. As she looked around in the darkness, she felt a void descend upon her—a sense of being alone in the world.

"Why did you come back?" Lamekins asked, groaning.

"For revenge and for my brother."

Lamekins crawled toward the darkness, reaching out with one arm for an embrace as he followed the sound of her voice.

"Things are different since you left," he wheezed. "Leave while you can. There's nothing here for you. The gold doesn't exist."

"My brother said 'I found it' in his note."

"Nonsense. Ramblings of a wild man."

"I know about the gold. I saw it myself when I was a child."

Lamekins pursed his lips and looked at the ground.

"You will end up a slave again. Or dead. Come with us to the forest, and we'll help you escape to safer lands."

He waited for a reply, but none came.

"Dzintara," Lamekins whispered.

"Find a piece of iron. Heat it up and press it against his wound. Otherwise, he won't live to see the sun up."

Dzintara slipped away under the cover of darkness. She knew who she had to find next.

FOG CURLED around rooftops and chimneys. The sound of hooves and creaking wagon wheels bounced from the stone walls of the buildings. Cargo-laden wagons inched down the street, with Varkelins riding alongside the lead carter.

As they entered the storehouse district, the wagons navigated between rows of towering, pyramid-roofed structures. Each store-house had small arched windows and four large wooden doors that extended from the top floor to the ground level.

The roofs sloped downward, with a beam jutting out from the peak, from which ropes dangled. Iron symbols of wine barrels, flour, and hemp adorned the walls, indicating the contents stored within.

The caravan halted.

Varkelins dismounted the wagon and knocked on the door. The door's small window slid open.

"It is I, Varkelins von Handelsberg of the Merchant Guild of Riga, here to store cargo from England on behalf of Albert von—"

The window snapped shut. The lock clicked, and the arch doors swung open.

The lagermeister, tall and imposing, stepped through the doors. Varkelins stepped back and looked up at him, retrieving a parchment from his person and handing it over. The lagermeister took it and read quietly.

"The cargo is to be stored on behalf of the Archbishop of Riga, Albert von Buxtheoven. The order for storage, along with the levy exemption, is here." Varkelins retrieved and extended another folded parchment towards the man, who barely gave it a cursory glance.

"It's all right here." Varkelins pointed at the parchment.

"He may be the high holy man, but he's not exempt from storehouse levies."

In the thin candlelight of the building's interior, Varkelins saw movement.

"There must be some confusion," Varkelins' said, his voice quivering. "If you read this, it will be clear." His finger battered the parchment. The lagermeister ignored it and stepped onto the plank road where the wagons rested.

"Oats, wheat, wine?"

"Some, yes, some wool."

"Leave it here and be gone," the lagermeister said.

"For storage?"

"No, for his debt."

Two men emerged from the darkness of the storehouse. Their blades flashed.

"There is another storehouse not too far off," the carter said.

Varkelins pulled the parchment from the man's hand and put it in his satchel.

"I think my carter is right, we best seek another vendor."

"Stay. We'll put this on the third floor."

"I think His Holiness has made other arrangements," Varkelins said, heading towards the perch.

"This is ours," declared the man with an eye patch, smoothly unsheathing his blade as he stepped in front of the carriages. One gestured for the first wagon to advance, and the one-eyed man stepped aside. The carter clicked his tongue, and the horses took six steps forward. A whistle echoed, and rope from the top beam floated down, stopping just above the wagon.

"This cargo is protected by the Merchant Guild. This theft will come back to you," Varkelins insisted.

"It's only theft if it doesn't rightfully belong to you. This wagon covers his Holiness' debt to the Storehouse Guild," said the lagermesiter and motioned to the other two. They placed a hook at the end of the rope, tied another rope around the barrel, and secured it on the hook. One whistled, and the barrel floated up into the fog.

"This is robbery," Varkelins said, angry now.

"Years of levy, tariffs, and tithing with no representation. No help. No recognition. He has committed robbery, that swine of a man."

"This will not go unnoticed."

The lagermeister stepped to Varkelins, towering over him, and smiled.

"These two here can easily gut you and leave you in the river to freeze over. Maybe they'll find you in springtime," he said, pulling on his pants.

Resigned, Varkelins joined the carter on the perch and waited while the men unloaded his cargo. He stared ahead, afraid to even blink. Once finished, they hopped off the wagon and vanished through the doors.

The lagermeister stepped onto the wagon, put his hand on Varkelins' shoulder, and spat.

"You let Albert know we appreciate the overdue payment. If he has any concerns, he can come visit us here." Then he turned and left, and Varkelins nodded to the carter, and the wagons began to roll again.

Varkelins brushed the dirt off his shoulders.

"The disrespect," he said, his voice thick with worry.

The carter shrugged and paid no attention.

"Can you believe this is what this great city has come to? Common theft and robbery?" Varkelins continued.

"And you," Varkelins looked at the carter in disgust, "you might as well have helped them load."

The carter looked at Varkelins and shrugged, and they rode off towards Turaida.

CHAPTER TWENTY-ONE

Ako's estate lay half a day's walk from Riga, hidden amidst trees and brush. A narrow dirt road wound its way through the forest, leading to a wide clearing where four buildings stood clustered together. The main house was a grand three-story log structure, accompanied by a barn, a lodge for servants and workers, and a rectangular hall for gatherings. It was all much larger than when Dzintara was a child, back when it was just a small log cabin nestled in the woods. She remembered watching her father ride off to Riga early in the morning and waiting for his return late at night.

As she stood at the edge of the forest, the sun began to set, casting long shadows across the frozen ground. Dzintara gazed at the familiar rooflines, remembering the days of her youth when she ran freely through the forest. But now, the main house was overrun with vines, and the once vibrant flower beds lay dormant. The estate was devoid of any signs of life.

Suddenly, the door of the servant's lodge creaked open, and an elderly woman emerged, wrapping herself in a fur pelt against the chill. She wore worn boots, a swishing skirt, and a kerchief over her gray hair. The woman gathered a bundle of wood from the shed and carried it to the main house. Soon after, smoke spiraled from the chimney. Leaving the house once again, the woman opened the barn doors. Inside, the pens were empty. The woman distributed fresh hay into the stalls and called out to the animals. A lonesome neigh called out. After tending to the barn, she moved to the dining hall, where a stream of smoke rose not long after. The woman lingered in the dining hall, and Dzintara stealthily made her way through the tree line and towards the main house. To conceal her identity, she'd wrapped her face with a strip of fabric torn from her shirt. She peered through the narrow windows. The house seemed empty. Moving around the building, she came to the front door and pushed inside.

A flood of memories overwhelmed her. She remembered the day she last saw her brother, the anger in her father's voice, and a distinctive gold coin. Shaken, she returned to the present.

The great hall, with its three chairs positioned near the hearth and a long table extending across the room, was draped in dust and cobwebs. She moved slowly towards the staircase, each step heavy with nostalgia. The door to her father's room groaned as she gently pushed it. The bed was made of strong, thick wood. The faces of Perkūnas, Māra, and Laima had been carved into the posts, protecting him and maintaining the balance between chaos and peace.

His desk was as heavy as it was wide. She traced her fingers along the carvings on one of the legs. It was the likeness of Velns, with a long nose and eyes and a frown and horns.

She remembered the story her father had told her as a child.

A powerful, greedy king captured and held the sun and the moon in a tower. The people in the kingdom were plunged into darkness, and they suffered greatly as the days went by without sunlight. Crops began to wither, and the once lush and fertile land turned into a cold, desolate place.

Hearing the desperate pleas of the people, Velns decided to help them, but not out of pure goodwill. He saw an opportunity to create chaos in the kingdom and amuse himself with the king's downfall. Velas entered the tower, where the sun and the moon were imprisoned under the cover of darkness. He freed the celestial bodies and returned them to the sky, bringing light and warmth back to the kingdom.

As the sun and the moon resumed their journey across the sky, the crops began to grow again, and life returned to normal for the people of the kingdom. However, Velns' actions also led to the king's eventual downfall, as his people, angered by his greed and tyranny, rose against him.

Parchments littered Ako's desk as though he was coming back any moment to retrieve them. She looked intently, without touching. A record of interested purchasers. Sketches of three-masted cogs. She carefully lifted one, reading the script, then opened a drawer and meticulously felt through the bowels. A knife. More papers bundled by string. Wax parchments. She found a necklace with a symbol of five circles within each other. She pocketed it, then searched under the bed and in her father's heavy wooden closet. Once she'd looked everywhere, she made her way back downstairs.

At the bottom, she was met with a blade to her throat.

"You want this day to be your last?"

The edge of the blade pierced the skin, and she raised her arms to show she was unarmed.

"I seen you out there in the forest lurking around. Didn't think an old woman would catch and kill a robber, did you?"

She pressed the tip against Dzintara's skin, drawing blood. "Empty your pockets."

Dzintara slowly took out the necklace and held her palms open.

"You ought to feel ashamed, you thief. Robbing a family that has suffered nothing but misfortune. Hide your face no longer, coward!"

Dzintara slowly unwrapped the cloth from her head. It fell.

The woman turned white, her eyes widened, the blade dropped from her hand, and her eyes rolled to the back of her head as she fell over. Dzintara caught her before she hit the floor.

Cradling the old woman in her lap and gently stroking her head, she began to sing "Līgaviņa," the very childhood melody once sung to her by Liga, now returned in a tender echo of care and memory.

A short time later, the old woman came to. Still startled, the old woman ran her fingers over Dzinatra's face, touched her hands, and ran her fingers through Dzinatra's hair.

"Tante Liga," Dzintara smiled.

Liga leapt to her feet and hugged Dzintara tightly. The old woman cried, kissed, and embraced her. Dzintara held back her tears as best she could, gripping Liga's clothes. She clung to her like she did the day she was sent away. Liga then stepped back, looked at Dzintara once more, and, overjoyed by her return, hugged her tightly again. She pressed a clean rag to Dzintara's throat, stopping the trickle of blood.

Liga led her by hand to the kitchen, seating Dzintara at the large wooden table. The old woman disappeared outside and came back with a pot of water. She picked a couple of stones from the fire with a metal tong, placed them in the pot, and sat.

Finally, Dzintara asked the question she'd wondered ever since she'd received her brother's note from Saladin.

"How did he find me?"

"He never stopped looking. I don't think he ever forgave himself for letting your father give you away."

"I was in a distant land. No one knew me or who I was. I was starting to forget who I was."

The water boiled in the pot. Liga took a set of clay cups decorated with vines and circular patterns and filled them with herbs wrapped in linen. She poured the hot water into the cups.

"For years and years, he looked for you. Your father told him to cease the foolishness. But he didn't listen. He wanted to find his sister," Liga sighed, and a tear rolled down Dzintara's face.

"One day, he found the merchant your father sold you to. He damn near killed the merchant, but he finally told your brother you were somewhere east. Armed with that piece of information, he left. He told no one. When your father returned that evening, I told him I thought Krists was out riding...but he was gone. For a while, we thought he had died during his journey. Then, one night, out of the darkness, Krists entered the front door. Your father was filled with anger and joy all at the same time," Liga laughed and cupped her face.

"We sat by the fire, and he told us of his travels. He talked of strange lands and men who tamed snakes. Your father wanted to hear none of it, so he left and went to bed. He told me he was so close to finding you and that he gave that note to someone who would get it to you."

Dzintara sat in silence. She drank her hot water with herbs. It tasted like childhood.

"How did he die?"

"Well, your father forced him to the Brotherhood. They rode North to convert the tribes, and he was caught alive at the Battle of Ice. The rest is too hard to talk about," Liga shook her head and wiped her eyes.

Dzintara sipped the hot water.

"Krists never forgave himself. He hated your father for it, but he was too weak to stand up to him. After he returned, your father took control of his destiny by sending him to the Brotherhood. Krists slowly morphed and became like them, the Christians of Riga, just as your father intended."

The two went silent, sitting for a moment, drinking their tea.

"I'll get us some more water," Liga stood, breaking the silence. The old woman disappeared, and Dzintara reached into her pocket and read the note again. When the old woman returned, she put the pot back on the stove and sat down once again.

"That coin is burnt into my mind. The gold," she said without looking at her.

"Your father was afraid that people would come looking for

the source of that coin, and at the source, they find a wealthy heathen. Your father always kept his identity hidden. Afraid others would find out who he was. Over time, Ako rose to great heights in Riga. But now it is different than it was. Riga was young. Lawless. They would have killed him and all of us and took the wealth. Your mother's passing—"

"Don't talk about that," Dzintara interrupted.

Liga smiled and leaned across the table to caress Dzintara's face, running her fingers along her scars.

"You never met her. Shame," said the old woman.

"I keep having these dreams about ice, the same coin my brother took to Riga that very night, and barrels of gold and silver with that same mint, and then a great fire on a cog with men a-burning."

"Sounds like Velns is playing tricks on your mind," the old woman smiled, refilling her cup.

Dzintara looked out the window into the dark.

"No, it's real. It's not just dreams, but I remember things. It's all tied back to that coin."

"It's not. Children's memories are vivid."

"I know my father hid something away. Gold and silver."

The old woman gave a dismissive chuckle and waved her off.

"Dzintara. Those are fairy tales. The truth is they can't accept one of us rising to wealth. They have to make up stories, ya know."

"But I remember—"

"Dzintara, there is nothing. Let it go," Liga took Dzintara's hands and looked her in the eye.

Dzintara sighed and stood and paced around, searching for answers.

"Last I saw of this place, it was a log house."

"The reward of your father's hard work."

"What of him?" Dzintara asked.

"I haven't seen him. He's been at the shipyard building away. No time to head back. It's been me by my lonesome self."

"Rumor is he has been taken prisoner in Turaida."

"Not your father. He practically keeps Albert's coffers full," Liga laughed.

"The shipyard was burned to the ground. I saw Lamekins. He was dying."

Liga put her cup on the table, looked up at the ceiling, and put her hands to her face.

"Oh no. Albert knows," she whispered to herself.

"Knows what?"

Liga looked around and rubbed her hands.

"Knows what?" Dzintara asked again.

"About your father's true identity," Liga lied.

The old woman stood and forced a smile.

"Let me make up a bed for you."

"I can't. I have to find him. I came for revenge and to claim what belongs to me," Dzintara stood and placed the cup on the table.

"What is it that belongs to you?"

"The gold. All that gold will help us fight them. Defeat them," Dzintara said.

"It's a myth, Dzintara," Liga shot back.

"It's not. That gold is the answer." Dzintara said.

"Defeat who?" Liga asked.

"The Crusaders...the man who killed him," Dzintara said with a clenched fist and tears flowing.

"Who?" Liga asked in confusion.

"You don't know him. He was everything to me."

"Don't be foolish, child. You'll end up like your mother."

"I will find it."

"Listen to me," Liga pleaded, "stay the night. That's it. When the sun is up, you can do what you please."

She cocked her head sideways and gave Dzintara a wide smile.

She took Dzintara upstairs to her father's room and laid her to bed. It was the first safe, warm bed Dzintara had lain in for many months. When the old woman left, she lit a candle and searched

her father's desk once more. In the back of the top drawer, she felt
something metal and round. She pulled it out and held it in the
candlelight. A gold coin with a pope on it. The outer rim read
HONORIVUS. She pocketed the coin and reached back into the
desk but found nothing else.

As she lay in bed, she took the coin from her pocket and
examined it. The coin glowed against the light. She ran her fingers
along the mint. She soon fell into a deep sleep. She dreamt of gold
and a cog engulfed in flames on frozen, desolate ice.

CHAPTER TWENTY-TWO

A small, desolate inn nestled in an alley close to the city square, by the House of the Blackheads. Wulfric had arrived two nights before, drenched and cold from the river. Seeking shelter, he requested a bed, paying with a few coins he had clutched tightly as he faced the peril of drowning.

When he woke up, he discovered himself in a tight room with three snoring strangers. Despite the brazier's efforts to warm the room, Wulfric could still see his breath mist in the cold air, and ice glazed the window.

He put his boots on and walked out into the early morning city square. A brown stray dog sniffed around for scraps, and when Wulfric saw it, they locked eyes. The dog pushed its chest out and tail up to the sky. They stared at each other for a while, and then the dog returned to its search for scraps.

For the third consecutive day, the river remained frozen solid. Wulfric wandered through the streets and the maze of alleyways, eventually making his way to the harbor. Looking at the dock, he stood where Varkelins' ship had been moored just two days earlier.

By midday, the sun had just edged above the horizon. While reflecting on the night's events, he found it difficult to accept that

Varkelins had planned Krists' murder and Marble Jaw had escaped with the ship.

Wulfric's aimless steps led him to a dim, decrepit tavern nestled in the storehouse district. Rough men huddled around a flickering fire in the hearth, nursing their ales. Ordering an ale, Wulfric settled near the meager warmth, rubbing his hands together over the flames as he surveyed the room's shadowy corners and its dispirited occupants.

A tall, imposing figure and his two companions sat a mere whisper away. One of them sported a makeshift patch with a filthy cloth tied over one eye. Catching Wulfric's gaze, the patched man briefly met his look before lofting his drink in salute.

"Skoal."

Wulfric returned the salute and continued to stare at the fire. Outside, the darkness crept in, and snow began to fall. With his third ale, time became a blur. His trance shattered when he caught the name "...Varkelins..." through the sudden burst of laughter at the nearby table, the sound drawing his full attention.

"He was laughed out of the Blackheads a couple of nights ago," said the man with the eye patch.

"And to think, the archbishop's ship vanished right from the harbor. Let's see how long Varkelins and Albert can keep their alliance afloat," added the tall man, then they all shared laughter at Varkelins' expense.

Wulfric silently repeated to himself, "Blackheads..." while carefully avoiding any appearance of eavesdropping.

"A corpse washed ashore yesterday. Likely Varkelins, the wretch. Must've crossed someone for coin," the man with the filthy eye patch added sarcastically.

"Hardly," countered the tall one, pausing his drink. "Varkelins, that sea coward and defiler of stable boys."

Their laughter filled the room, but Wulfric's involuntary chuckle gave him away.

"Hey! You!"

Wulfric turned to see the man with the eye patch, holding his knife and playing with it menacingly.

"Fancy our chat, do you?"

Wulfric's head shook in a panicked denial, his eyes darting away.

With his one good eye, the man squinted at Wulfric. "Time you left."

Wulfric paid the innkeeper after he had downed his ale with the coins he salvaged while drowning. Then he vanished into the snowy night.

DZINTARA WOKE in the morning and breakfasted with Liga, asking her for a horse. Once they were done eating, they made their way to the stables. A brown mare with a white spot on her forehead stomped in the back. Dzintara saddled the horse like she'd done so many times before.

"The woods is a dangerous place. If you get caught, they will not show you mercy," Liga warned.

"I won't get caught."

"Is there anything I can say that will make you stay and live out the rest of your life here with me and your father?"

"He's in a dungeon."

"Then with me?"

"I have to do this."

"I don't know why I even try. I know the answer already. Maybe it makes me feel like I have done everything I can."

"I will send for you," Dzintara gazed into Liga's eyes.

"Perkūnas showed me how this ends. Stay."

"Maybe it was Velns," Dzintara said, trying to lighten the mood a bit.

"Here," Liga said, walking around a corner to the barn and returning with an embroidered saddle pad. "It was a gift to your father."

Dzintara looked at it. It depicted a wooden boat. To the right, a bearded face blew wind into the sails, while to the left, a half-man, half-fish calmed the waves.

Dzintara approached her mare with the embroidered blanket. Placing it over the mare's back. Then, she secured the saddle, ensuring it was snug.

She kissed the old woman's forehead.

"When you were a child, you would disappear into the forest for hours. I told you so many times about the dangers of wolves, of other tribes, but you didn't care. You followed your ignorance."

"Bravery."

The old woman watched as she bridled the mare, adjusting the bit and straps.

"If he is in a dungeon like you say, then he's north. In Turaida."

"Then that is where I will go," Dzintara said, rubbing the horse.

"What do you expect to happen when you get there?"

"He will tell me where he hid the gold and silver."

"You're going to get yourself killed."

The old woman looked into her eyes. She knew there was no stopping her. Stubborn. Just like when she was a child.

"At least he will see who his daughter has become," Dzintara said, a quiver of sadness in her voice.

Smiling, she gently grasped the old woman's hands. The old woman did not return the smile.

"There is an opening in the rocks that leads to a bad place. If you see it, turn and go the other way," Liga said.

Dzintara kissed Liga on the head a final time. They embraced, and she led the horse outside and mounted it.

"I will send for you."

Liga reached into her pocket and gave her the locket Dzintara had taken from her father's desk. Dzintara fingered the gold locket and then placed it securely in her pants. With a click of her tongue, she kicked her horse and galloped into the forest.

She turned the horse north and rode hard through the trees. The winter sun hung low in the sky, casting a blood red glow through the trees. Dzintara rode late into the night, stopping without making fire. She tied the horse to a tree, and with her khanjar in hand, she laid on the saddle pad behind a rock, keeping herself hidden from passersby.

CHAPTER TWENTY-THREE

She opened her eyes as an arrow buried itself into the tree next to her. She scrambled to her feet, grabbed her satchel, untied, and mounted the skittish mare mid-stride. Nearby, she could hear the clash of steel against steel. She pulled her horse left. Then suddenly, "Off the horse!"

A man dressed in a white robe embroidered with a red cross held his bow aimed directly at her. Looking around, she weighed her options. The mare stomped her hooves and shook her head restlessly. The knight followed the unsteady horse with his crossbow. Dzintara dug her heels into the mare's sides and took off. An arrow swooshed by her head as the mare's hooves pounded the forest floor.

The mare let out a loud squeal and disappeared from under her. Dzintara flew into the air. When she hit the ground, everything went black for a moment. Foamy sweat and blood stained her mare's hide, the arrow wound at its neck pulsing with each strained breath. She squinted as her vision came back into focus.

The soldier was on her, bow pointed at her chest. "Where is the ambush?"

She pushed herself up to her knees. A shin met her chest. She fell over, arms hugging herself in pain. She felt the tip of a blade at the back of her head.

"Are you with them? Where is the ambush coming from?" a deep voice asked.

Broken glass bottles of elixirs and potions lay scattered about her satchel.

"Just kill the fucker," said another voice.

"Wait," she put her hands up, kneeling, "I'm not with them. I'm a traveler. I am alone."

Glass cracked under his boots as he laughed, crushing the unbroken bottles.

"Stop! Those are healing potions."

"Who are you with?" the blade pushed further into the back of her scalp.

A horn blew in the distance. With a quick swing, she slipped the blade off her scalp. Jumping to her feet and grabbing her khanjar, she drove the crusader's sword to the ground and drove the khanjar into the soldier's neck. His companion stared, dumbfounded. She sprinted off, determined to survive.

With the sound of the battle well behind her, she finally stopped running. She crouched, gasping, between a cluster of pines and scanned the nearby trees. Not a rustle of leaves or chirp of a bird.

Then, a war cry pierced the air, swiftly followed by the haunting call of the horn. Arrows whistled past Dzintara's head, dangerously close. From the dense underbrush, an army of tribal warriors erupted.

A host of fierce fighters charged forth. Their torsos were either bare or covered in hides, their limbs adorned with ancestral markings and sacred symbols. Fragments of armor from past skirmishes were intertwined with their tribal attire, with patches of leather and chain mail protecting their vital spots. Some bore headpieces crowned with the antlers of stags or the snouts of wolves. Together, they charged with a primal vigor that seemed to raise the ancient spirits of the land.

Behind her, a company of mounted crusaders charged into the fray.

With no time to reach for her khanjar, Dzintara looked for a place to hide. The horses had difficulty maneuvering between the trees. The tribesmen were on them, slaughtering both men and horses.

Dzintara crawled through the chaos, past scenes of slaughter, and through blood-soaked mud. Ahead, she spotted a rock formation, massive and imposing. With a mix of desperation and relief, she squeezed herself underneath it, pressing her body face down. Concealed and safe, her breaths were quiet and measured in the cool, earthy darkness.

Suddenly, she remembered. The white snowstorm. The cog frozen in the ice, brown obscurity in the middle of the white desolate ice. Her father, dressed in wolf skin, instructing men to take the barrels and chests on sleds to land. When the men left, it was just her father. He made his way into the belly of the cog and, a while later, appeared as the men with sleds returned. The men spoke among themselves of gold and no more worries. Her father asked all of them to retrieve one last thing from the belly of the ship.

When she came to, all was silent. The war cries and screams faded into a not-so-distant past. She crawled out of her hiding place, her refuge. The sun lingered just above the horizon, long shadows of trees. She walked, her breath misting the air, until she came to the edges of the battle.

Birds of prey circled above the forest canopy, attracted by the blood and flesh. The ground was littered with fallen warriors, tall, fair-haired men with wooden helmets. Beside them, the Saxon invaders lay sprawled, their white robes now stained crimson.

Then she heard a sword clatter in its scabbard. She turned and faced a white robe. His sword was stuck, and he struggled to pull it out.

"There is a live one here," he shouted.

She sprinted away into the arms of five other brothers. She raised her hands.

"Take him," ordered a voice from under an iron helmet.

Two men tied her hands in front of her and delivered a blow to her face. She felt her cheekbone crack. She felt blood flowing from her eyebrows and nose. She fell forward, and the men laughed. They stood her up and began marching away from the battlefield. The other three men went from body to body, going through pockets and driving swords through hearts to guarantee death for each Curonian.

They marched a short while until they came upon a clearing. A pyre blazed, and one of the warrior monks fed it with large tree branches. Above, a rope hung from a thick birch branch. Others huddled in prayer as Anno recited a chant from loose leaves of parchment.

Along the tree line, bound tribesmen sat across the blazing pyre. One lay on his side, his life's blood weeping from his gut. Another's face was so swollen and distorted that his eyes were naught but slits. The remaining captives bore the scars of battle upon their bodies.

In a pile in the middle of the camp were the spoils of the battle; wooden helmets, spears, swords, and shields. There was a crown of antlers and several wolf snouts. Two of the warrior monks admired a sword cast in iron with inscriptions carved into a blade and engraved with gold. On one side of the blade, two lines twisted in opposite directions, creating a spiraling pattern. This intricate design of hundreds of stacked, twirling lines ran the entire length of the blood groove. Gold bracelets, one-headed idol necklaces, leather tunics.

Dzintara was thrown to the ground, away from the others. Her captors approached the Curonian tribesmen. She couldn't make out their muffled conversation.

The flame was finally high enough to satisfy the crusader's bloodlust. A knight pointed to one of the captives. Two robed figures strode forward and seized him. They forced him into the armor of a fallen crusader. The tribesman offered no resistance, his expression blank. A sense of familiarity crept over Dzintara as she watched.

Anno folded the parchment and walked over to the defeated enemy, who was being readied for the pyre. His crisp white robe, with the vibrant embroidered red cross, swayed as he walked.

"Where is the village? Point to it," Anno demanded.

At that moment, she knew it was *him*. The voice rang in her head like a thousand bells repeating. Her heart raced in her chest. She was now looking at the man who executed Muhammad.

The tribesman's blue eyes gazed past Anno as if he had already joined the world beyond.

"Just point, and you will live," Anno's words were calm and low.

Anno calmly reached out for the last piece of armor, an iron helmet.

"At the Battle of Ice, your kind burned the surviving knights alive in their armor."

The tribesman smiled, and Anno rammed the iron helmet onto his head. The captive fell to his knee from the force. Someone looped a length of rope beneath the man's armpits, tying several firm knots and throwing the end of the rope high over a tree limb. Two other crusaders pulled the end of the rope caught, readying for the hoist.

"Up," Anno ordered, and the armored captive rose into the air.

The rope creaked as he swung back and forth, and the fire popped. They tied the rope off to the trunk of a nearby tree.

Anno strode towards a tent that contained a crucifix. He emerged carrying a thurible, its chains clinking softly. As he ignited the incense, smoke began to coil and curl upwards.

He swung the thurible, moving among the captives,

humming in a low tone. The incense blended with the smell of roasting flesh. Monks yanked the tribesmen to their knees, forcing them to watch. After Anno finished the ceremony, he returned the thurible to his tent and then joined the captives. He strolled, looking at them.

"Don't close your eyes," Anno warned. "You are beholding your fate. The only question that remains is where you will go from here."

The Curonians watched on in silence.

"Wait for it. They always scream," Anno mused with a half-smile.

But he never did. He never made a sound as his feet sizzled and his armor smoked from the joints.

"Which way is the village?" Anno asked again.

He loomed over the captives, his hands on his knees as he brought his face close to theirs, striding down the line of men, querying each with a guttural growl, delivering slaps across their faces, or a hard yank on their braids. One broke. The young warrior began to weep. Anno sauntered over and bent near the boy's face. He gently lifted his chin.

"A boy in a man's game."

Anno's dirk slid through the bindings, and he lifted the boy to his feet. Placing his hands gently on the boy's shoulder, he held his dagger in his right hand, pointing the blade at the boy's face.

"All you have to do is point," Anno whispered softly in his ear. "Show thy village."

The boy slowly turned right and extended his arm, and then his finger uncurled, pointing into the woods. Anno smiled.

"Thank you."

With tear-filled eyes, Anno thrust the blade into the boy's heart. The boy crumpled to the earth. Anno knelt, prayed, and made the sign of the Holy Trinity over the boy.

"Why did you kill him? He told you what you wanted," Dzintara cried out.

He replied without turning. "Mercy. To spare him from suffering."

He wiped his dagger in his white robe and turned to face a sitting Dzintara.

"Is this your tribe?" he pointed at the tribesmen with the dagger.

She shook her head.

"Stand."

Rivulets of red dripping down from her broken brows and face, she stood.

"Search him," Anno ordered.

One warrior walked over, running his hands over her body. Her khanjar was found instantly. Anno took the khanjar out of his hand.

"Where did you get this?" Anno demanded.

"I found it during my travels," she responded.

"Impossible. Where are you traveling from?" Anno rebutted.

"Northumbria."

Anno unsheathed the khanjar, dropping the scabbard.

"What brings you here?"

"I am a merchant who got robbed in the woods."

"What's your name?" Anno fired.

"Krists."

"What ship did you arrive on?"

"Captain Gorm's," she blurted in a deep voice.

"No Captain Gorm vessel has docked as of late. No vessel at all."

"We arrived just before the freeze."

Anno held up the khanjar in front of his face. The sunlight bounced off the clean, decorated steel.

"In darkness we come, so in light we may prevail," he read the Arabic writing on the blade.

"Have I read those words right?"

They gazed at each other in silence.

"I don't know. I found it," she replied.

"A merchant from Northumbria, traveling with a dagger used by the infidels of the Holy Land, who got robbed in the woods and just stumbles upon Christian knights converting pagans."

Some men chuckled at this. Anno faced his men and pointed the khanjar at one of them.

"Do you believe his story?"

A head shook. He pointed to another.

"Do you believe him?"

He chuckled and shook his head.

"Do you believe these lies?" he pointed at one captive.

Silent, devoid of any reaction, the captive stared ahead.

"I don't believe it," Anno said.

He grabbed her face and examined the scars, turning her head in all directions.

"I believe you're not one of them."

Dzintara gazed into his face.

"Strip him and hang him over the fire."

Two men grabbed Dzintara as Anno picked up the scabbard and placed the khanjar in his waist belt. They dragged her next to the pyre where the armor still steamed.

"Wait! Wait! I will tell you the truth."

Anno turned and smiled. They released her, and she fell to the ground.

"Are you not the least curious how I deciphered the script upon your blade?," he asked, standing next to her.

Dzintara watched the fire spark, and one log gave, crumbling, sending embers high toward the forest canopy. She looked towards her fate, remembering the dream in which she was drowning.

"I found the dagger. I swear it," she insisted.

Anno stayed silent. He stared at her, smiling.

"I was there. An infidel taught me how to speak," he said.

She glared at Anno and the others gathered around the cooling armor.

"We are the light. And nothing defeats the light," Anno gazed at her, then turned his back to her and motioned. The white robes grabbed Dzintara by the arm. They ripped her pelt off.

"What was his name?" Dzintara yelled.

Anno turned to her and paused.

"The infidel who taught you to speak," she continued.

With years of interrogation and conversion by the sword, Anno understood that every question had a purpose. It struck him as odd that a merchant from Northumbria would inquire about a man's name so far from home. But the reaction to the answer always gave away the truth.

He approached her, "Saladin".

She swallowed hard, searching desperately for anything she could use to kill him on the spot. Inches from her face, Anno stared into her eyes as if to taunt her.

The knight brothers erupted into a cheer in the distance. A wagon carrying sacks and barrels was rolling slowly towards them. Two men sat in the driver's seat. A man on horseback accompanied the wagon. Anno watched as the wagon came to a halt.

"I take it we need not worry about Curonians anymore," Varkelins said, standing on the perch of the wagon.

"How did you find us?" Anno asked as Varkelins climbed down from the wagon and extended his hand.

Anno cautiously took his hand and looked hard at Varkelins.

"Artur at the fort said you rode along the coast looking for the Curonians." Varkelins pointed to his escort on horseback.

"This lad led us here. We left what cargo we could at the fort and brought you some to help along the way."

Anno smiled and clutched Varkelins's shoulder.

"You lost a lot of men?" Varkelins asked, scanning the camp.

"It was a hard battle, but we press on."

"I'm no battle strategist, but it seems—"

"Then, no need for your thoughts," Anno interjected.

An odd silence settled between the two.

"Hunger can be hard in the winter," The glow of the khanjar

in the sunlight caught Varkelins' eye. "Where did you get that?" Varkelins asked with sudden interest, gazing at Anno's belt.

"The infidel who carried it is about to burn alive."

Varkelins looked at Anno and the khanjar. He forced a smile.

"Do you mind if I watch?"

Anno motioned for Varkelins to join.

They walked over to the fire. Varkelins walked slightly behind Anno, hiding his face.

"Strip the man, then place him in the armor," Anno ordered once again.

"I will tell you the truth! Wait!" Dzintara yelled.

Dzintara clenched her fists and gritted her teeth as the rough hands continued to tear away at her pelt, bruising her.

"Anno, let me buy the dagger and the exotic," Varkelins said, pointing at Dzintara.

"What would you want with them?"

"I'm a collector," Varkelins smiled, put his arm on Anno's shoulder, and gestured to accept.

Anno stepped a pace away, twirling his mustache. Then, he took the weapon from his belt and set it in Varkelins's hands.

"The man stays. He is an infidel. An enemy."

The warrior monks pushed Dzintara face-first into the ground. One of them then took out his knife and began cutting away at her already-torn leather tunic.

Varkelins shot a glance at Dzintara and blurted, "The man sailed with me from Northumbria."

Anno turned sharply. "What?"

"He's a skilled physician," Varkelins continued, his voice steady despite the tension. "You've lost too many men already."

Anno's eyes narrowed. "An infidel who deserves to burn alive."

"He can treat your wounded," Varkelins pressed. "Look around—another battle, and you'll have no men left to fight."

Anno scanned the camp, and the weariness of his men was

evident in every movement. Varkelins had a point. If they lost any more, they'd be forced to retreat, defeated. His mission to eradicate the Curonian village was crucial for gaining favor with the Merchant Guild.

Varkelins seized the moment. "Use him as a physician. If he survives, I'll buy him and make him a slave in Turaida."

Anno hesitated, but the weight of his decision was palpable. "Halt," he finally ordered.

The warrior monks yanked Dzintara to her feet. Her face was streaked with mud, and the silk she used to bind her breasts peeked out from beneath her pelt. Anno's gaze lingered on her, the implications of the situation sinking in.

Anno grabbed the khanjar from Varkelins hand and unsheathed it. He slowly approached Dzintara and pointed the knife in her face. Dzintara exchanged glances with Varkelins. He cowered, just like he did on the ship.

"You're a physician?" Anno asked.

"Your men crushed my potions and vials."

"This man has pleaded on your behalf," he said, pointing the blade towards Varkelins.

"You will march with the captives. When we make camp, you will attend to the wounded. If I catch you doing anything suspicious, I will have you beheaded. Take her over there," Anno said.

They put Dzintara with the rest of the Curonian captives. She stared at Varkelins as she passed him, trying hard to avoid eye contact. Anno returned the khanjar to Varkelins, who admired it and tucked it in his tunic.

He whistled, and moments later, the carter appeared from the woods. The driver took the perch, and Varkelins sat next to him. The trio that rode into camp with rations rode back out the way they came.

Dzintara was in a daze as she tried to grasp what just transpired. The mud and blood dried on her face and cracked. In her mind, she schemed when and how she would kill *him*. All she needed was one opportunity, even if it meant sacrificing her own life. She looked up at the sky, and the circling ravens looked like black blurs against the gray sky. She felt naked without her khanjar.

CHAPTER TWENTY-FOUR

Winter's arrival made the sun a rare sight, casting the city into a perpetual dimness. When Wulfric returned to the inn, the innkeeper informed him it would close for the season. He had until day's end to clear his debts and leave.

Wulfric spent his days keeping warm in an abandoned barn outside the city or wandering Riga's streets, and at night, he spent his time watching the Blackheads, waiting to see if Varkelins would show his face.

Food became scarce, and his appearance changed. A beard grew on his once clean-shaven face, making him look more like a beggar than a former second in command.

That night, he stood in the icy darkness, warming his hands with the breath of his mouth.

Fumbling in his pocket, he extracted his dwindling coin purse, revealing a meager three pfennigs, a single denier, a few denaro, and a lone denarius. His fingers traced over the silver coins in his palm, his teeth worrying his lower lip.

An opportunity arose as a group of men neared the entrance and engaged in conversation with the guard. Seizing the moment,

Wulfric quickened his pace and slipped past an unnoticed shadow.

"Ey," yelled the guard, who grabbed Wulfric, shoving him against the wall. "You again."

"I am looking for my friend."

"Like I told you last time. He ain't here."

"Varkelins. What about Varkelins."

"He ain't here either."

"I just want to go in and look. That's all."

With a swift motion, the guard shoved Wulfric, sending him sprawling to the street. The group of men chuckled and made some inaudible remarks. Wulfric pushed himself up from the frozen dirt and wiped the blood from his lips. The guard crossed his arms and scowled.

Wulfric walked away.

The snow fell lightly, and the gray clouds hid the moon. The dwellings all around were quiet, with the occasional faint candle glow coming from the window. In the distance, he heard drunken laughter and muffled conversation. It was rare for someone to wander the streets at night. He stopped to listen.

"We must go meet my father at the Blackheads," the voice laughed.

"The leech hasn't attended in a while. I wonder if something ill has begotten him," said a second voice. A crude belly laugh bounced off the frozen stone.

Wulfric heard piss hitting the snow.

"My father thinks Albert will make his move. He said we could use the leech for information."

"I'm sure he'll do anything for a nibble at the power teat."

They shared a laugh, and the piss stopped.

"Empty your pockets and put the contents on the ground. Slowly," a third voice suddenly hissed. Wulfric edged closer to the corner to get a better look, drawing his blade. He could make out three men, one wielding a blade at a smaller man's throat. The third man made a run for it, disappearing into the far darkness of an alley.

"Your friend is a coward. Take your coat off. Give me everything," the robber demanded.

The man began to strip, first removing his cloak. Wulfric rounded the corner, and when he was within three arms-length, he stopped and watched.

"I'll give you everything. Just don't kill me."

"Your dagger."

"Anything but this. It was a gift from the Merchant Guild to my father. It's priceless."

With a swift motion, the thief sliced the man's forearm open. The man screamed.

"I said, give me the dagger. Or the next one will be your throat."

Wulfric leapt from the darkness, wrapping one arm around the robber's neck. He pressed his blade into the thief's side, squeezing his arm tightly on the man's throat. The brigand fell limp as the small, thin man nursed his cut arm. Wulfric dropped him to the ground, retrieved the man's cloak, and handed it back to him.

The man took it from him, stood, and then turned to kick the unconscious bleeding robber repeatedly.

"Satisfying?" Wulfric asked.

"Very," the man answered. A final kick, and then he turned, swung his pelt over his shoulder, and put out a hand.

"Friedrich," he said.

"No one wanders these streets at night. At least, no one other than me," Wulfric responded.

"Who are you? I've never seen you before," Friedrich asked.

"Why? Do you know everyone in the city?"

"Just about. Worth knowing anyway. I spend a lot of time in the harbor and have never seen you."

The snowfall ceased, and the gray clouds broke open, a sliver of moonlight shining through.

"Hmmm," Wulfric grunted in response.

"Well, you look like you have seen better days," Friedrich said as he glanced at Wulfric's overgrown hair and beard, his gaunt frame, and his ragged clothing.

"This land is cursed," Wulfric said.

"You handled yourself well. I never saw you coming," Friedrich changed the subject.

"It ain't my first. A man of the sea gets plenty of practice," Wulfric said, flicking the tip of his blade toward Friedrich.

"Merchant?"

"Not quite."

Friedrich broke his gaze and looked up into the alleyway.

"Fucking Wilhem," he spat. "A cowardly Baron, unworthy of his sire's name, but a friend."

"What do you want done with this scum?" Wulfric asked, nodding to the thief.

"Leave him. He'll freeze overnight. What about you? You look like you need some coin."

"I'm not looking for charity," Wulfric said.

"I could use someone like you. Commoner. Knows how to handle himself."

Wulfric sheathed his blade and looked down at the humped thief, weighing his options. He needed to find Varkelins and find a way home. He'd need money either way.

"Look, take this. You saved my life," Friedrich said, taking a leather pouch out from under his shirt and handing it to Wulfric. The coins weighed heavy in Wulfric's hand.

"I'm no one's errand boy."

"No one said that. You can always find me at the House of the Blackheads. Know where that is?"

"Aye."

"You need work. Just come and ask for me when you're ready. In the meantime, consider it my thank you."

Wulfric pocketed the purse, glanced up at the moon, and disappeared back into the shadows.

CHAPTER TWENTY-FIVE

The warrior monks traveled through the dark pine forest, leading captives tied together like animals, thick hemp ropes cutting into their wrists and around their throats. The Brotherhood entered the unknown, surrounded by long shadows and the eerie creaking of tree limbs. The Brothers looked around cautiously, gripping their weapons. Some knights rode on horseback, their nervous steeds' breaths visible in the cold air. Others marched alongside, guarding the supply-laden animals.

Dzintara looked at the tribesman in front of her. She dragged on, one weary foot after another, the worn leather of her footwear threatening to give way at any moment. Anno rode tall on his horse, his armored chest draped in a white robe emblazoned with the stark red cross.

"We venture into Curonian territory. Remain vigilant. Have your blades at the ready."

As they quietly moved through the forest. Anno stopped and pointed to a brother on horseback, carrying a satchel instead of a sword.

"Brother, mark this newly entered land so that Albert can be informed of the Brotherhood's rightful claim. Do it quickly, before nightfall."

The balding knight dismounted and sat at the base of a pine tree, placing a cloth on the frozen earth. From his satchel, he took an inkpot, a quill pen, and a parchment and began to map the area they had crossed.

The rest of the Brothers halted as well and started to pitch camp for the night. Dzintara and the rest of the prisoners were staked at a distance from the Brothers lest their heresy be contagious.

Dzintara examined her fellow prisoners, taking note of one who stood out. His long hair was intricately braided, and a wooden talisman hung from his neck on a worn leather string. The talisman, with three distinct holes, functioned as a whistle.

The captives' faces were tired and worn. One was gravely wounded, and his cut had turned black. He wouldn't make it through the night. Anno dispatched a scout as the others went about making camp. The Brothers had removed their armor and had built a modest campfire. They gathered around it, enjoying wine and passing around meager camp rations.

Anno knelt beside the cartographer. "Brother, your skills are unparalleled. You wield the quill with the precision of a warrior," Anno said, praising the man.

Laughter erupted from the group around the fire, drawing a sharp glance from Anno. "Fools," he muttered under his breath.

"These men will lead us to our demise," the cartographer remarked, without taking his attention off the map.

A loud burst of laughter followed a snap from the fire, making Anno leap to his feet. "What the fuck are you doing?" he demanded, striding toward the group.

The circle parted, revealing the campfire that was now a bit too lively for stealth. Anno kicked the logs and stamped out the flames.

"You wretched fools. Might as well invite death over for an ale," He scolded them, his voice full of contempt for their carelessness. The knights scrambled like rodents, each finding a quiet tree to rest by.

A guard dragged Dzintara to tend to the wounded. Most wouldn't last the night. She knelt beside a man with a stomach wound, his face pale in the flickering torchlight. As she examined the wound, her eyes darted to a sword lying just a few arm's lengths away, propped against a tree, unattended. The guard behind her, torch in hand and sword drawn seemed distracted, staring off into the distance. This was her chance.

Dzintara inched closer to the sword, her heart pounding. The dying man's breath turned from rapid panting to wheezes. She kept moving, each shuffle of her knees bringing her closer to the weapon.

"Ahhh!" the wounded man cried out, his voice filled with agony. The guard snapped back to attention, his gaze locking onto her.

Dzintara quickly returned to the knight's side, pretending to tend to him. "What are you doing?" the guard demanded, raising his sword.

"I was looking for herbs," she said, her voice steady.

"The ground's frozen," he replied, suspicion in his eyes.

She reached down and grabbed a handful of moss from the ground. "We can use this to soak up the blood," she explained, stuffing the wound with moss and dirt while the guard watched her. Her chance was gone.

The knight took his final breath, and when he did, the guard roughly bound her hands and led her back to the captives.

Dzintara sat and turned to the captive with the braided hair, who was laughing quietly, amused by the recent events.

"Muḷki," said the tribesman as he tapped his head. Dzintara smiled.

The moon hung high, shining through the forest canopy. Some of the warrior monks had fallen asleep, their snores mingling with the night sounds. The prisoners lay on the ground, sleeping fitfully, but the one with braids stayed seated, upright, and alert. He gazed at Dzintara and opened his mouth as wide as he could. Between his cheeks and teeth was a shiny, slim object. He reached for it with his hand and pulled it out. It was a small needle with twine wrapped around its base, used for repairing fishing nets. With quiet focus, he worked on picking apart the ropes binding his hands.

Dzintara leaned against the tree, staring at the moon through the forest foliage. Memories flooded her mind: receiving the khanjar and fearing to disappoint Muhammad, the lustful face of the merchant her father sold her to, the childhood fear of the world beyond the woods, Muhammad's expressionless decapitated head, and waking up to Gorm's calloused hands around her neck. All of it had led to this moment. Except, at this moment, something was missing: fear.

Where fear usually lived, she experienced a growing sense of curiosity about what awaited her, whether it was death, escape, or even victory. She couldn't bring herself to envision what that victory might look like.

A shadow emerged from afar, growing larger as it approached. Dzintara narrowed her eyes, trying to see it in the moonlight. Soon, the scout in white appeared from the darkness, reaching Anno's side to wake him. They whispered urgently, their words lost in the night.

"We move dawn," Anno whispered aloud into the dark.

When Dzintara awoke, the moon had vanished. The grim troupe stirred, fastening their armor for the journey ahead. The tribesman with the talisman sat despondent, the small knife needle broken and discarded on the frozen forest floor. Dzintara slid closer to him, tenderly resting her head on his shoulder. They exchanged a final smile.

"Krists," she said.

"Alvydas," he tapped his chest gently.

A knight with a limp struggled over and kicked the sleeping captives awake. The wounded one did not wake. The knight untied him from the pack, leaving him unburied.

The group, brothers and prisoners in tow, marched deeper

into the forest. After a time, Anno ordered a halt, motioning his soldiers to silence.

Anno dismounted, whispering orders to several of his knights. Arrows were placed in a pile. They built a small fire, shielding it from view.

Beyond the forest, across an open meadow, a village was slowly coming to life. Roosters were crowing in the early morning sunlight, and cows and goats were pleading to be milked. Candlers were flittering to life in the log homes of the villagers. Anno made the sign of the cross and quietly began to chant:

"Te Deum laudamus:
te Dominum confitemur.
Te aeternum Patrem,
omnis terra veneratur.
Tibi omnes Angeli,
tibi Caeli, et universae Potestates:
tibi Cherubim et Seraphim incessabili voce
*   proclamant."*

Silently, the captors lined up the prisoners in a row and cut their bonds while holding them at sword point. Several brothers hurriedly forced the prisoners into the bloodied white robes of fallen knights. A memory of Acre flashed through Dzintara's mind.

"You're using us as bait," she accused the knight nearest her.

"Sanctus, Sanctus, Sanctus
Dominus Deus Sabaoth.
Pleni sunt caeli et terra
maiestatis gloriae tuae.
Te gloriosus Apostolorum chorus,
te Prophetarum laudabilis numerus,
te Martyrum candidatus laudat exercitus—"

"Just like you did in Acre," she shouted, interrupting Anno's prayer.

"Skrieniet un glābiet savas ģimenes," she screamed to the Curonians.

One tribesman rammed his shoulder into a crusader's chest and bolted toward the open meadow. He attempted to sound a battle cry, but an arrow silenced the cry almost instantly.

As one, the tribesmen bolted toward their home village. A line of archers bent in towards the fire, tipping the arrows to the flame, then stretched straight again, a wall of flame. They lifted their bows skyward.

"Fire!" Anno order.

"Save your families!" Dzintara screamed at the top of her lungs as she ran toward the village.

The fiery arrows ripped across the clearing, landing on roofs, in the long grasses, and against the wagons on the street.

Villagers rushed from their homes, beating back flames. Thatched roofs crackled. Another round of arrows descended, pinning villagers to the ground and burning them alive.

She heard Anno scream, "Kill them all!"

Alvydas blew the whistle around his neck, sending villagers to flee to the forest. Arrows whistled past. Dzintara dropped to the ground and counted. When archers began reloading, she jolted to her feet and continued her sprint.

She dropped to the ground as another set of arrows sent another rain of fire. Log houses were now engulfed in flames, black smoke rising to the sky.

She heard a loud roar from the warrior monks and looked back. Alvydas lay face down with an arrow planted in his neck. The knight charged towards the village.

Villagers lay on the ground, trapped and burning. The White-robes, both on foot and horseback, surged, crossing into the heart of the chaos. Dzintara needed cover. She ran from one log house to another for cover, and she made a sharp left and then a right. A blade swung close, missing her. She rolled to the ground, kicking the sword from the boy's hands.

"I'm not one of them!" she pulled her wrist from the loose binding, then pulled the robe off, showing her plain clothes beneath.

As the White-robes rampaged through the village, cutting down everyone in their path, one on horseback noticed the Dzintara and the boy and charged toward them. She grabbed the boy and dragged him and his sword through the smokey streets until they stumbled upon a log house that was at the edge of the village. She looked back and had no sight of their pursuer.

INSIDE THE HOUSE, she lay on her back, gasping for breath.

The boy beside her coughed, fighting for breath.

"You need to leave! Just run! Or hide," she said, panting.

The boy stood before her, his young, innocent face framed by blonde hair falling over his eyes. His hands were barely big enough to grip a sword. Outside, screams and chaos filled the air. Black smoke choked the village's narrow dirt streets. Amidst the screams, the conquerors' occasional laughter rang out.

"Slēpies vai skrien mežā!"

The boy watched her silently. He pointed at her left thigh. Dzintara looked down and noticed that she had taken a cut from the boy's sword. She stood and peeked out the window. No sign of them.

She opened the front door. "Go hide in the forest," she repeated. Again, he just stood there.

"I can't help you," she said, touching his face as she walked out the door.

Sword raised, she crept down the street. Curonians lay in the street, limbs akimbo. Creeping from one house to another, she searched for survivors. As she crouched by a barrel, watching the street, a stray horse neighed and charged around the corner toward her. She leapt aside and fell face-first to the ground. She watched the horse gallop across the clearing toward the forest. A sharp pain shot from her wound. Touching the back of her thigh, her hands were covered in blood. She stuck her finger into the wound to see just how deep it was. Just a surface wound, thank the gods.

She rolled over, stood up, and continued her search. A grunting noise caught her ear. She followed the sound toward one of the homes that hadn't burned to the ground. The grunting was rhythmic and angry. She pushed the door open. The back of a White-robe, his breeches at his knees and weapon out of reach, on top of a girl either unconscious or dead.

The man's grunting became louder and more frantic. Dzintara crept up behind him and plunged her sword into his back. He startled, choking on the blood that filled his throat. She yanked the sword from his back and kicked him to the ground, pushing his lifeless body off of the girl.

The girl's eyes were closed, and there was blood between her legs. The girl's hands were still warm when she touched them. The girl's body was limp and heavy. Dzintara attempted to hoist the girl onto her shoulders, but her leg gave out. She set the girl back down and moved towards the door, cracking it open. All was clear. She grasped the girl beneath her arms and hauled her out the door.

"Burn everything!" Anno ordered from somewhere in the distance.

Her leg felt numb as she dragged along, but she kept at it. For a moment, she stopped at the tree line to catch her breath. Dots of white came pulsing before her eyes. Looking back towards the village, the White-robes went from house to house, setting everything on fire. She continued to drag the girl, and she saw that there was life in her as her eyelids moved.

"Almost there."

When she looked down, her leg was soaked in blood. And then everything went black.

CHAPTER TWENTY-SIX

The last wagon from the caravan rolled to a stop in front of the heavy wooden gates of Turaida Castle. The moon hung above the horizon. Varkelins shivered as he waited for the guard to appear.

"Name yourself!" shouted the guard from the tower above.

"Varkelins. I am bearing merchandise from Northumbria for His Excellency, Albert the Archbishop of Riga."

The gate lifted, and the last cart of merchandise from Riga, spared by the storehouse guilds and not given to the brotherhood, entered the courtyard. Sleep-weary servants began unloading the remaining cargo. Varkelins led the effort while Albert emerged from the house to inspect the commotion. Albert's heavy coat swayed with each step, and his feet crunched the snow below.

"Your excellency," Varkelins gave a quick bow.

"Hm," Albert grunted, looking over the cargo. Then asked with an accusatory tone, "This is all of it?"

"Indeed."

"Seems a bit thin to me."

"I have everything recorded, so we can go over it together."

"*Scheiße*, it's freezing out here. Come inside once they're done."

Albert lumbered back into the stone house built into the wall of the castle. Varkelins sighed, bracing for Albert's inevitable excuse for the delayed payment. His thoughts turned to his own dwindling resources; without additional funding, bankruptcy loomed.

Inside, the table overflowed with an abundance of meats, poultry, bread, and wine. Albert, seated at the head of the large table, was engrossed in devouring a chicken leg. He gestured for Varkelins to join him. As Varkelins moved past the hearth toward the dining hall, he felt warmth envelop him, not just from the fire but from the saint-adorned tiles lining the walls. Each tile bore the image of a saint, their expressions tranquil despite the chaos of their stories, silently observing from within their ceramic confines. Varkelins stared as Albert's teeth tore away at the meat. When he was done, he chucked the bones onto his plate. The saints stared at them both.

"Sit. Eat. You haven't eaten," Albert said with his mouth full.

"I'm trying to work up an appetite."

Varkelins quietly stepped over to Albert and handed him a stack of parchments. Then, he walked over to the hearth and ran his fingers along the tiles, admiring them. Albert sucked his teeth and wiped his hands with a cloth, and grabbed the parchments with his fat fingers, squinting to read the small script. Some time went by in silence, save for the occasional *hmmm* or cough.

"This is barely going to get us through winter," Albert finally said.

"There was double when I got—"

"I see that. I can read," an annoyed Albert interjected without looking up.

Varkelins tapped on the painted tiling along the mantle of the hearth.

"Don't tap on that," Albert ordered.

"Your debt to merchants and storehouse guilds in Riga is not going unnoticed," Varkelins spoke without looking at Albert.

"Ah — to hell with them. Most of them don't tithe unless they need something," Albert rebutted without looking up.

Then Varkelins shifted and met Albert's large dark eyes. The candlelight from the chandelier above flickered in the darkness of his eyes.

"Half the cargo went to pay your debt," Varkelins said. "The storehouse boys almost fed me to the Dvina."

"Ah! A little toughening up would do you some good," Albert said with a hint of jest in his tone.

Varkelins cocked his head in disapproval, and Albert could see his initial approach wasn't working.

"So be it. Make another trip," Albert suggested, quickly switching strategies.

Varkelins refrained from speaking for some time. The pelt-covered floor held a bear that caught his attention, and he walked over and fidgeted with its head using his feet.

"I can't make another trip," he finally said.

"Why?" Albert asked.

"Your debts were my profit. I don't have enough to fund another commercial voyage, neither do you."

Albert threw up his hands. "Ah, goat shit!"

Pieces of meat flew from his mouth as he spoke, and he slammed his fist on the table and spilled his mazer.

"I have everyone squeezing me for money. You, the Brotherhood, the guild. I am the archbishop. Everything — " Albert's teeth seethed, "everything that is Riga would not exist if it wasn't for me. What if I have debt? Forgive it, like how God forgives your sins."

"Trade requires upfront coin. Crew. Boat. Port levies. Shall I go on?" Varkelins spat back.

"Men who conquer find a way," Albert said.

Varkelins forced a smile.

"Albert, I am penniless. I outfitted this last voyage with the last bit I had. You promised me an appointment. I could have easily sold the cargo and made two times, three times what I put up."

Varkelins marched over to Albert and leaned into his face. Albert arched backward.

"I need this appointment—bishop or city official. Something!"

"Well, no one wants a penniless official," Albert said, laughing

"No one wants a penniless archbishop," Varkelins rebutted.

Albert sighed and wiped the grease on his hands on his robe. He motioned for Varkelins to sit, but Varkelins refused.

"*Setz dich. Mein Freund...setz dich.*"

Varkelins straightened his back, walked to the table, and sat. Albert smiled at this.

"*Du bist so weit weg, mein Freund.*"

"I can hear you just fine. And don't call me your friend," Varkelins responded.

He shifted in his chair. An old woman came from the darkness of the adjacent room and set a plate for Varkelins. She shuffled back and forth, bringing utensils and a mazer, and then she poured him some wine. When she was done, she looked at Albert, and he motioned her away.

"I am working on something. I have recently—" Albert searched for the words. "I acquired knowledge that the shipwright knows where the gold and silver are hidden. So, I had him arrested." Albert said, impressed with himself.

"What gold and silver?" Varkelins asked, perking up.

"About thirty years ago, a vessel made its way to us carrying gold and silver to fund our Crusades. The sea froze over, and the ship was stuck. Everyone onboard froze to death. By the time the cog was found, it was burnt to crisp. Charred skeletons in the hold."

Albert took a moment for a drink and to let Varkelins take all of this new information in.

"I think — I've learned that Ako had his people loot the ship, and he hid it all. Once they were done, he burnt the ship."

Varkelins rolled his eyes and sighed, "Albert, these are tales that drunken man warble about in a tavern."

"*Es ist wahr,*" Albert insisted.

"How do you know it's true?"

"The pope sent me a letter saying that this gold was coming. It just never made it here. A note from the captain made it back to the Vatican."

"*Vielleicht war es eine Lüge und er wollte dich ersetzen,*" Varkelins responded, an edge in his voice.

Albert slammed his fist onto the table and stood. "It was not a lie! And I cannot be replaced! Never! I am respected at the Curia!"

"What is your plan then? To find this great hoard of gold? Torture Ako?" Varkelins asked with a raised voice.

"I will get it out of Ako where he hid it. That will open opportunities for us both. Expansion! Expeditions! Trade! We'll stomp those scum Brotherhood into the ground. We won't need them. We'll buy our own army!"

Albert raised his hands to the heavens as if he were asking God Almighty for all of this. Varkelins stared back quietly, then sighed to himself. He forced a smile at Albert.

"Where is the Ako?"

"In my dungeons."

Hans rushed into the dining hall, interrupting, "You excellency, there is something outside the gates!"

Albert jumped in his seat. "Well, what is it?"

"The messenger said it is to be delivered to Varkelins," Hans said.

Albert eyed Varkelins. "Expecting something?"

"I'll go inspect," Varkelins, refusing to answer the question.

Hans led Varkelins just outside the wooden gates where a sack lay.

"None of the guards have dared to go near it," Hans said with a shiver. "They said that you lost a bet, and they expect payment."

Varkelins knelt beside the sack and pulled it open. The unconscious face of Dzintara stared back at him, prompting a whispered, "Krists." He drew back the sack further to reveal her entire body. A groan escaped her lips, and Varkelins heaved a sign of relief. She was alive.

CHAPTER TWENTY-SEVEN

Her eyes took a few long moments to adjust to the darkness. For a while, she lay there face down with her cheek touching the frigid stone. Eventually, she rolled over on her back. Although her vision was still blurry, she could make out the torch fire bouncing off the glistening stone walls. When she squinted, the iron bars became clear. A feeling of nakedness descended on her, and she gasped. Her identity was no longer a secret. She ran her hands down her body, and a linen hemp tunic covered her. The wound on her thigh had been cleaned and dressed in lard and honey, then wrapped in clean linen. The silk she used to bind her breasts was gone.

A sudden cold draft howled, cutting through the thin linen. She shivered, then sobbed quietly to herself.

TO KEEP warm in the endless days that followed, she curled up into a fetal position at night, covering herself with a. flea-ragged, moth-eaten pelt. She got a sense of the dimensions of her cell by feeling around in the darkness, patting the floor and walls.

Food came once a day in a bucket. A thin porridge of barley.

At night, she listened to the rodents scurrying about. Occasionally, she thought she could hear faint breathing. Her cell bars were spaced out unevenly. One morning, she crawled across the wet, cold stone floor and put her thumb on one of the cell bars and her pinky on another. She repeated this until she found one where her pinky didn't reach. Cold to the touch, she grabbed onto two adjacent bars. Her ears scraped against the corroded surface, pushing until her head stuck out of her cell. Next to her middle cell were two others.

"Hello. Anyone else down here?"

The echo of her voice bounced through the small dungeon. She crawled back into the darkest and hugged her knees. She waited, listening in the darkness, but no response came.

Not knowing whether it was day or night, she slept to no rhythm. As time passed, she developed a ritual upon waking. First, she unwrapped her wound to let it breathe. Next followed a series of exercises and stretches to keep her body from deteriorating. She then paced her cell and recounted the events that led up to here. Sometimes she cried, and sometimes she screamed, and sometimes she laughed. Her dreams became lucid. Time became a void.

She had recurring nightmares of her father standing in front of a cog, frozen in ice, bursting up in flames. In the dream, she watched her father watching the burning spectacle. She could hear screams from the belly of the vessel. She screamed out to her father, but he couldn't hear her. Then, he turned towards her, his eyes glowing red.

In the delirium between her dreams and waking reality, she sometimes heard a rasping breath, unsure of which world it belonged to. She realized she wasn't alone.

The bucket arrived one day, each time carried by a man she couldn't make out.

"Wait," she said, "Who's in the other cell?"

The guard stood still for a moment, watching her. Without answering, he receded, and she heard his steps up the stairs. The dungeon door opened and shut. Dzintara pushed her head through the cell bars, trying to look into the cell next to hers.

"I know someone is in here. Talk to me," she called out into the cold, wet misery, "who are you?"

No one answered.

To measure time, she counted each step she took from the time she awoke until the bucket came. It was about fifteen thousand steps. One day, on the thirteen thousandth step, the shadowy figure of the guard stood in front of her cell, holding a bucket.

"You're early."

The guard opened her cell and slid the bucket in her direction. Instead of the liquid barley gruel, she found two chicken legs. Crouching in the darkness, she sniffed at the roasted chicken, then snatched a piece with both hands, biting into it as hard as she could. Tearing meat and ligament from the bone, she closed her eyes on the first bite and let out a deep sigh. When she looked up, the guard was gone, but she didn't care much. She sucked the bone smooth of the first chicken leg, then reached for the other piece. As she was about to bite, she hesitated.

Dzintara stood and approached the cell bars. She held the chicken leg by the end of the drum and stuck her arm out between the bars, tossing the leg near the adjacent cell. It slapped on the cobblestone, within reach of the other prisoner. Waiting patiently, she watched. Time went on. The air in the cell was chilling, so she knew that night was coming. Soon, sleep came over her eyes, and her waiting slid into the darkness of half-dreams.

SHE DREAMT of her young brother standing by their father's desk, admiring a gold coin minted with Honorius and then pocketing it. Then, she saw images of men coming to her father's house, inquiring where her brother had acquired such a coin. She woke to the sound of clanging against the cell bars. Groggily, she turned her head just in time to see an arm stretch out from the adjacent cell, fingers straining to grasp a chicken leg lying just out of reach. The arm trembled with effort, muscles taut. Inch by inch, the hand inched closer until, with a final desperate lunge, it closed around the chicken leg and pulled it back into the darkness of the cell. She heard the faint sound of chewing. "Where am I?" she eagerly asked.

No response. Just the sound of chewing.

"Where am I? Who are you?" She asked again.

Whoever was in the cell next to hers must be deaf or mute, she thought.

With a defeated sigh, she pulled her head back through the bars and sat down, resting her back against the iron bars. She curled her knees to her chest.

"I just want to hear a voice," she whispered. "Any voice."

Silence. The flames flickered and danced on the stones of the wall. Then, a loud sigh came from the cell.

"Welcome to the dungeon of the Archbishop of Riga."

Her eyes widened, and she sprung to her feet. She knew that voice. Tears sprung to her eyes, and she gasped repeatedly, searching for air. She wiped the tears away, but they kept coming.

"No point in crying, my daughter. We'll both be dead soon enough," the voice responded from the other cell.

CHAPTER TWENTY-EIGHT

Varkelins sat with a full tankard of ale, watching as merchants laughing, drinking, and negotiating. The merchants were poring over parchments, pointing and arguing loudly. One merchant drunkenly accused another of being a thief. The sound of a fiddle filled the hall, a cheerful tune that belied the cold and ice-locked city. Mazers in front of each man stood filled with midus or ale.

He quickly scanned the room in both directions. He found Hendricks, sitting in a dark corner, two empty seats at his table. His gaze wandered, as if in search of someone. Varkelins stood and walked through the bustling merchants, taking one of the empty seats at his table.

"What do I owe the pleasure?" Hendricks asked.

"I've been thinking about our last encounter."

"My sincerest apologies, but my son can be quite the fool at times. I assure you he meant no harm."

"I'm not here to talk about your son or his buffoonery, Hendricks. I'm here to talk about the future of this great city. And its rulers."

Hendricks drank and sized up Varkelins. "Careful, Varkelins. The ice on the Dvina is still yet thin, friend."

"Fact is, Albert's coffers are empty. He'll surely continue to raise levies on goods coming into and leaving Riga. Come spring, you'll be paying so many levies that no one will trade with this city."

"Don't speak ill of your master," Hendricks warned.

Varkelins hesitated for a moment, unsure whether he would be able to obtain Hendrick's support. But then he remembered sometimes the cunningest thing was just to turn the tables.

"You're right, friend. Forget I said anything. Albert did mention something about the export of amber, but it was not important."

He stood, as if to leave. Hendricks raised his arm to stop him. "Wait, just sit."

Varkelins paused, appearing uncertain, but it was a calculated hesitation meant to provoke a stronger commitment from Hendricks.

"I want to hear you out, Varkelins. Forgive me for my initial reaction," Hendricks gave a surfaced apology, but that was good enough for Varkelins to know that he's got Hendricks right where he wants him. Varkelins slowly lowered himself back into the chair. "Apology accepted," Varkelins said.

"Continue."

Varkelins looked about, dropping his voice, as if he was about to unveil a great secret. "Albert's grip on the city is slipping. His once abundant coffers are now empty, and he's desperate to refill them. Unfortunately for me, my merchandise fell victim to his insatiable spending and his endless debts. The storehouse guild seized two-thirds of it, and they claim there's still owing."

"And? What about the amber exports?" Hendricks asked, almost impatiently.

"Well, it's only a matter of time before he empties the guild's pockets, too."

"Come now, Varkelins, don't spin yarn at the House of the Blackheads. This is a place of trade, not hearsay," Hendricks warned.

"The winter is long and dark, Hendricks. And barren."

"The guild is too powerful. He wouldn't risk us turning our backs on him. This is our city. He's a mere figurehead," Hendricks tilted his chin pridefully.

"I can see why you would say that, sitting where you are," Varkelins said, leaning in. "But if he rekindles his relationship with the Brotherhood, then winter for you may be longer than for the rest of us."

Varkelins leaned back, crossing his legs, letting this piece of news settle in. Hendricks sipped his ale in thought.

"Albert is insatiable, but he's no fool. The Brotherhood is weak. Anno is struggling to gather new recruits. His numbers are thin. If Albert strengthens his relationship with the Brotherhood, then, I say, let them come," Hendricks reasoned.

"You may be right," Varkelins said, baiting Hendricks. "Unless, maybe, The Order wants to strengthen their position here. Some say the dawn of the northern crusades is coming. They will need an outpost for their northern campaign. Riga could be their chosen location. This is what some say. I don't know who, but some," Varkelins said, winking at Hendricks.

Hendricks couldn't find words. They sat silently for a while.

"What exactly are you implying, Varkelins?" Hendricks said, hissing.

"I'm not here to spin yarn, Hendricks. All I can say is that with your support, I can make sure that when the time comes, you and your guild are on the winning side."

Hendricks reached over and grabbed Varkelins by the collar. "You scum! How dare you come to my table, you swine, and threaten me with your lies."

The commotion drew concerned looks from neighboring tables. Varkelins gently placed his hands on Hendrick's clenched fists and pulled them away from his collar. Hendricks leaned back in his chair, and Varkelins adjusted his tunic, then smiled at the concerned fellow merchants, putting them at ease.

He glared at Hendricks with disgust. "Look around, you old

fool. It doesn't take a prophet to see what's coming. The Battle of Ice was lost. The tribes run free, taking what they want. And Riga is just a day's ride from the sea, with access to the entire north by ship."

Varkelins stood and looked down at Hendricks. "You have a choice to make."

Varkelins walked through the great hall as the merchants gazed on. But he didn't turn his head as though none of them were there.

CHAPTER TWENTY-NINE

The Dvina was completely frozen over, preventing any ships from coming or leaving the port of Riga. Hungry men walked out onto the river, cut holes in the thick ice, and fished to feed their families.

Anno settled back into his fortress. He sat at the head of a large table in the dining hall. A large fire filled the room with light but little warmth. Anno leaned over a parchment of paper, hunched under a doubled pelt. On the table beside him, a candle had burnt halfway. He would occasionally look up and run his hand through his beard.

He heard the rattling of the chains that opened the fortress gates, followed by the commotion of greetings and hearty laughter. As the dining hall door opened, snow burst in, swirling around a dark-robed figure.

"Willkommen, Bruder Markus. Wie war deine Reise?"

Markus rubbed his hands together. Anno watched him move swiftly across the hall to the hearth, bending low to warm his hands. Markus stood and stared silently into the flames for some time, turning his outstretched hands as if to melt the ice from them.

"Gut dich zu sehen, Bruder Anno."

"I apologize for the lack of hospitality, but rations are tight, and the winters are long. There won't be another ship for months to refill supplies. Have you heard about the success of our campaign?"

"Campaign?"

Markus's beard, which reached down to his chest, was dripping with melting snow. Snot dribbled from his thick nose, and the firelight reflected in his wide, dark eyes.

"We've been pressing for converts in the region and expanding our territory. Our commitment is to you and the order."

Markus nodded softly, hands resting over the fire, "I have news."

Anno turned his chair to face Markus and leaned in with curiosity.

"Hochmeister von Salza achieved something that was unthought of before," Markus said with a joyful tone, "The Teutonic Order has been recognized of equal status as the Templars and the Hospitallers. The church has offered spiritual and financial support for our order. That means a crusade here in the north to convert all subjects and rule this land under God."

The white teeth behind his beard flashed as Anno smiled widely.

"Dem Gott Allmächtig sei Dank," Anno responded to the news.

Markus took his pelts off and hung them out to dry next to the fireplace. He wore a white robe underneath with a black cross embroidered on the front. Anno stood, and they grabbed each other by the forearm and hugged each other with congratulations. Then they sat, silent for some time.

A wet log hissed, its embers bursting out of the grate. Markus gazed at Anno, tilting his head in search of words.

"Markus, I see there is something on your mind. That is not all that you have come here to say."

"Brother Anno—I bring more good news, but," the man

pursed his lips, "it comes with sacrifice. Like how our Savior had to sacrifice in order to save us all."

Anno leaned back in his chair.

"I gave Salza the letter and asked for his consideration. He asked about your brotherhood."

"He did? In what way did he inquire about me and my band of mercenaries?" Anno said with a slightly sardonic tone.

Markus forced a nervous smile and chuckled.

"He asked about the brotherhood's loyalty and where it may lie."

Anno nodded, motioning him to continue.

"You see, the Hochmeister knows that you were commissioned by Albert to convert and subjugate the heathens of this land—and claim it for the Holy Mother Church—"

"After all this time of me begging for amalgamation, squirming, pleading, and shedding blood just for a moment of his attention, you come to me and tell me that he has inquired about us," Anno spat tersely. "And now, the Hochmeister is asking you about our brotherhood?"

"Yes. It's Albert."

Anno's dark eyes widened.

"What about Archbishop Albert?"

"Salva is petitioning His Holiness to remove Albert and transfer his authority to the Teutonic Order. However, His Holiness is hesitant, fearing retaliation for favoring a military order over a man of the Holy See. Despite Salva's repeated requests and pleas, His Holiness maintains that bishops should have supreme political and spiritual authority, with our order serving the bishops."

"And where does the Brotherhood of the Sword come into all of this?" Anno inquired, rubbing his hands together.

"The Hochmeister asked me to come here to tell you that the Livonian Brothers of the Sword have strong considerations about becoming part of us. One of us."

Anno snickered and smiled, but Markus didn't return the smile. He stared hard at Anno.

"Markus, years of negotiating and begging with no results. Now, suddenly, this? But there's more, I'm sure, so out with it," Anno demanded.

"The Hochmeister was very pleased with the progress you and your brothers have made. We are servants of God and his Holiness—"

"Enough with the bullshit. What is the sacrifice, Markus?"

"The Hochmeister needs to know that your loyalty is with us and not with Albert. Once Albert finds out, he will make a move against us."

"Our loyalty is where it has always been. With the Ordo domus Sanctae Mariae Theutonicorum Hierosolymitanorum."

"The Hochmeister will be glad to hear this. But it's not enough."

The sound of his chair scraping against the stone echoed through the hall as Anno pushed back and stood to face the hearth.

"Isn't what we've done enough? We made a claim to this land and converted the heathens. We have stood against Albert. Men have shed blood."

"The Papal courts are discussing a Crusade to Prussia and into the Semigallian lands. You and your brothers are not bound by any allegiance and can act as you please. We have allied with various kings and sent Brothers to serve in the campaign in Prussia. However, no one is daring enough to venture into the tribal lands of Semigallia."

"There it is. The sacrifice. You and Salva want me and my men to go," Anno said.

"Going into that territory and laying claim to it will strengthen our position for these lands. Your Brothers will join our order. His Holiness will have no choice but to grant us absolute power."

"You want me and my brethren in arms to supplement the

cowardice of your men and of your superiors?" Anno said, scoffing.

"Anno, you know these lands better than anyone. If there is a band of knights who would succeed, it would surely be yours, The Livonian Brotherhood of the Sword."

"Salva wants to send us to our deaths," Anno said.

"No, if we make the first move, it would look like a betrayal to the pope."

"The request is a tremendous one. I will have to take most of my men with me and leave our fortress vulnerable," Anno countered.

"Of course, the amalgamation comes with a handsome fee. The conquered lands would cover it. It will be shared with you. The fiefs will be split with the Order. Including you, as Provincial Master of Livonia."

"What if I refuse?"

"That is an option. However, the Hochmeister's stance would be that you are self-interested and that your loyalty lies with yourself, not with the order. Once the Papal courts approve the funding of a northern Crusade, you and your men will essentially be in the way, thus making the Brotherhood an enemy of ours."

"Essentially an order, then," he muttered.

He paced the hall, his footsteps echoing in the large stone chamber. The altar loomed silently. Suddenly, a loud crack from the dying fire broke the stillness, signaling its fading life.

Anno touched the cold iron ring of the door and stepped into the cold night. Snowflakes fell like ash from the sky. In the courtyard, a young Brother in his undergarments was restrained to a pillory and flogged repeatedly by the courtyard master.

"What has he done?" Anno asked.

"Got into the rations."

"Enough. We'll need every man in the best of shape."

"Aye, Grandmestier."

A small wooden shed stood behind the fortress. Anno opened

the creaky door, gathered firewood in his arms, and walked back into the empty hall where Markus was waiting.

"Brother Anno, you've wanted this for years. Your skill in organizing men for war is unmatched. You will have unlimited resources and won't have to beg Albert for scraps. You'll also govern. Expanding these lands isn't cheap, and the returns from fiefs are significant."

Anno knelt in front of the hearth, placing logs upon the fire.

"These lands are barren," Anno said quietly.

"As a brother, I ask you to go south to Semigallia and prove to the Hochmeister that the Brotherhood is the right choice."

"We have proven ourselves for years. What you ask of me is mortal sin."

"I don't understand. Mortal sin?" Markus asked, perplexed.

"A man of the cloth knows that suicide is a mortal sin. That's what you and Salva are asking of me and my men."

"Anno, you are the only ones who can defeat the Semigallians. There is no one else. It's now or never."

"There is always another Crusade. Another call for service to Christ and his kingdom. In this endeavor, there is no such thing as never," Anno said angrily.

"I have made your case to the Hochmeister and have pleaded as you requested. The time is now," Markus begged. "You must give to get."

"The Curonians have attempted to conquer the Semigallians but were entirely unsuccessful. They were completely routed. The Semigallians are magnificent fighters; so formidable, in fact, that none have survived to recount any tale of successful conquest against them."

"Brother," Markus whispered, "you will be the first."

Anno flashed a dismissive smile. He shifted his weight in the chair and gazed at the fire. "The Hochmeister will not hesitate to find someone else. The time for Crusades in this land is upon us. We will act now, with or without you. Without you, you and your brothers will be seen as obstacles."

Anno shot an angry glance at Markus.

"Can I count on you?" Markus asked.

Anno rose and stepped toward Markus, extending his hand. Markus met his gesture, and they embraced in a hug and firm handshake.

"Why," Anno asked, his eyes locked with Markus's, "are you so quick to send me off to my death?" Markus said nothing in response but glanced away.

Anno nodded. "If I die in battle, you will honor this agreement?"

"I will honor our agreement. I swear it upon our friendship. The Brotherhood will be amalgamated. But also, I pray you'll stay alive, my brother."

Markus took up his pelt, wrapping the warmed skin around his body. "The cold is hard in these parts."

"It's unforgiving," Anno said, smiling.

Anno embraced Markus like a younger brother, gently touching the back of his head. Markus broke the hug and stepped into the frigid darkness, the door creaking shut behind him. Anno turned back to warming his palms by the hearth, listening for the gate to rattle open. Markus, the Provincial Master of the Teutonic Order and his longtime confidant, rode away. As Anno gazed into the flames, a creeping sensation settled within him. He knew this was the final farewell to his cherished childhood friend.

CHAPTER THIRTY

I t had been five days since her father last spoke to her. She refused to be the one to break the silence.

Meanwhile, her leg wound was healing. Every morning, she cleaned it as part of her daily ritual. She noticed that her treatment was much better than her father's: better food, clean water, more frequent meals, and a change of clothes. She felt more like a lower-class guest than a prisoner. During the day, she sat by the iron bars of her cell, waiting. The only sound from her father's cell was his snoring. On the sixth day, she received a tray with enough roasted pig for four men, while her father got no food. She ate loudly, savoring the fatty bits with audible sighs, and threw the scraps out of her cell, out of her father's reach.

Beyond the prison doors, the wind howled. Her full stomach kept her warm and sleepy. She slumped against the stone wall, staring at the platter with enough pig left for two men. She sucked her teeth, searching for leftovers with her tongue. The smell of roast pork lingered in the cell. She rested her head against the iron bars, remembering the day her father sold her. It felt both long ago and like yesterday. Slowly, she dozed off into a deep sleep.

❄

TALL PINE TREES SURROUNDED HER, making the land feel foreign. She looked down and saw she was dressed as a man, just as she had been when she hitched a ride on the cog. The silk wrapped around her chest was so tight she could only take shallow breaths. She wore baggy trousers and held her khanjar. She started running. The forest seemed endless, and every time she saw a clearing, it vanished as she reached it. She felt trapped, the silk tightening with each stride, making her gasps for breath more desperate.

Turning around, she saw black mist flowing towards her, pushing past the trunks and rising into the canopy, consuming everything it touched. Gripping the khanjar, she ran as fast as she could, but the black mist was always behind her, pursuing her relentlessly.

Then, she saw a clearing through the pines. The sun was shining brightly, and the birds sang cheerful sounds. She plunged forward. Acorns pierced her feet through her leather footwear, and twigs and branches hit her face, drawing blood at every step. The smell of pine turned to rot, overwhelming her with the scent of decaying flesh. She tumbled at the edge of the forest line, free from the prison of the pines. She could breathe again.

She lay on her back, staring at the bright sun. She laughed, her face warm, her fingers clenching handfuls of dirt. She looked down and saw that she was naked. Her fists tingled as if the earth was moving. The fresh spring scent gradually turned into a rotten smell that crept into her nose.

The sun turned dark orange without moving from its peak, then bled into dark red. The smell of rotting flesh filled her nose, making her cough. She looked around and saw she was sprawled on top of a mountain of corpses, the faces of her tribesmen. Among them was the braided-haired tribesman who had tried to escape. He opened his eyes, and she gasped. Her hands turned into maggots. She struggled to stand on the hill of bodies, her breathing heavy. As she ran down, the corpses became more decayed. Her legs sank knee-deep into the rotting flesh, making it hard to pull them out.

"Help!" she screamed.

The eyes of the corpses all opened at once, staring calmly as if reassuring her she was in the right place, and there was no need to fear. She pushed herself out of the rotting mud with both arms and reached solid ground, finding herself in the village. Knights with red crosses on their white robes stood in a circle. She couldn't see what was in the middle, but she walked toward them, khanjar in hand.

"Hey!"

She held up her khanjar, ready to fight. None of the knights turned. She threw a stone, hitting one on the helmet. She bent her knees and held the khanjar in front of her, her naked body casting a long shadow in the dark red sun. The knight didn't react. A slow, synchronous humming began from the circle. She approached the nearest knight and stabbed him in the back. He didn't move. Then, she saw what they were focused on: the knights were in a trance, slowly chewing through the flesh of the living.

Then, she saw her brother tied down and writhing. His severed legs were being passed around to hungry mouths. She took her khanjar and stabbed one of the knights in the throat. As the blade pierced the corrupted flesh, the knight turned to dust. She cut the throats of all the knights until none were left. She looked at her still-living brother, his arms and legs amputated. His lips moved in a whisper.

"I can't hear you!" she screamed.

Then, he began to fade behind black clouds. He continued to whisper, louder and louder, but in a language she did not know.

"Dzintara," her brother mouthed in breathless horror, "Dzintara, Dzintara!"

She was back in her father's chancery on the estate. The top drawer of his heavy pine desk was open, with gold coins spilling to the floor. Her brother entered the room and tried to explain, but she couldn't hear his words. Then, the black mist returned. Her young brother, not even four feet tall, pointed out the window at a black mare. The mist swallowed him, and he vanished.

Her father emerged from the black fog. His face was angry. He was pleading with the gods for the city men to not come and search for him. But they did.

Out of the black fog emerged the merchant who had purchased her. The last thing her father mouthed to her, though she couldn't hear him, was that she was not to be trusted and that this had to be done to preserve the family's future.

Images of memories flickered in the fog: the slave markets of Kyiv, her trip east. Then the mist lifted, and she was alone in the darkness, somewhere between the living and the dead. Her breaths became fleeting, and she grabbed her throat.

She woke, gasping for breath and weeping.

"You kept repeating your brother's name," her father's raspy voice called out. She pulled the pelt over her head, just as she had done as a child. "He died in the Battle of Ice. Fell with the rest of the knights," Ako's voice continued.

The thought of her brother becoming one of the murderers she'd spent her life fighting was appalling.

"And you let him," she yelled into the darkness.

"I had to."

"You had to," she scoffed. "Do you have any idea what they do to us?"

She paced the cold, wet stone of her cell.

"My loyalty to the guilds and Albert—"

"Don't talk to me about loyalty. You sent your only son to fight us. You betrayed us."

Silence fell.

"You're one of them," she sobbed. "I saw it with my own eyes. Everyone told me it was a dream, but it's true. I've had the same dream for the last twenty years. You killed them all. You took the gold and lured them back into the cog and let them burn alive. I remember it as clear as day."

"There was no other way," Ako replied. "It was a matter of time before word got out, and other tribes would be hunting me and our family. I did what was necessary for a father to do."

"A father," she let out a laugh. "Sell your daughter off to the markets of Kyiv and send your only son to die murdering your own people? A fine father you are," she spat.

"I gave you to the merchant to protect you."

"To protect me?" Dzintara laughed bitterly.

"They were looking for you. A heathen girl running around with gold coins. If I hadn't given you away, they would have found you, and all of us would have hung in the square."

"It was Krists who took the coin, you fool. I said it was me so he wouldn't get a beating. But what I got was worse."

"Until you passed by my cell, I hadn't seen you for twenty years. You look different. You sound different. But you're still the same little girl."

Dzintara shot a look at the cell wall in the direction of her father's cell and pointed at the wall like he was there in front of her.

"You have no idea who I am, Ako. Or what I am capable of. Choose your words wisely with me, old man."

Ako sighed. "Did you come back to kill me?" he asked.

She laughed until tears came to her eyes, and then she sat down next to the iron bars of her cell, wiping them away.

"What would you need such a vast amount of treasure for? Someone would kill you for it."

"To fight them."

"The fruits of the tree don't fall far. She was just like you. It's like listening to a ghost or a memory," Ako said.

"Don't talk about her."

"At least your brother followed orders. He listened, and he understood. He saw the vision of what I was creating. He believed in it," Ako's voice trailed.

"Did you ever tell him the truth?"

"He doesn't know about the gold."

"About me," she growled.

"No," Ako sighed.

"Did he ever ask about me?"

"He loved you. Thought he would find you one day. Wore your necklace wherever he went. Krists did what needed to be done for our tribe."

"For you," Dzintara's hands trembled though she had no more tears left to shed. Looking into the torchlight, she had many questions for her father, but the words wouldn't come.

"I think you're the reason Krists never took a wife. He was afraid to lose her. In the end, he died alone on the battlefield. Albert held the most grandiose ceremony the city had ever seen in his honor. He will be remembered. He made me proud."

The door to the prison creaked open, and footsteps trailed down the stairs. An old guard limped to her cell and put his index finger to his forehead with his palms extended as if he were searching for something through the iron bars. Dzintara emerged from the blackness, and the veteran guard recoiled, taken aback.

"Where is the other guard?" she asked.

"You're a woman," the veteran sentinel said. He grinned and shined on his slash of raw gums.

"You do for me, and I'll make sure you're well-fed," he said as he grabbed the front of his pants. Dzintara curled a sly grin, her white teeth shining back at the aged guard.

"Come back later tonight."

The old guard grinned lasciviously.

CHAPTER THIRTY-ONE

K neeling in agony in front of the altar, he prayed, demanding answers from a God who had abandoned him. Outside, snowflakes descended, a bitter offering to Anno's men as they prepared their horses for the journey.

"On you go, you bloody bastards. Most of you aren't coming back anyway," the courtyard master shouted as he paced around the men.

"Cowards stay behind like the courtyard master," said one of the warrior monks. The men laughed as the large courtyard master spat in their direction.

"All he can do is flog little boys," yelled another with a thin face and a scar around his throat. The men baited each other loudly.

The jeers and taunts of his men drifted to Anno as he knelt in front of the altar in the dining hall. The flicker of a spent taper cast its gloomy light across the vast hall. Wraith-like shadows danced across the stone walls, a heathenish mockery of the state of his soul.

Anno looked up at the cross above the altar. The effigy of Christ was meticulously detailed: a wound in his side, a crown of thorns on his head, his face hanging down with eyes closed, and a thin red line of paint resembling a tear. Anno's father had sought God's words before battle, or so he told Anno. With each skirmish, words dimmed. Each life taken stripped away the language justifying his work. Now, the words had utterly abandoned him.

"Just give me an answer," he demanded.

No answer came.

"Why?" he yelled at the cross, his voice echoing through the cold stone chamber. He gave up and crawled on his hands and knees to a spot beside the cross, leaning against the stone wall to rest. Snow seeped in through the slits like unwanted visitors. Only a fool would lead his men into war during winter unless the path seemed illuminated.

"This was my calling," he whispered into the dark. "I watched my father serve you. I've followed his path. I vowed to make this world a place of your kingdom and peace."

Anno scratched his beard and ran his fingers through his hair. "I can't do this alone. It's weighing heavy on my soul. In my dreams, I see their faces. Their souls."

Doubt sprang its roots like a poisonous weed, growing faster every moment.

The heavy wooden door swung open, and the wind screamed. " Grand Master, we are ready to make our way south."

Anno rose to his feet and stared at the man in silence. "Grand Master, we are ready. Did you hear?"

"We leave tomorrow," he answered.

"Grand Master, I can't hear you."

"We leave at dawn!" Anno shouted, then turned his back on his brother. The man closed the door, and Anno prostrated himself before the altar once more, searching for an answer that would not come.

A WALL of snow cascaded from the sky, disorienting him and pushing him in all directions. Varkelins plodded through a dense pine forest, snow crunching underfoot. He raised his forearm to shield his eyes from the wind and saw a faint light flickering in the distance. He headed toward it and reached an opening surrounded by pine trees on a wind-battered slope. The trees seemed to bow in homage to a long-forgotten sun god, leaning forward as if yearning for their deity's return.

In the middle of the broad clearing, a hooded rider sat on horseback. Varkelins lifted his lantern and called in the fashion of a Jackdaw: chek! chek! chek!

"It is I, Varkelins," he shouted over the wind.

The hooded stranger dismounted, waiting. Another man, shrouded in darkness, approached, keeping his distance. Brother Markus broke the silence. "I was beginning to doubt you'd show," he said.

Raising his lantern, Varkelins called out against the howling wind, "Markus, has a decision been made?"

"Our loyalty to Albert remains uncertain," Markus responded. The lantern's glow illuminated his face. Varkelins edged a few steps closer, his gaze shifting between the shadowy, hooded figure and Markus. "Don't worry about him. He's with me," Markus said.

"The weather is unkind this evening," Varkelins said, easing the tension.

"The Hochmeister has decided."

Varkelins stood there with the lantern by his side. "I take it it is fair news."

In the flickering glow, sorrow weighed heavily in Markus' eyes, visible beneath his thick beard and within the shadows of his dark hood.

"I feel torn between my duty to the cause and my loyalty to a friend. Anno and I grew up like brothers, but our paths diverged —he chose war, and I chose the chancery."

"And where does your heart lie?" Varkelins asked.

Brother Markus turned his back and looked at the pines, bowing in the wind.

"The cause is greater than any of us," Markus finally spoke, turning back to Varkelins. "Anno is a great warrior. What the order needs is a great man of diplomacy. One who can rise above the archbishop and unite the merchants and the guilds under one rule, the knights. Anno thinks with the sword. His tongue lashes out in poor judgment and anger. His eagerness for conquest makes him drunk."

Varkelins's eyes narrowed, and his head tilted slightly to the left as he stared into Markus' eyes. Varkelins felt a growing suspicion that Markus was about to ask him to kill Anno.

"What am I to do of this?" Varkelins asked.

"Nothing. Anno has been dealt with. He will ride south where his chance of survival is doubtful, even with God on his side. What the order needs is a man who can speak the language of the merchants and who knows Albert's weaknesses. A man loyal only to the order, balancing the display of power with pleasing his Holiness. The Hochmeister believes that man is you."

"That is a blessing to my ears."

"We ask only the following. Keep Albert on your side as long as you can. Make him feel safe and powerful. But persuade the merchants to turn against him. Chaos will ensue as the merchants seek to depose Albert. A three-way war, out of which the Teutonic Order will be the victor. And ruler."

"Divide and conquer."

"Out of chaos comes order. We must rid the region of Albert and show the people of this land a new and better order."

Varkelins straightened and tilted his chin towards the sky. Snow fell and melted on the lantern glass. "This, I can do."

"One final matter remains. You will be in a position of great power. The Hochmeister and the Order need to know you are loyal and faithful."

"I'm betraying the archbishop, my one single ally at the moment, mind you. What more loyalty do you want?" he protested.

"A challenge for you, perhaps. There are whispers of your

insolvency. Loyalty comes in the form of hefty dues. Upfront and ongoing. Power requires resources."

"Talks of my insolvency are lies designed to undermine me. The sum will be paid in full," Varkelins said, scoffing.

Brother Markus looked into his eyes. The snow beat down, and the branches on the pine shivered. He reached inside his heavy robes and retrieved a pigeon, its small body held fast in his grip. Markus cupped the trembling bird like a precious treasure.

"Take this. You must not jeopardize losing control of the city or the situation getting out of your control. You will know the right time to use it," the brother said.

Varkelins cradled the pigeon in his hands, tucking it safely within the folds of his fur tunic.

Anno woke up shivering on the cold, hard stone floor. His breath fogged in the icy air, and the taper by the altar had burnt out. The hearth fire dwindled to embers. Outside, it was pitch dark. Anno stood, aching from the cold, and limped to the hearth. He squatted by the dying fire, wrapping his legs around his knees to keep warm.

Uncertainty still lingered, eating away at the blind conviction that had once filled his soul.

"I can't do this unless I have Your blessing."

He grabbed onto the table, pulled himself up to stand, and walked over to the table where his armor and robe were laid out.

He suited up, piece by piece. Over the armor, he carefully donned his white robe with the embroidered Red Cross. He scowled at the cross, his lips tight. With a fierce bellow of rage, he overturned the altar, casting a final gaze at the fallen Christ. Then, he prepared to depart with fifty of his men, all awaiting his command.

He stepped out into the courtyard. There were fifty men, all awaiting his command, their breath hanging heavy in the cold air. "Saddle up. We move out," Anno ordered.

The men mounted their horses, murmuring in the early

dawn. Just before Anno reached the gate, the one-eyed crusader yelled, "No prayer before battle?"

Halting his horse, Anno glowered at the men.

"We are fighting children with wooden sticks and stones. You need prayer? Stay behind."

Anno spurred his mare and motioned for the gate to open. He rode out of the fort, seeking vengeance. The brothers followed in single file into the narrow band of the sun's first light.

CHAPTER THIRTY-TWO

Dzintara lay awake on her cell floor, listening. In the darkness, a door creaked open. She heard soft steps descending the stone staircase. The old jailer shuffled over, carrying a torch. He waved the torch in a circle, causing the flames to flicker in the air.

"Where are you?" the old guard whispered in a playful tone.

Dzintara stepped forward into the torchlight. "Stand close to the bars. Put your ass against 'em."

He fumbled with his breeches, struggling to keep a grip on the torch. In the dim light, Dzintara slipped back into the shadows, where his failing eyes could no longer find her. His braies hit the floor with a soft thud, and when he finally looked up, she had vanished, swallowed by the darkness.

"Where are you?"

"Come in here," she said, making her voice girlish.

"I'm no fool."

No answer. He swung the torch, squinting to see her in the cell.

"I'll piss in your food. I swear it."

In the shadows, she quickly undressed and grabbed one end of her cloth robe with each hand, twisting the linen.

"Come here now, girl!"

Naked, she stepped forward into the light, smiling at him. She presented her bosom as if offering. He reached forward through the bars, eager to touch her. She moved forward, pressing herself against the bars, suppressing a shiver of disgust.

Like a lover, she slipped her arms around his neck, leaning in as if for a kiss. But in one swift motion, Dzintara whipped her twisted robe around his head and yanked it hard against the back of his neck, slamming his face into the cell bars—once, twice, three times. He crumpled to the floor. She reached through the bars, unhooked his keys from his girdle, and unlocked the cell. Grabbing the wooden lavatory bucket, she brought it down on his head, over and over, until his skull cracked with a sickening crunch.

Breathing heavily, she kicked his limp body onto its back and stripped him of his stinking clothes. Slipping into his foul linens and breeches, she dragged him by the feet into a dark corner and locked him in the cell.

"Fool."

She approached her father's cell and paused, her steps faltering as memories crept in—fragments of happier days when he would lift her onto his knee, his laughter warm, his hands playful and affectionate. But that man was gone, replaced by a hollow figure lying in the dark void before her, a stranger draped in the shadow of someone she once loved. For a moment, she turned away, ready to leave the past where it belonged. But as she took a step, the memory of her own second chances—those rare moments of grace and unexpected kindness—made her stop. Slowly, almost reluctantly, she turned back toward the cell, her heart wavering between the man she remembered and the one he had become.

"I know you're awake," she said, softly. "I can free you, and we can leave together."

The howling wind filled the silence. It was her last attempt to find any trace of a father in him. His silence lingered, and she gave a lonely nod in his direction.

"I wish you luck," she said.

"You are your mother's daughter," he replied, in a tone somewhere between admiration and disdain.

Dzintara stood there, dressed in the sentinel's clothes. A man once again.

"I will find the gold."

"You'll die trying," Ako said.

OUTSIDE, snow fell in heavy sheets, blurring everything around her. Dzintara squinted through the thick white haze, trying to decipher where she was. A well. Stone walls. Towers looming overhead. The distant groans of laboring beasts echoed faintly, almost swallowed by the storm. Beneath her boots, the snow crunched as she circled the courtyard, her breath quickening.

Suddenly, a sharp voice rang out through the storm: "Old man!"

Dzintara spun, her heart leaping into her throat. A hooded figure raced toward her, their footsteps muffled in the snow. Panic surged through her veins. She bolted, her boots slipping on the icy ground as the cold air bit at her lungs. The snow cushioned her steps, but it was treacherous, slowing her with every slippery stride. The castle walls loomed ahead. She scanned the battlements—no guards in sight. She raced toward the tower door, fingers fumbling on the cold iron handle before slipping inside.

The narrow stone walkway stretched around the outer bailey, snowflakes swirling in the open air. If she could just make it to the postern gate unnoticed, she might escape. But behind her, the crunch of footsteps grew louder, closer.

Inside, the hallway was dim, flickering torches casting dancing shadows on the stone walls. Hugging the wall, Dzintara crept along, avoiding the light, her ears straining for any sign of guards. A sudden noise behind her—the heavy slam of the door she'd come through—made her freeze.

"Old man, I know you're in here!"

She stiffened, the voice cutting through the cold air like a knife. Then recognition hit her: Varkelins. Her pulse slowed for just a second, and she let out a shaky sigh of relief. But the sound betrayed her. Before she could slip deeper into the shadows, Varkelins was on her, his hand gripping her arm like a vise.

He grabbed her by the throat, hissing into her ear. "Did the woman confess? Did she tell you about the gold?"

A guard, alerted by a slamming door, came running down the tower stairs."Halt! Who's there!"

Varkelins released her and moved into the light. At the sight of Varkelins, the guard visibly relaxed."Varkelins. So sorry to alarm you, brother."

"I needed to walk, and the weather outside. Well, one can hardly move about the courtyard in this sort of snowstorm."

"Freezing by bloody arse up there in the tower," the guard grunted in agreement.

Varkelins lowered his voice. "Well, the truth of the matter is that I was planning on sneaking to the kitchens to get some warmed wine. I could bring some up to you if you like?"

"Much thanks. Would do me good, brother." With this, the guard trundled back up the stairs and out of sight.

Varkelins turned.

"Enough with the games, old man. What did she say?" Varkelins asked.

Emerging from the darkness, Dzintara grabbed Varkelins by the collar, looking directly at his face.

"What did you tell that bastard to ask me? Did you think you could have me raped, and I would tell him all my secrets?" She pulled back her fist and punched him in the jaw.

"What the hell?" Varkelins yelped, holding his face. Then he smiled.

"It's you. I suspected you would figure out a way to escape."

"I saved your life on the ship."

"And I saved yours in Anno's camp. Even though you lied to me. Deceived me. Tried to seduce me, even "

Dzintara glared at him, tempted to punch him again. "You need to help me get out of here,"

"Twice. I saved your life twice. You owe me."

"I have nothing of value for you, Varkelins."

Varkelins reached into his pocket and held a closed fist in front of Dzintara. "But I think you do." Slowly, he uncurled his fingers, revealing a gold coin.

Dzintara gasped, "Where did you get that?"

He pocketed the coin and pointed at her. "You, when the Brotherhood dumped your body in front of the gates. Who do you think cleaned you up? Made sure you stayed alive. Those idiots never found the coin or this." He reached into his pocket. "Open your hand."

When she did, he dropped the locket she got from Liga into her palm.

"What is to become of my father?" Dzintara asked, pocketing the locket.

"Most likely hung."

"I don't know where it is," she said.

"I am confident you will find it. When you do, we will split it."

"I can disappear. You'll never find me."

"A risk I'm willing to accept. I have ears everywhere, Dzintara," he said, smiling at her. "Or should I call you Krists? I will find you."

He pulled her khanjar out from under his shirt.

"Don't forget this," he said, handing her the khanjar.

She stared at her knife in disbelief, then tucked it into her belt.

"Come. Hurry," Varkelins said. "I'll get you out."

He led her down the dark walkway toward the unguarded postern gate. In such a storm, no one would expect visitors coming or going through the small, concealed door. Varkelins unlocked it and pushed it open. A fierce wind blasted a flurry of snow into the hall as Dzintara stepped out into the blizzard.

She turned to Varkelins. "No promises."

"One more thing. If you find Anno, kill him," Varkelins said, smiling as he shut the gate. The snow outside came halfway up her thigh. The tower loomed over her as she looked up. A horse's whinny reached her ears from nearby. She followed the sound and found a mare, saddled and tethered to the castle walls, untied the horse, mounted, and rode off.

As she moved on, the blizzard receded, clearing her path. Snow crunched under the mare's hooves as she rode hard through the Gauja valley. The river was partially frozen, but where it wasn't, it roared. She found a calm spot to cross. She stripped and held her clothes above her head as she crossed the icy waters, her horse breathing hard beneath her, nostrils flaring.

Shivering, she changed into dry clothes and continued through the virgin snow to find Lamekins, the sole surviving man with any knowledge of the gold. Suddenly, she pulled the reins, and the mare halted with a powerful force, almost tossing her off. Fresh tracks of horse shit lay in the trampled snow. Turning her horse, she searched for the source of the tracks. They ran to the south. She looked north, across the valley in the direction of Brotherhood's fort, to the bright moon hiding behind the grey clouds. The horse neighed.

Anno was heading south to where the unconquered tribes lived. A raven croaked in the tree, then flew south into the night.

CHAPTER THIRTY-THREE

T he Gauja valley glared bright white as the sun reflected off the freshly fallen snow. Icicles hanging from the roof dripped beads of water. The new blanket of white clung to rooftops, bent over the tops of trees, and buried doorways. In the Turaida Castle's courtyard, the servants worked hard, clearing the snow and ice to make way for the horses and carriages that came and went.

Varkelins awoke to a loud bang on his bedroom door. Hans stood in the doorway to inform him of the official news of Dzintara's escape.

In the courtyard, he'd overheard soldiers speculating about the incident, suggesting that Dzintara possessed some demonic powers with the ability to fly over the high walls.

Varkelins listened to the men in the courtyard, relieved that none seemed suspicious of his involvement.

Hans led him to the old sentinel, lying dead and naked in Dzintara's cell. Varkelins pretended to inspect the body. The head had been nearly crushed. The lavatory bucket lay on the floor, splintered and covered in blood. The old man's grotesque, flaccid cod and hairy stones were swollen, as if Dzintara had taken pains

to crush the man's cod as well as his skull. Varkelins hid a sly smile
and then made for the archbishop's rooms.

The warmth of the bear pelts comforted Albert in the crisp,
icy cold of his room. The ornamented bed was carved from Pinus
Nigra. The hangings from the canopy were thick red fabric decorated with embroidered gold crosses, doves, and swords. In the
center of the hanging embroidery, Albert's seal of Riga was
prominently displayed. It featured a city wall with open gates and
two towers. At the midpoint, situated on the cross pole, was a
mitre. Alongside the key, on each side of the embroidery, additional intricate details complemented the central image.

A large bear pelt covered the stone floor of his room. Silk and
embroidered damasks were placed so that guests could sit and talk
to him while he lay in bed. A heavy gold cross stood in the center
of the room, directly across from his bed. Under the cross was a
prie-dieu with soft velvet padding for kneeling.

Varkelins watched Albert as he slept. He recalled last night's
events in his head and formulated a story in his mind about how
Dzintara had murdered the jailor during a rape attempt and then
made a daring escape—most likely with the help of her heathen
gods.

Albert let out a snort as he awoke. Varkelins let out a cough,
and Albert jumped at the sight of him.

"God of Glory, Varkelins!"

Varkelins smiled.

"Good morning."

"Why are you in my chambers? What do you want?" said
Albert, annoyed.

"Hans let me in. I have news you must hear at once."

Albert sat up in bed and rubbed his eyes. He turned and sat at
the edge of the cloth-wrapped feather mattress and groaned with
every movement. His feet rested on one of the furs covering the
stone floor.

"What is this important news that you awaken me...with your
presence?"

"The girl escaped."

Albert looked up at Varkelins with a tilted head.

"Her father?"

"Still in the cell."

Varkelins crossed his legs and swayed the resting leg back and forth.

"How did this happen?"

"That old horny fool fell for her tricks. Locked him in the cell. How she escaped after, I do not know. "

Albert hacked and stood, shuffling his feet across the fur over to the wooden door of his chambers. It opened with a creak.

"Water!" he screamed down the hall and shut the door.

He shuffled back to the bed and lay down, placing his forearm on his forehead.

"Your plan failed. You didn't get any information about the gold?"

"We didn't get the right information."

"I knew your plan wouldn't work. Putting father and daughter together, hoping they'd rekindle after twenty years. Idiotic. Now we lost the girl."

Varkelins stayed silent.

There was a knock at the door, and a servant entered carrying a bucket of water. He set it on the dark wood dresser and left. Albert walked over and dunked his face into the freezing water. He lifted his head back and let out a deep breath. Water dripped from his face onto the floor. He breathed heavily for a few moments.

"I shouldn't have let you bring her here. You should have just left her with those swine." He motioned in the direction of the fort of the Brotherhood.

"Now I owe them more gold thanks to you, and we have nothing," Albert continued. "That's coming out of what I owe you."

"I said we didn't get the right information. I didn't say we didn't get any information."

Albert splashed water on his face and turned to Varkelins. He raised his eyebrow, motioning for him to continue.

"She confirmed that, indeed, the gold does exist. I found this on the floor of the cell." Varkelins reached into his pocket and flicked the gold coin at Albert. The archbishop watched as the gold flew through the air to land at his feet. Albert's eyes widened.

"I told you," Albert shouted at the top of his lungs. "All this time, you doubted, but I knew it existed. The church wouldn't leave one of their own stranded,"

"Before he went to question her yesterday, the jailor had overheard her speaking to her father. She had told her father that she remembered helping haul the gold. And Ako burning the cog. Apparently, he used tribesmen to haul it somewhere and then burned all of them alive."

Albert began to smile. "I want men searching every place from the sea to this castle. I want every dead village searched, through and through until it's found. These herring eaters — impossible. They couldn't have dragged it far from the shore."

"With what men would you entrust this search?" asked Varkelins.

"Servants, our soldiers."

"I fear we haven't enough men, and we need here to keep you safe from the Brotherhood. They mean you ill, Albert."

Albert slammed the top of the dresser, causing the wooden bucket of cold water to spill onto the floor. The furs soaked up the water like a sponge, their hairs turning from dark brown to ink-black.

"Do something! We must find that gold! What about the old man? He knows where it is!"

"I'll set another jailor on him. Perhaps more torture will loosen his tongue. And, in the meantime, I will see what we might do about the Brotherhood." Varkelins took a pause as if thinking. "In the meantime, let's give the Brothers some trouble. I'll spread rumors that those vultures are planning to take control of the city and lay heavy burdens against the guilds."

"I don't understand."

"We paint a picture that the Brotherhood is behind all the levy increases. Merchants will be outraged and will turn on the Brotherhood. This gives us time to search for the gold and ready ourselves for battle."

Albert pondered the statement, "Let the city wipe out the swine."

"Either way, we win. The Brotherhood is wiped out, or they kill citizens, strengthening our position with the merchants and the residents of Riga."

Albert seemed pleased with this proposal. After a while, he smiled. "Just don't fuck this up."

ALBERT AND VARKELINS, accompanied by a guard of enormous size, made their way down the winding steps to the dungeon. They stood in front of Ako's cell. The guard banged his sword against the bars.

"Show yourself."

Ako stayed in the darkness.

The guard banged his sword harder. "Step into the light."

An old man with gray hair and an unkempt beard stepped forward. His robe was torn, and his eyes were sunken deep into his skull. He looked frail, broken, and obedient, standing with his head bowed slightly, as if awaiting further orders.

Albert smiled. "There you are, old friend."

CHAPTER THIRTY-FOUR

Winter's black void and icy desolation faded into the light of spring. The ice caps on the Dvina cracked and broke away, clearing a path for cogs and barges to navigate. The early spring sun brought brief delight, but soon, rumors of deadly Curonian raids spread through the northern lands. Maritime trade dwindled to a trickle.

The markets of Riga opened, drawing crowds as winter reserves dwindled. Slow trade led to low supplies. Harbormasters and job seekers filled the berths, awaiting trading ships. Wagons lined up outside the city gates, but few ships arrived.

Merchants began calling in their debts. Those unable to pay surrendered what property they could. The House of the Blackheads, once filled with music and laughter, now echoed with accusations and desperate merchants seeking answers. The great hall buzzed with wild conspiracies and attacks against the powers that be.

Varkelins took a seat in the corner and ordered an ale. The House of the Blackheads sat eerily quiet, with only a few men scattered around its tables. To boost the flow of money, the House made room for other guilds. Each guild voluntarily divided into pockets spread out across the Great Hall. Varkelins listened attentively to the conversations around him while his gaze wandered. Merchants sat on one side, and on the other were the masons, the lagermeister, and the port keepers, each group eyeing the others with suspicion. He listened.

"Another levy is coming; I know it in my bones. No trade, yet Albert takes what he can." A rumble rose among the grumbling crowd.

"Albert squeezes every piece of silver he can get."

"Nay, it's the bastard Anno and his thieves." Another voice said.

A heated argument in a corner turned to shouting. Varkelins glanced over and saw Friedrich sitting with a stranger.

A loud slam of ale was followed by two men taking to fists. Men cheered while others struggled to break up the fighting.

"Friends!" Friedrich shouted.

"Times are uncertain. We've faced ups and downs before. It is not the nature of noblemen to spin yarns and lie in this great House of the Blackheads," he said.

The hall's attention turned to Friedrich. Merchants around him nodded in agreement while members of the storehouse guilds booed and hurled their wooden cups of ale at him. A cup landed at his feet, and Friedrich calmly picked it up, placing it gently on the table.

"What is it that ails this great city? Why do our kin go hungry, our commerce suffers, and our once-prosperous streets now run with the filth of despair? Why has the Lord seen fit to curse us? Do you want to know the reason?"

The hall rang out in a loud "Yes!"

"The Brotherhood has poisoned this city! The very men who swore to guard us, to secure our trade, to protect our wealth—they are the root of our suffering. They have threatened our archbishop, the father of this city, and forced his hand to raise merchant levies. They seek to rule us with an iron fist. To take what little we have left and squeeze us for every last coin."

Shouts and catcalls echoed through the hall. Men began pounding their wooden steins on the tabletops.

"Anno the 'Conqueror'? No, Anno, the scum, and his band of brigands," he spat on the floor. "They would steal from us and enslave us. But we will not let them break us. We refuse to be ruled. We will cast down the Brotherhood and any who would conspire with them."

The merchants in the hall rose with a roar of approval.

"The time has come to reclaim our city, our homes, and our futures. The Brotherhood must fall!"

A member of the crowd started rhythmically slamming his cup on the tabletop. Others followed, and the hall rang in a rhythmic drumbeat.

Friedrich looked pleased and continued. Varkelins sunk deeper into his seat. The merchants, lagermeisters, and port keepers jumped to their feet, shouting for Friedrich to continue. Varkelins slowly pushed his chair back and made for the door slowly and quietly.

"You, Varkelins," Friedrich yelled. The hall became silent.

Varkelins slowly looked at Friedrich. The hooded stranger stood up. It was Wulfric. He quietly gasped. Wulfric was alive.

One merchant cried out, "Sodomite!"

The hall rang out in laughter and jeers.

"Your loyalty to the Brotherhood is a well-known secret," he sneered.

"Who paid you to spread these lies?" Varkelins asked.

"I tell no lies. Only the truth," Friedrich replied.

When Varkelins looked around the room, Wulfric had vanished.

"I am one of you. I have worked side-by-side with you for decades. We've traded together. I have tithed and been levied, just like you. I have shown my loyalty to the Great Archbishop Albert," Varkelins insisted.

"The snake hisses when it's threatened," Friedrich shouted.

"I have nothing to hide. My loyalty has always been with this great city."

"Varkelins, we all know you would sell your own mother for a seat at the table of the merchants' guild table."

A wave of mocking laughter followed, filled with blood lust.

"I have no need for such things. I wish to live well in a great city. That's all," Varkelins responded, desperately afraid.

"The little bastard has raked up much debt among the storehouses," a yell hurled from the crowd of lagermeisters.

"Bankrupt! What other choice would he have then to align himself with the bloodthirsty thieves of Livonia?" Another, from a murderous crowd.

Varkelins stood before them, outwardly unmoved but trembling inside. He contemplated his next move, unsure if he would leave the Great Hall alive. If the guild members uncovered his allegiance to the Brotherhood, he would be as good as a slaughtered pig.

"Enough of this madness!" he yelled. "I will prove my allegiance to this great city and show you that I have no other ties than the one to His Holiness and this great city."

Varkelins looked at Friedrich.

"The Brotherhood rode south."

"You swine! We know this already," Friedrich said.

"You don't know that the fort now holds less than twenty men, maybe thirty." Varkelins paused as the room went quiet, finally listening. "The men Anno left are frail. He took the warriors with him and left behind the old, fat, and stupid."

The merchants hung on to his every word. Whispers grew into heated discussions, each word adding fuel to the fire.

"The time to act is now before they return. Take the fort. Kill the swine that have held this city captive," Varkelins urged.

Varkelins and Friedrich's eyes locked. Friedrich smiled slowly.

"Gather your best men! Tonight!" Friedrich commanded, fanning the flames.

Varkelins took a deep breath and walked towards the door. He turned and looked back at the crowd, now preparing for battle.

When he left the House of the Blackheads, he walked the meandering streets, staying in the shadows of the night.

He was being followed. He could hear footsteps behind him on the wooden walkways. Varkelins pulled his dagger and ducked into an entryway, ready to strike. A shadow walked past him, and the footsteps receded into the distance. Sheathing his dagger, he let out his breath.

As he walked onto the street, a fist greeted him with a blow to the face. He glimpsed a blade in the corner of his eye and prepared to defend himself. Another blow from a fist, hard into his ribs. Varkelins grunted in the dark, and the figure grabbed his collar and shoved him against the wall. Wulfric's scar shone in the darkness.

"Wulfric, what are you doing?" Varkelins wheezed as Wulfric's hands closed around his neck.

"You killed Krists."

"Wait...Krists?" Varkelins coughed.

As Wulfric's hands tightened around his throat, Varkelins felt the veins in his eyes bulge and saw spots. He delivered a swift, hard kick to Wulfric's groin. The hands dropped, and Wulfric cried out in pain while Varkelins bolted into the darkness. When he was no longer pursued, he stopped, lungs burning. After collecting himself, he checked into a nearby inn for the night.

CHAPTER THIRTY-FIVE

In the middle of the camp, a small fire struggled to survive the tumultuous early spring weather—scorching days followed by sudden freezing nights. The sun's warmth thawed the snow, turning the road to mud.

Holsteiners, horses known for their strong backs, powerful hindquarters, and arched necks, were ill-equipped for such terrain. They trudged onwards through the mire, sinking deeply into the mud. At night, the mud froze again, turning the ground into a different kind of treacherous terrain, so ungainly that their mounts would be in danger of breaking their legs should they try to travel in the dark. The bitter cold seized the flesh of the men, biting deep into their bones. When morning came, the men realized that their armor had frozen together, and they had to wait for the spring sun to thaw it.

The men gathered around the warm fire to clean their bloodied swords and piss on their armor to keep it from rusting. Deep red stains covered their white robes.

There were no prisoners because they took none. Anno restricted the men from drinking and ordered prayer twice a day. If any warrior monk refused, Anno would have them flogged. The men were told to sit in groups of three and to spread apart. He heard the discontent in their voices from inside his tent. He wondered how much farther he could push them. Had his father led his men into such glaringly bad conditions, would he also have followed in faith? The answer, of course, was yes.

He looked up from the cartography he was studying by candlelight. Arturs stood over him, staring at the map. He was missing the nub of three fingers on his right hand. When he pointed at the map, he did so with a stump.

"We can't push on into marshlands. We need to wait for the full spring. Even one week's time would greatly enhance our odds."

"Artur, we must. Rations are low. We don't have a week."

"We are in the land of the Semigallians. These men fear no death. They have rejected subjugation time and time again. This tribe are strategists and slow thinkers. Their thoughts are focused on how to deliver the most efficient and deadly punishment on their enemies. Warriors at the truest. They are fearless. Violent and bloodthirsty. As the legend goes, they once spent a full day executing prisoners of their enemies. From sundown to sunup, heads rolled, and blood covered the dirt. When they were done, the ground had turned to mud. Blood mixed with dark brown earth."

"I know these men," Anno spoke in a soft tone. "We once fought alongside them."

"Then you know we are outnumbered. Our men are not trained for this terrain. Ambush may be right around the corner, and we have nowhere to hide."

"God is with us," Anno said, doubting it within.

"Even with God, we must grasp every advantage. Now, we have none," Artur said.

Anno dipped a thin steel pin into the dirt below him and made a mark on the map. Laughter rang through the night. He shoved the map aside and stormed out of his tent.

Several men gathered around the fire, holding cups of ale.

"Enough!" Anno hissed, approaching from the dark, kicking over the cup nearest him.

The men dispersed, leaving him alone beside the flickering fire. He surveyed the surrounding darkness as his crusaders fled like rodents into the dark.

"The dangers of this land are many, but none so great as the retribution I will bring down on any of you who disobey my orders. Understood? Be vigilant. Fools, we are not."

The men responded in a chant from the safety of the dark, "Yes, Hofenmeister."

The fire cracked in the silence.

"We move at dawn and press south."

The men acknowledged his orders. Anno returned to his tent.

"Artur, you may leave," Anno dismissed him.

Artur let out a heavy sigh and nodded in assent.

Anno lay down on his makeshift bed, holding the map in front of his face, staring at the lines and symbols. There wasn't anything he was looking for. Once he grew tired of staring at the world confined on the parchment, he fumbled around in his pocket and retrieved a silver cross.

A dying Christ rested on his palm. He turned to his side to reflect on it. He thought about how the winter had turned against them. How the melting snow made it hard for his men and the horses. They could no longer use the river ice as a way of traveling. He thought of the marshlands and how difficult they would be to cross.

He scoffed and pocketed the crucifix. An owl howled in the distance. As he lay on his back, the cold gnawed at him. There was something else gnawing at him—an emptiness, a sense of abandonment. The notion that God had forsaken him.

"This triumph will be mine and mine alone, unshared with you," Anno said through his teeth.

He didn't remember sleeping, but when he turned his head, bright red and orange light peeked into his tent. Birds chirped, and water dripped from icicles. Anno opened the tent flap and stood. The spring sun chased away the darkness on the horizon, its fiery hues conquering the night, only to be consumed by shadows again soon, as if ordained by God.

Anno stared at the horizon and thought about the last time he'd seen his father. His illustrious father was a founding member of the Knights of Hospitallers. When word came back with news of his father's death, it was said that he had died bravely on the battlefield.

He had long believed the story about his father, which was why he sailed with Albert and established his own order. But he learned the truth in the Teutonic Knights' library. His father was a drunk and a gambler, killed in Jerusalem by a man to whom he owed money. His throat was cut, leading to a local uprising that the Knights Hospitaller eventually quashed. The archives also revealed that his father was nearly expelled from the Knights multiple times for insubordination, blood-thirst, drunkenness, and accusations of sodomy. The list went on, bringing into focus scenes from his childhood he had long avoided.

"Let's move out," Anno yelled to his men. Artur approached.

"How does it look out there?"

"Quiet night. Just some animals. Nothing worth mentioning."

A warrior monk ran towards him.

"Hochmeister, you must come and see," said the monk, who wore only a light pelt over his armor. He led the way for Anno and Artur.

"I woke up and found him like this."

The corpse's face was purple. Frozen hair hung like thawing icicles from his head. His hands were clenched into fists, and his armor was coated in splintering frost. Anno knelt and touched the face. "Stupid fool," Anno muttered.

"I told him not to sleep with his armor on. He kept pissing himself to keep warm. I warned him. I did."

"Drag this body to the center of the camp," Anno ordered.

"Yes, Hofmeister."

Artur grabbed the frozen corpse by the leg with another crusader and pulled it next to the dying campfire. Anno called his men to him.

"Look at this." Anno pointed to the body. The newly woken men gathered around.

"Look at it!" Anno's scream echoed through the forest, and a murder of crows took flight, their screeches piercing the morning sky.

"This is the result of disobedience. One less man to watch your back. One less man to stand next to you in charge."

Uneasy, guilty whispers spread among the cloaked, shivering men.

"No more warnings. Only Prayer and deep thought are permitted. And no more ale. No more wine." He stomped over to the pack mule carrying the rations and rummaged until he found the wine sac.

"No more bloody wine or ale!" He screamed, spilling the wine from the sac onto the frozen earth. "Water is your only friend now."

The men responded affirmatively but unenthusiastically. "Strip the armor and leave the body," Anno said as he motioned for them to carry on.

"What about his burial rites? Would you deprive this man of seeing the kingdom of God?" asked one of the men.

Anno turned and faced them. "You are welcome to stay here and wait for the earth to thaw."

Anno left them and walked back to his tent.

Artur ordered the men to be ready for the march. The men kicked the fire and broke down Anno's tent. Several crusaders struggled to dig the frozen earth, and eventually, they forfeited. One nailed two sticks together and left the cross in the middle of the camp next to the thawing body.

Anno stared out into the forest as sunlight broke through the canopy. Anno lifted his face and closed his eyes, letting the sunshine warm his face. All the snow would soon turn into mud.

The rivers would run higher. Anno spat into the dirt and pressed his boot against the ground, feeling the frost yielding to the warmth of the sun. When he arrived back at camp, the men were ready to move out. He motioned, and the caravan of warrior monks began to walk out in single file. Anno walked over to his Holsteiner, cloaked in white with an armor plate over its muzzle. They looked at each other and the horse neighed. He mounted, clicked his tongue, and joined the caravan of men.

CHAPTER THIRTY-SIX

Dzintara woke with the sun warming her face. She was covered in dirt, her stolen clothes filthy, torn, and threadbare. For weeks, she had followed the tracks of the Crusaders, unable to catch up to them. They moved more swiftly than she had expected.

All she found were horse manure, blood, human feces, and leftover embers. Each campsite was barren except for a red wooden cross, its branches tied with string, standing fifty arm's lengths from the center, with divots in the mud where men had knelt to pray. Every cross marked a newfound territory claimed by the conquerors on behalf of the Holy See.

Determined, she mounted her horse once more, tracking the white robes like a hunter stalking a wild animal. She ate small game and rodents and foraged berries and greens to stay alive. After the sixteenth day of riding, she came dangerously close to the invaders. A rough cough had given them away. She'd pulled hard on her reins, then circled around them, keeping out of sight. When she was clear, she rode toward Lamekins' village as fast as her beast would allow it.

Her mare was wearing down from being ridden hard day after day. Deep within Semigallian territory, she knew she was only a couple of days ahead of the warrior monks, who were stuck in the mud and forced to move on foot.

At dusk, she stopped to rest. She made a small fire for warmth and fell into a deep sleep, her body still weak from the months in the cell below Turaida. The neigh of her mare woke her. It was past dawn. In a panic, she realized she'd slept through the night. The fire had died out; the embers faded to black, a thin trail of smoke upwards. Her horse neighed nervously, stamping its hooves. In a hurry, she kicked the fire and adjusted the saddle on the horse. Suddenly, she realized she wasn't alone. The birds had ceased chirping, and there was no rustling in the underbrush. All she could hear was the soft draw of the wind, her own heartbeat, and the horse's nervous breathing. She felt eyes watching her.

A twig snapped, and the mare's ears cocked. Dzintara pulled her khanjar and turned. Scanning the forest. Nothing moved. The horse huffed, and she placed her hand on its nose.

Another twig snapped. When she turned, she saw a shadow slipping past. She heard footsteps running from behind. She snapped her head around and saw a warrior in a wolf's head coming for her, a club held high. She ducked as the club missed her ear. She struck a fist to the heart of her attacker, knocking him to the ground, where he gulped for air.

"*Stuok!*" a familiar tongue shouted from the shadows. "Stop!"

Wolf-men, carrying clubs and lances, emerged from the trees. She crouched and extended her arm with the khanjar, shifting her feet as she eyed them all. The horse huffed and reared.

"*Ėk kovotis!*" Dzintara threatened the wolf-men.

A large wolf-man stepped into the light, lifting his snout. Lamekins flashed an enormous smile at her.

"You're alive," she said with relief and lowered her khanjar. She ran to Lamekins, wrapping her arms around him. "I thought you were dead," she said, crying with relief.

"*Berneli, tu mane matéi.*"

"I know. I didn't think you would pull through. The wound was deep, and you didn't have much time," Dzintara said, smiling.

Lamekins lifted his shirt. A scar ran from his armpit to his hip, muddled and melted like wax, wrinkled into streaks of canyons and high plateaus where the skin had burned.

"The Curonians heard of our misfortune and came to our rescue. Now, why are you here, my niece?"

"Danger is coming. I tracked the white robes. They are two days behind, and they are murdering everyone in their path."

Lamekins regarded her. "How many?"

"I didn't get close enough to count, but I think about thirty, with horses and full armor."

Lamekins nodded and stared ahead. Lamekins' lack of urgency surprised Dzintara. "With so many men, the mud should give us time. We need to lay an ambush and finish them."

"No, you need to warn the tribes. We need to run."

He smiled at her serenely. "No. We need to fight."

Lamekins turned and whistled. Two wolf warriors approached, and he gave them orders. The warriors ran off and disappeared deep into the woods.

"It is done. They will call the tribes. It is done."

Dzintara nodded, knowing the conversation was closed.

"I saw my father," she began.

He glanced at her, then down at the forest floor. After a moment's pause, he gathered the courage to ask, "How did he look?"

"I only spoke to him. He stayed in the shadows," she replied.

"His spirit?"

Dzintara's eyes drifted to the canopy, where slivers of sky and clouds filtered through the leaves. "Different. As if I never really knew him," she admitted.

"How did you get away?"

"I escaped with some help," Dzintara said, a playful smile dancing on her lips.

Lamekins let out a hearty laugh. "Some things never change, just like when you were a child."

"He said you knew about the coins," she lied.

Lamekins shifted his weight, his smile forced and eyebrows furrowed.

"You're thinking of what to say next," she observed, cutting into his thoughts.

With a sigh of defeat, Lamekins grumbled. "Your father was secretive. He never mentioned those coins to me," Lamekins lied in return.

"So, he never spoke of them? You weren't part of the crew that hauled them ashore?" she asked. "You never went looking for them?"

Scratching his beard, Lamekins's face stretched into a long, wolfish grin.

"I tried but found nothing. Eventually, I accepted it was just a myth."

"You never wondered how father amassed enough wealth to build a shipyard? How did he, a tribesman, come to be accepted as an equal among Christians?"

"Those coins would have been recognizable to anyone in Riga or near," Lamekins rebutted.

"But Father was clever, resourceful. He could have melted them down, sold the gold by weight."

Dzintara waited for Lamekins to respond, allowing an awkward silence. He said nothing.

"Unless, of course, there were too many coins to smelt down safely." She waited. He refused to answer.

She needed to get through to him. "He sent me away because Krists had used one of the coins in Riga. He thought it was me. I saw the fear in his eyes that last night I spent with him as a child. He was afraid I knew his secret. He sold me, Lamekins. To protect his precious gold, he sold me!"

Tears were forming in Lamekins' eyes. Still, he refused to tell her. "I'm going to check on the men."

"No!" Dzintara shouted, frustrated. "I need to know this, Lamekins. That gold will help us fight them."

He walked off.

She collapsed to the ground, defeated. She wept softly, remembering being sold at the slave markets of Kyiv and the merchant who bought her as he would a cow or a donkey. She remembered being loaded into the hold of a cog, sailing east—and of the horrible things the sailors did to her. A child, used, raped, subject to their cruel lusts.

She thought about the day of her rescue when the cog was attacked near Acre. Then there was Muhammed, a physician who took her in, healed her body and her mind, and taught her medicine.

Now, she was back home, walking through her tribe's forest.

IN THE HEART of the dense wood, they came upon a village fortified with walls made of pine reinforced with birch. The wooden gate opened, and they walked in. Thatched huts were scattered about haphazardly, smoke curling from the roofs. Chickens pecked at the dirt, and goats roamed freely. The villagers went about their daily tasks, tending to their crops and livestock, weaving baskets, and preparing food. In the center of the village stood a fort made of wooden planks and sharpened poles, a symbol of protection against outside threats. They were greeted by running children and low, rhythmic drumming. A river flowed behind the village where women were washing garments and cleaning off the carcasses of dead deer.

"Home," Lamekins said somberly.

"We didn't used to live this far from the sea," noted Dzintara.

"It's protection from the outsiders. We keep fighting them off, but we have to go deeper into the forest."

A venerable matron, her head adorned with a crown of intricately intertwined twigs, leaves, and vines, danced forth to greet them, trailed by a trio of rhythmic drummers. Her words baffled Dzintara, echoing from a distant past. With vigorous shakes, she brandished birch branches toward the returning warriors. Each combatant advanced and bowed low before her. She struck each in turn with a bundle of branches, ceremoniously removing their wolf-skull headdresses. When Dzintara's turn came, she knelt to receive the old woman's blessing. The scent of birch branches evoked memories of her mother's blessing. She took a deep breath and let the memory linger.

Lamekins left, and Dzintara sought refuge by the river, finding a hidden corner of tranquility. She stripped off her clothes and waded into the biting chill of the running water. A symphony of bird calls filled her ears as she shut her eyes. Opening her eyes, she cast her gaze skyward.

Two cloud formations loomed, their shapes evoking formidable armies on the brink of conflict. As the wind guided them into an inevitable collision, the aerial armies clashed in a silent, ethereal battle. Then the breeze shifted, nudging one cloud formation away from the other—an army in retreat.

She floated aimlessly on her back, her thoughts drifting to her mother and aunt. Both burned with relentless fire and passion, seeking to remake the world as they saw fit. Each met a violent end. She couldn't help but ponder her own fate.

The river's relentless cold numbed her body and turned her lips to blue. Shivering, she paddled to the bank and shook herself dry.

She made her way to Lamekins' house, which was made of rough-hewn logs and covered in moss. She opened a loose wooden door and entered. The log walls inside had intricate symbols and depictions of nature and wild creatures carved on them. She traced her fingers along their grooves with a delicate touch. She hadn't seen such elaborately rendered symbols in a long time. Lamekins appeared from a second room with a wooden cup and touched her shoulder. She turned, smiled, and accepted the birch tree syrup.

"I made up a bed for you. It's in the other room."

"Thank you."

In the corner, a wooden doll with a birch twig crown rested on a table.

"Old memories," Lamekins said.

"I remember," she said and touched Lamekins' beard. She entered the adjacent room, finding a straw bed awaiting her. She lay down, staring at the thatched roof. She heard Lamekins leave through the outer door. As she dozed off, she listened to the children chanting and playing outside, the wind sweeping through the trees, and the river flowing downstream into the sea.

CHAPTER THIRTY-SEVEN

The meeting hall was within the grand cathedral of Riga, its towering stone walls reaching towards the heavens and its conical peaks piercing the sky.

Varkelins handed his horse off the stable hands.

The entrance doors painted the hue of dried blood groaned as Varkelins pushed them open, entering the desolate cathedral. Light filtering through the small alabaster windows cast a pale glow upon the ground, illuminating motes of dust swirling in the air.

Varkelins approached the altar, bowing deeply and crossing himself in reverence. Gold candelabra, a wooden cross, and rolled parchments on a stand adorned the altar. Behind the altar rose a life-size Christ, nailed by the hands and feet. Varkelins stopped, turning to look at Christ as if drawn by an unknown force.

Many times, he had passed the altar without so much as a glance, but today was different. He stood before it, staring as if seeing it for the first time. His gaze met Christ's, whose lips curled into a wry smile beneath the crown of thorns. Varkelins then turned to the ordinary door to the left of the altar. He opened it and descended a spiral staircase lit by torches mounted on the walls.

Varkelins entered the chamber. Two dozen nobles stood socializing, draped in rich velvets and fur. They wore masks with elongated snouts and wild animal features on their faces. They stared at Varkelins as he moved through the room, his face bare and unmasked.

A large table covered in purple satin stood at the back of the room. On its surface, silver chalices and goblets glimmered in the candlelight. Suckling pig and roasted pheasant glistened with grease. Varkelins took his seat at the table, his eyes surveying the room as whispers slithered like serpents through the gathering of masked nobles.

Moments later, Albert emerged from the back chamber. Dressed in a dark purple cassock, he made a striking appearance. A mozzetta, a short cape reaching the elbows, was worn over the cassock to symbolize his position in the church. A pectoral cross was prominently displayed around his neck. On his finger, the gleaming Episcopal ring symbolized his authority.

The room fell into a respectful hush as the scrape of chairs echoed across the floor as the nobles stood, waiting for Albert to take his seat. The fire in the hearth crackled fiercely, casting flickering shadows on the stone walls. Finally, Albert took his place at the head, and the nobles sat, removing their masks.

Albert spoke. "As we near the season of Lent, our great city faces its heaviest burdens. The Brotherhood has failed to protect us from Curonian raids and has put a curse upon us, turning against us and leaving our great city vulnerable. They have taken some of our best men. I ask you, in exchange for what? To rule? To take more and give less? We asked them to protect our cargo upriver. Did they?"

The nobles shook their heads.

"Instead, they bring upon us this curse that only God can deal with. This stops today. The Brotherhood must be defeated. We are no longer in a position to stand against one another. We must be united against the oppression of the Brotherhood."

Albert angrily slammed his fist down on the table. The startled nobles in the room looked to each other, whispering under their breath.

"We will imprison all conspirators and collaborators of the Brotherhood and put them on trial for treason against our city, against our God. We have reports that the Brotherhood's fort is vulnerable. It is guarded only by those left behind by Anno, as he took his most capable men south."

The room went quiet.

"I will gather an army," Friedrich said, his young face burning with anger and vengeance. "I called this meeting. As many of you know, my father recently passed. Now, I manage the family affairs. I can organize and deploy an army. Our coffers are full, and our bravery proven time and again."

Albert smiled and looked around the table, acknowledging the nobles. They sipped their wine, waiting for his response.

"Few men in history have the courage to change the world. From a young age, they stand out for their sense of duty and sacrifice. I was one of those men. My uncle tried again and again to make this land flourish and attract trade. But it was when I convinced His Past Holiness to let me sail with a hundred knights and take this fruitful land that Riga was born. Young Friedrich, I see myself in you. Your devotion and sacrifice are exemplary."

Friedrich stood. "I will lead. We will win. In exchange, I want the shipyard and a seat in the government." His voice rang out across the room. With a steely gaze, he locked eyes with Albert, daring the archbishop to challenge his bold proposition.

The nobles looked between the two men, waiting to see what Albert would do.

"Ako has been imprisoned and will face trial for treason," Albert said at last, an edge of malice in his voice. "He conspired with the Brotherhood. The shipyard belongs to the church."

Friedrich carefully placed his chalice in front of him and twirled the stem between his thumb and index finger.

"Which one of you is willing to sacrifice life and silver for this cause?" His voice filled the chamber. The nobles seated around the table cowered, shrinking in their chairs and avoiding eye contact. He planted his knuckles on the table and leaned forward with fierce determination.

"These men poised on the precipice of time's abyss, shielded by their reputation and affiliations, are reluctant to surrender anything beyond what can be written with pen and paper. Albert, are these the ones hailed as Riga's great saviors? Your saviors?"

As he spoke his accusations against the nobles, Varkelins shrank back in his seat, trying to vanish. He knew Friedrich knew he'd been conspiring with the Brotherhood. Albert also knew that Varkelins supplied the Brotherhood with rations last winter. Soon, the two would turn on him.

"Great sacrifice must be met with great reward, beyond the promises of the afterlife. I will have the heathen shipyard and a chance to do good for this city. Ruling side by side with Albert."

Albert regarded him for a moment, then nodded.

"Execute the heathen conspirator," Friedrich ordered. "Each of you must provide twenty of your finest men from your families, along with a contribution from your coffers. This will prove your commitment to the future of our great city."

Friedrich approached Albert, and the two embraced, signaling their alliance. Varkelins watched, sensing the shift in power. As Friedrich whispered to Albert, the archbishop's gaze fixed on Varkelins, sending a shiver through him. Realizing the change, Varkelins broke from tradition, rose from his seat, and left the room. Friedrich then gestured to a nearby masked figure, who approached and removed his mask, revealing Wulfric.

"Follow him," Friedrich said, whispering.

Varkelins knew he would be pursued. Weaving through the forest, he made his way to an old sheep stand, pulling his horse in after him. Time passed. Once certain that he'd lost his pursuer, he fled back to Turaida Castle.

Upon arrival, he burst through the door of his room. He struck a flint and sparked the wick of a candle. Ripping a piece of parchment and dipping a quill in a black ink well, he wrote a concise note. He retrieved the pigeon Markus had given him from under his bed. He rolled up a scrap of parchment, placed it in a small sheepskin pouch, and tied it to the pigeon's legs. The pigeon flapped its wings and cooed in protest. He walked to the window and released the pigeon into the air. It twisted in the wind, then regained its form and flew away. Varkelins sat on his bed, wiped his brow, and stared out into the darkness.

CHAPTER THIRTY-EIGHT

"They're here," Lamekins said excitedly, abruptly pushing the door open.

Springing from her bed, Dzintara stepped into the brightness of the day.

The chieftains of the Semigallian, Latgalian, and Curonian tribes sat on their makeshift thrones around the bonfire, its radiant blaze providing warmth through the billowing smoke.

The villagers gathered around. The shrill scream of a suckling pig suddenly pierced the air, restrained by a trio, while a fourth slid a blade through its throat, draining its blood into a bowl. The men speared the piglet, hoisting it on a spit over a blazing fire.

Dzintara's gaze swept over the villagers before settling on the chieftains. Bauska, standing to the right with his thick beard and dark eyes, caught her attention. His hemp headdress was embroidered with diamond shapes, and a gold circlet with a dangling chain symbolized past tribal unity. He wore a finely embroidered tunic beneath a reindeer hide robe, and resting beneath his palms was an ancient sword carved from mammoth tusk—a relic of the Latgalians' strategic warfare. Known by all for his self-interest and impulsiveness, Bauska's reputation was as prominent as the symbols of power he carried.

Next to him sat Vilnus, the eldest, an aging Curonian chieftain renowned for his wisdom. His long hair framed a trimmed beard. He dressed simply in a homespun tunic with a cloak of bear fur. His iron sword bore Viking motifs, reflecting the Curonians' seafaring expertise and victories. Dzintara recalled her father learning shipbuilding from this wise and cautious man.

On the left sat Rinda, a formidable figure dressed in deerskin with a waist-long braided beard. His simple attire, paired with a fur hat and a long spear, underscored his tribe's reputation for repelling invaders. Their fearless combat tactics were famed among Christians and non-Christians alike.

The rūgėjas, the shaman of the tribe, moved in a circle around the chieftains, humming and chanting in a low tone while shaking birch tree branches in a ritual of respect and invocation. She blessed them and their gathering.

Lamekins walked over to a large birch tree standing at the edge of the commons. The tree had an iron tap, which Lamekins turned and poured a cloudy liquid into four wooden cups. He gave two to Dzintara, holding the other two himself. They walked back to the fire, offering the cups to the gathered tribal leaders.

"May the trees watch over us and ravens carry our souls when we pass."Lamekins raised his wooden cup, and the chieftains followed suit.

Lamekins glanced at each elder before scanning the entire assembly.

"Labdėin, and welcome to each of you and your families. These are perilous days, and we must make haste. You may remember Ako, son of Kaupo."

A murmur in the crowd. Bauska spat on the ground in disgust.

Lamekins paused, momentarily thrown off by Bauska's reaction. He gathered himself and continued. "His daughter upholds our traditions. This girl, Ako's daughter, was bartered as barbarians trade their daughters. She has battled Christians in far-off lands. Now, she has returned to us to bring news from Riga, informed by her extensive travels in Saracen lands. I vouch for her truth with my father's blood as my witness, Now, let her tell the rest of her story "

"There is an evil arriving in a few days' time," Dzintara said, approaching the elders.

"Apologies, brethren. The girl has been gone a while and has forgotten her manners."

"Do not apologize for me, Lamekins. I have no time to bow and scrape. If we don't act now, These traditions will die along with us."

"Let the girl speak," Vilnus said.

Dzintara looked at the other leaders as they shifted in their seats and placed their cups aside. "The Christians are coming, and they intend to annihilate us."

Nervous chatter scattered through the crowd.

"I have spent my years fighting these men in the distant east. Before that, I endured slavery, sold by my father, Ako."

Lamekins, ashamed, looked away from Dzintara.

"Returning home, I found myself for several moons in a cell beside my father. I escaped. Fleeing, I stumbled upon the tracks of Christians heading here. I rode with all haste to bring this warning. I overtook them two days ago. I've witnessed their brutality firsthand—villages set aflame, the young mercilessly killed, women violated, and our kin used as bait."

She paused and stared at the three.

"We cannot defeat them alone. We must unite and end their journey southwards before they reach your villages. We need every warrior for this fight."

"They will win eventually," Bauska said, interrupting. "Isn't that why your grandfather betrayed his own kin? The pope himself converted him. He returned and then turned against his own people. Your father is the same. They both knew the inevitable, which was that the Christians would win."

Dzintara's stomach dropped.

"They are superior in terms of weapons, tactics, and armor.

Their ability to unite men for war is unmatched. We must seek an alliance with them," Bauska continued.

A quick murmur rippled through the crowd.

"Of course," Rinda said, his braided beard swaying as he spoke. "You feel safe in Latgale believing they won't reach you—"

Dzintara interrupted. "But they will. And when they arrive, they will slay you, they will rape your women, and enslave your tribe. I've seen it many times. It's only a matter of days."

"The girl is right," Rinda said.

"You fools would send us to slaughter before seeking an alliance. And for what? Pride? Glory?" asked Bauska. "The Latgalian tribe sue for peace."

"These men will not make peace! We are no better than animals in their eyes. They will end us and send our women to the markets of Kyiv." Rinda's deep bellow echoed through the crowd. "We fought them and kept them out. They don't seek peace. They seek conquest."

"We offer them trade, coast access, and safe passage through our lands," Bauska said, countering.

"You will subject your people to these murderers? To conquest?" asked Dzintara in disbelief.

"If that's what our survival means, then yes. It's better than annihilation"

Dzintara spat. "Coward!"

Bauska sprang to his feet, sword in hand. "Stupid girl, dare call me a coward? I've spilled more blood than your father ever did. You're a troublemaker like your whore mother."

Instantly, Rinda's spear was at Bauska's throat. "Your words are poisoned with deceit. You sit comfortably in the south, far from danger. You're not after peace. You're buying time. Our villages will face the Christians first, shielding yours. Tell me why I shouldn't slit your throat this instant, coward."

Dzintara didn't so much as flinch.

Vilnus sat in quiet contemplation, watching the commotion unfold before him.

"I have spent the better part of my life fighting these men," Dzintara said.

"You carry that sword today because your father and forefathers made hard decisions. Ones that cost the lives of men. Today, you must make a hard decision."

Rinda lowered the tip of his spear.

Bauska lowered his mammoth sword and placed the tip into the ground. "Your father, the greatest traitor of all. Look at how well he did by making peace with them."

"Only to end his days in a dark prison, under torture," she said. "He's to be executed. Let's fight them. Together."

He cocked his head right and looked at her silently for some long moments.

"I've made my decision. We seek peace." With this, he turned and motioned for his men to follow. As he walked away, his cloak dragged in the dirt behind him.

Dzintara yelled after him. "Those men, your forefathers, they were deserving of that mammoth sword. It seems for you it's merely an accessory."

Bauska raised his hand, and his men immediately halted. A heavy silence fell over the village as he turned to face the other elders. "I pray to the gods for your survival," he said, his voice carrying through the stillness.

Bauska and his men mounted their horses and swiftly departed through the village gates. Vilnus rose, his gesture dismissive towards the retreating Bauska. "Latgalians, ever shortsighted, blind to the greater good."

The village hushed as Vilnus began to speak.

"Let there be no doubt," he said, "the girl speaks truth. We've seen their trade vessels increase on the river every harvest. We raid the weaker villages and camps to instill fear, yet they persist. But it's not just their goods—it's their people. They keep coming. The city will grow, and with it, their hunger for our land and resources. They will overwhelm us, pushing us from our homes and erasing our way of life."

Approaching Dzintara, Vilnus faced her squarely, arms crossed. "The branches of the birch tree, each unique, all stem from the same trunk. Your father and grandfather brought great misfortune to our lands. Yet here you are, standing before us, seeking redemption."

"I am my mother and father's daughter. I own their legacy of misfortune. I have been gone a long time, and I am the last of my kind. I am prepared to sacrifice my life to stop this evil march once and for all. By the word of the great Diev, I will fight them, or I will die trying. The Semigallians are the greatest fighters of this land." She looked at Rinda and bowed.

She turned to Vilnus. "The Curonians are the greatest seafarers in all the lands."

Vilnus Nodded.

"We cannot win without each other. Will you join us?" Dzintara asked.

"Your father killed my men and took all the gold and silver for himself," Vilnus responded.

"As you said, no branch of a tree is the same," Dzintara responded, staring hard at the Curonian.

Vilnus exchanged a look with Rinda, who simply shrugged. Together, they retreated into a cabin to deliberate her proposal.

The village lapsed into silence, awaiting the elders' decision. The only sound breaking the stillness was the crackling of the roasting pig.

Dzintara turned to Lamekins, opening her mouth to speak. But Lamekins raised his hand, cutting her off. He smiled and placed a finger to his lips.

The sun had set, and the moon hung high in the sky. As the pig was pulled from the fire and prepared for carving, the elders emerged from the cabin.

Rinda and Vilnus stood in the center of the circle, surrounded by the villagers.

"The Curonians are with you. I will have my men here in a day's time," said Vilnus.

"As are the Semigallians," said Rinda.

The village broke out into a loud cheer.

Dzintara hugged both elders and then Lamekins. The villagers feasted on the roasted piglet. The Wolf Warriors danced their war dance, the fire casting a silver glow on the snouts of their masks.

She ran her khanjar across the sharpening stone, watching the young men circle the fire, their movements wild and full of energy. Boys, she thought, the sight tugging at a distant memory. Her brother had been just like them once—too young for a mask, so he had painted his face with wolf blood instead. She could still see him as a boy, howling at the moon, growling and snapping at the other boys as they danced around the flames.

Sadness rent her spirit, knowing that many of these men would die in the coming days.

"Join them. You are the greatest warrior of them all here. Your place is there," Lamekins said drunkenly, "I know you don't believe me."

"About?"

"That I don't know anything about your father's doings with the coins. If I did, I would tell you."

She glanced up at him as she sharpened her blade.

"You worked for him all those years, and he never mentioned it?"

"Never," he said, raising his ale.

"Trust me. I would tell ya. All this time, the guilt I dealt with. The day he gave you to that merchant, every day I go back and replay in my head how I should have done more and acted differently. No use. No turning back."

She stood and faced him. His head reached her up to her chest, seated. Dzintara put her blade away. With her hands resting on his head, she said: I absolve you of your guilt.

Wrapping his thick arms around her. He hugged her and lifted her off the ground.

"Ah! Put me down," she laughed.

"Time for you to dance with us warriors. In place of your brother."

They joined the Wolf Warriors, dancing and howling around the pyre, moving like the wolves they claimed to be. For a moment, she forgot what lay ahead. Lamekins' drunken smile, the scent of the village fires, and the rhythm of her native tongue made her feel as if she had never left. Somewhere in the darkness, her father and mother were waiting for her to come home.

CHAPTER THIRTY-NINE

Stomach-deep in mud, the scout squirmed as Anno and his men approached. Relief washed over his face. Anno dismounted, the mud sucking at his boots as he trudged toward the scout. He glanced up at the pines, then around the marshland. The scout pleaded for help, but Anno only stared.

"Pathetic," he muttered under his breath. Then louder, "Get him out."

The men exchanged glances, muttering amongst themselves, until Anno heard the snap of a branch and the clang of iron against wood. He turned to see his men cutting down a thick limb. A crusader extended it to the trapped scout, who grabbed hold. Two others pulled him free from the mud, and the scout, drenched and panting, thanked them.

"How far did you make it?" Anno asked.

"I got stuck on the way back. The mud's neck-deep all the way through. The next village is half a day's ride in good weather. I don't know about now."

"God will guide the horses. They can make it."

"Hochmeister, you'll exhaust them," Artur said quietly from behind him.

Anno gazed across the swamp, a forsaken wasteland stripped

of God's grace. Brackish water and tangled roots sprawled endlessly before him.

"Move out! Follow me and the Lord, or perish," Anno commanded, his voice cutting through the silence.

They mounted. The scout climbed onto the mule with the rider at the back of the line. Anno led the men forward, but after only fifteen strides, his horse abruptly halted, its hooves sinking deep into the muck.

Anno kicked the horse's ribs. It wouldn't budge.

"Move!" he snarled.

He spurred the horse again, but the beast stood firm. Frustrated, Anno dismounted. His boots sank into the mud as he grabbed the reins, pulling with all his strength. The horse remained rooted.

"You, take the lead," he said to Artur.

"Yes, Grandmaster."

The second in command urged his horse forward, but it too sank into the mire. One by one, Anno ordered the men to try, and each time the result was the same—the horses refused to move. Frustrated, Anno approached the lead horse, locking eyes with the beast. It whinnied and stepped back.

"Leave the horses. We continue on foot," Anno commanded.

"That's madness," Artur protested, his voice sharp with defiance.

Anno shot him a glare sharp enough to silence any further objections.

He pressed on, the mud and mire sucking at his boots, each step heavier than the last. Reluctantly, his men followed. The rot of the earth seeped through his armor, and with every stride, he scanned the landscape for a glimmer of hope. There was none. His gaze lifted to the pine trees, where thin shafts of sunlight pierced the canopy. The grim truth settled in: without the horses, they wouldn't survive.

He touched the red cross on his blood-stained white robe,

seeking solace in the familiar symbol. But no answer came. He turned to face his men.

"We'll head for higher ground and camp for the night. Tomorrow, we move east to the river and follow it south," he said, gauging their reactions. "It will delay us, but we need the horses."

The men led their horses through the mud toward the east, seeking firmer ground. As dusk settled, they finally found solid footing and set up a modest camp. They stripped off their armor and stretched, relieved to be free of their iron cages.

"Hochmeister, where shall we pitch your tent?" asked Artur.

"Nowhere. We must be ready to move quickly. We sleep on the ground tonight. I'll make do in that clearing." He pointed toward a horseshoe-shaped gap in the trees.

"Put the horses in the middle of the camp, where they'll be safe from wandering off or being killed by wild animals," he ordered.

The darkness soon swallowed the light. Anno ordered the men to spread out in groups of three, staying within shouting distance of one another. He stripped off his armor piece by piece and laid it beside his small fire. He removed his solleret, then the cloth covering his right foot.

With the firelight flickering on his face, he examined his diseased foot. The sores, swollen and purple, had overtaken his toes. He gingerly tended to them, placing the foot cloth near the flame to dry.

Alone in the clearing, he knelt and prayed. The occasional rustle of branches or snap of a twig made him reach for his sword.

An owl's distant hoot and a sharp shriek filled the air. His eyes grew heavy, his prayers faltering. Rubbing his eyes, he lay back, staring at the pine trees lit by the fire. His mind drifted to the day the Crusaders left for Lower Saxony, when Albert asked him to stay and serve for land. He hadn't expected the pagans' resilience. Over the years, tribes had rebelled, reclaiming land. The financial toll of his campaigns—the Battle on the Ice and the defeat in Riga Bay—had drained the Brotherhood's coffers. Anno preached

poverty and battling inner demons, yet he found himself
consumed by greed for gold and land. Slowly, he succumbed to
sleep.

In his dream, he was naked and falling. Below him, a red river
churned. He crashed through the surface, the crimson liquid
enveloping him. Desperate, he kicked upward, breaking through
to the air. He looked around—nothing but desert on either side.

Something pulled on his leg. A hand grabbed his shoulder and
yanked him back under.

The current dragged him forward, more hands clawing at
him, reaching from the murky red depths. He kicked them off,
screaming. In the distance, gold shimmered on the river's surface.
The blood-red water carried him toward a canyon, gold floating all
around him. He tried to grab the canyon's walls, but they were
smooth. As the river rushed him around a bend, he spotted a low-
hanging tree branch. He reached for it, but pain shot through his
hands.

Thorns, sharp and unforgiving, pierced his skin. He looked
closer and saw writing carved into the branch: Iēsus Nazarēnus,
Rēx Iūdaeōrum.

Suddenly, a tribal boy stood at the canyon's edge, watching
Anno.

"Help!" Anno screamed.

"I accept your God," the boy said, lifting an axe. In one swift
motion, he chopped the branch, sending Anno plunging back
into the river of blood.

He woke in a cold sweat. It was dawn. A heavy fog had settled
into the swamp. He put his head back on the ground and took a
couple of deep breaths.

A sudden realization flashed through his consciousness: no
birds chirping, no men snoring, no men talking. The horses
weren't shuffling in their standing sleep. He looked around, but
all he saw was fog. He looked at his armor that lay on the
ground. He stood, and the pelt fell from his body. He walked to
his armor and wrapped the cloth around his leg. He was putting

on the solleret when he heard a low thud just beyond his campsite.

He drew his sword quietly and walked barefoot through the swamp, mud squishing through his toes. He held his sword with two hands, crouching low.

Through the white dawn, he saw men lying in a deep sleep, empty wine sacks next to them. He kicked them one after the other, and as they woke, he put his index finger over his mouth.

He gestured to them, pointing at t their swords. The men grabbed their weapons and followed him. Anno silently directed one man to the left and one to the right and gestured for the third to follow him.

The crusader following Anno made a shivering sound, and Anno spun around. Thud. Blood covered Anno's face. The warrior, with a spear through his neck, struggled to breathe as blood filled his throat.

Anno watched as life kicked out of him. The sword fell from his hand.

"What the fu—?!" he heard someone yell in the distance. A low whoosh, followed by a loud scream, then silence. Anno turned to find the horses pierced to the ground, bellies slack, and bowels emptied. He continued walking past the horses and came upon another three dead soldiers, pierced through the heart.

"Ambush! Ambush! Ambush!" The screams echoed from the distance as Anno heard the frantic sound of men scrambling for their swords. Then he heard it—a sound that would be etched into his memory for the rest of his days. The battle cry of the Semigallians. A wolf's howl, followed by a scream of death. Steel clashed; men grunted and fell.

Through the orange fog, a wolf-man lunged at him, club raised. Anno blocked the blow, swung his sword, but the warrior slipped back into the mist, vanishing.

"Today isn't my day. It's yours!" Anno shouted into the fog, just as a short spear whizzed past his head.

Another wolf-man attacked from the left, his club missing

Anno's head by a hair, but smashing into his shoulder, the crack of bone resounding. Pain shot through his body, forcing him to grip his sword with one hand. The weight dragged him down, but there was no time to adjust. He swung desperately, his blade meeting the club. Another strike—he blocked again.

The tribesman moved with brutal speed, raising his club for a final, crushing blow. Anno turned his head, eyes squeezed shut, his sword wedged in the wood as the wolf-man fought to free his club. Seizing the moment, Anno kicked the warrior square in the chest, sending him sprawling to the ground.

Anno yanked at his sword, but it stayed stubbornly lodged in the wood. The wolf-man staggered to his feet. Anno gritted his teeth and screamed in desperation, yanking again, but the blade would not budge.

The wolf-man steadied himself, raising the club once more. Anno realized in that moment this was a fight he couldn't win. With a last burst of effort, he twisted the sword, dislodging it just enough to spin and deliver a wild, sweeping strike. The combined force of the momentum and desperation sent the wolf warrior crashing to the ground, his chest ripped open.

But there was no time to think.

Anno ran, the branches tearing at his flesh as he tore through the underbrush, heart pounding in his ears. The mist swirled around him, and somewhere behind him, the howls continued. He didn't look back.

At some point, exhaustion overtook him, and he collapsed. When the fog cleared, he lay on his back, wheezing and coughing violently. His arms rested limp at his sides, and then he felt it—a sticky wetness seeping from his abdomen, trickling onto his hands. Blood—his own. His vision blurred. "Help," he prayed, fingers curling into the dirt.

But no answer came.

CHAPTER FORTY

Ako felt the bite of the iron shackles on his wrists, the corroded metal burning grotesque, blackened sores into his skin. His eyes were swollen shut, and he struggled to open them. With his tongue, he probed the bruised gums where his upper teeth used to be, feeling the jagged edges of his shattered bottom teeth. He mustered the strength to stand, a symphony of pain with every movement. His kneecap was shattered, and he could hear bone grinding against bone.

Each faltering step reminded him of his greatest sin—his inherent otherness in a Christian world. Once an insider, now a heathen, he clashed with their rigid dogmas. His existence was an affront to their beliefs, a blemish on their pious tapestry. No suffering could erase his transgressions; despite his past assimilation, he would never truly belong.

Repeatedly, he stumbled, his face meeting the unforgiving ground, yet he summoned an inner resolve, clawing his way back up, his bloodied hands finding solace in the jagged embrace of the weathered stone walls.

Outside the prison, the crowd roared, jeering his name: "Ako! Ako! Ako!" It felt as though the stone walls trembled.

A slender beam of sunlight pierced through a hairline fracture in the stone. He put his swollen eyes to the crack. Met with searing brilliance, he looked away in pain.

"...heresy, witchcraft, and betraying this great city..." Albert's accusations echoed through his cell.

The furious mob roared, demanding a victim to atone for their misery.

He sighed, wishing his death to come quickly. Holding on to the wall, he slid to the ground and squinted into the ray of light coming through the crack. His mind wandered, remembering the day he sold Dzintara to protect himself and his fortunes.

Dzintara's silhouette emerged in the blur of light.

"I regret nothing," he yelled. His daughter faded away.

He covered his face with his hands, trying to block the flood of memories. Yet they persisted, relentlessly invading his consciousness, denying him any peace in these last moments.

"You just won't let me be, will you," he groaned.

He remembered Dzintara, covered in blood, when all the boys in the village went hunting, and she snuck away and was the only one to come back with a buck. Next, the memory of the last time he saw her mother. His wife. The sudden pain of her loss knocked him over to his side. Tears mixed with blood flowed from his eyes.

"I regret nothing," a frail and defeated murmur escaped his dry lips. "The vessels, they were my creation. Most exquisite in all the lands."

With outstretched arms, he reached for the ghostly image of his dead wife, a hazy blend of fleeting awareness, deceiving an old man in these final moments.

"I did it for her. They would have found her. Found the gold and wiped our family from this earth," he pleaded with her.

His wife faded.

"Please, you must believe me; everything I did was for the tribe and our family. It's true."

She was gone, replaced by vast darkness and emptiness.

"I regret nothing." His feral growl bounced off the walls of his cage.

The cell creaked open, and Ako sat up to greet his last visitors. A guard, and next to him, Varkelins.

"It is time, my old friend," Varkelins said.

Ako struggled to stand.

"I can't walk."

Varkelins threw him a cane made of birch.

"For the king of cogs," Varkelins said softly.

The old man grabbed onto the wall and grasped the end of the cane. With a great struggle, he stood.

"Last chance," Varkelins said. "Confess to your treason. Tell them that you were forced to it by the Brotherhood."

Ako remained silent. Varkelins gestured for him to come forward like a father coaxing his young son to take his first steps. Hobbling on one foot, Ako moved out of the cell. In the torchlight illuminating the prison walls, he could finally see Varkelins' face. Varkelins greeted him with a smile and a respectful bow, looking Ako directly in the eyes.

"I truly mean this. I am sad to see you go. Your work was magnificent," Varkelins said.

"The best there ever was and ever will be," Ako replied.

Varkelins gently turned Ako towards the exit. As the mob's chanting grew louder, Ako's heart raced, and his breathing quickened with each step.

He stopped.

"All is well?" asked Varkelins.

Ako nodded as if to say he was ready.

Taking a deep breath and slowly exhaling, Ako pulled his shoulders back and lifted his chin. The cane thumped as it hit the floor.

"All is well. I'm ready. I regret nothing."

Varkelins touched his shoulder, a gesture filled with sorrow. The door swung open to the blinding light. Ako faced the angry mob with his chin held high. Rocks and spit assaulted him, striking his chest, shins, and skull.

The mob was filled with men who had relied on his vessels for trade and battle, merchants he had built for and hosted, and friends he had lent to without usury, never holding a grudge when they couldn't pay. The guard's shove directed him towards his fate. He heard a high-pitched laugh and felt warm liquid hit his face.

"You fool," Varkelins screamed, "I'm covered in piss."

As his eyes adapted to the light, Ako saw the hostile crowd. Guild members, fueled by hate, stood alongside hypocritical burghers, all united in fury and chanting, "Die, traitor!" Their malicious smiles gleamed as he stumbled forward, like a goat to the slaughter.

Ako heard a sickening crunch of bone and a man's grunt as the guard hit a bystander. He struggled to fully open his eyes, hindered by swelling and pus.

Then he saw the scaffold. A forceful shove from the guard sent Ako reeling towards the steps. Ako climbed, reaching the first, then the second, and then the third. As he stepped onto the platform, his broken kneecap gave way, sending him tumbling to the side. The crowd roared with laughter.

Crawling to his feet, he finally came face-to-face with the ultimate traitor, Albert. Next to Albert, Ako saw a man holding an axe. He turned away towards the blurry outline of the blood-thirsty crowd.

"As the Archbishop of Riga, I condemn you for heresy and treason. You conspired with the Brotherhood to take control of this city and exile the Church."

The mob called for his death.

"Ako the Heathen, do you admit to the charge of conspiring against the church with the Brotherhood, practicing devil worship, and unleashing a curse on this city, all to overthrow and oppress the city for your own enrichment?"

The crowd went quiet, waiting for the answer. Ako, with what strength he had left, squared his shoulders, locked eyes with Albert, and spit.

The mob responded with outrage. "Kill him!" he heard someone in the crowd yell.

"Let him burn in hell!" said another.

More stones and rocks clattered against the wooden platform. The carcass of a dead chicken landed at his feet.

"Ako the Heathen, I hereby sentence you to death. As your baptism was a lie, I will not, cannot pray to God for your forgiveness," Albert said.

The guard seized Ako's arm, dragging him towards the center of the platform. With a swift kick to the back of his knee, Ako collapsed onto the unforgiving wooden surface. Ako's head was forced down onto a carved wooden block, its hollow circle cradling his neck in an embrace. Albert approached, lowering himself beside Ako, his heavy wine-filled breath clouding Ako's ear.

"You were never one of us. You're a primitive heathen, and that's all you ever were," Albert whispered.

The horde screeched and roared. The scent of blood was in their nose, and they were salivating for it.

Closing in on Ako from all sides, the blurry spring sun faded, giving way to darkness and peaceful silence. Ako felt a blow to the back of his neck, and then everything rolled to black.

CHAPTER FORTY-ONE

The bodies, stripped bare, were dragged and heaped into a mound. Nearby, their armor was methodically arranged. Dzintara watched as one wolf warrior dragged an injured crusader out of the mud. The survivors huddled in a guarded circle next to their dead companions.

"That's all of them. None escaped. The Brotherhood has been wiped from our lands," Lamekins declared.

"Anno escaped," Dzintara said without taking her eyes off the pile of bodies.

"Let it go. Dievs will ensure his fate in the wilderness."

"They'll come back in larger numbers. I've seen it with my own eyes too many times. He needs to be found and killed."

"It's just one Dzintara."

"Don't be a fool, Lamekins. I need three of your men to help me hunt."

"I can't give any men. We need to hold the line here in case more of them come."

"They won't. Not yet," she said.

Lamekins stayed silent. One wolf-man took the surviving knights and started beheading them one by one. Dzintara and

Lamekins watched coldly. Arturs screamed and begged for his life before the wolf-man severed his neck,

"Give me two men," she asked.

"Dzintara—"

Lamekins watched as one knight tried to run. The executor caught up easily and cut his leg off at the knee.

Lamekins turned to her. "I can give you two. But come back. All of you."

"We will," she replied.

Lamekins whistled, "Visvaldis. Austras."

Two wolf-men, unscathed from battle, turned to him and approached.

"Visvaldis, Austras. Dzintara, daughter of Ako, granddaughter of Kaupo of Turaida. She is your leader now. Do as she tells you."

The two young wolves punched their chests.

"We need to find their leader," Dzintara said, pointing to the remnants of the Brotherhood. "Our people's future depends on this. Let's look one more time, then get ready to ride out."

Visvaldis and Austras nodded, moving off.

She turned to Lamekins. "I think your men would have found him if he was nearby. But please, have them search again."

Lamekins nodded, giving the order.

"You have managed to do something no tribesman has done in a long time," Lamekins said to Dzintara.

"What have I done?"

"You've united the tribes. Semigallian fighting next to Curonian."

Dzintara went silent a moment, taking this in.

"Lamekins, before I go, I need to know one thing. Why did the tribes take you back? You worked with my father. Did they not see you as a traitor?"

"In the end, we are of the same tree. When I was close to my death in the shipyard, the Curonians helped me. Even when I worked for your father, I always gave to the tribe. Silver, gold, food, whatever I could."

"You're a good man," Dzintara said, touching Lamekins' shoulder.

Austras whistled and waved to Dzintara.

"They've found something."

Dzintara stepped through the bloodied mud filled with amputated limbs, fallen swords, spears, and axes. Visvaldis and Austras had found what appeared to be Anno's campsite. They were inspecting the clearing. The embers of Anno's fire were faded to charcoal. She ran her hands just above the coals. Next to the fires, she found a cloth covered in droplets of blood. Kneeling down, she found a cache of parchments.

"Scribe of their faith," she said, tossing it into the embers.

She examined Anno's armor and scanned the surroundings.

She said, "This is the man we are looking for."

Varkelins entered Albert's chambers in the Riga Cathedral. Albert was removing his cassock. He looked at Varkelins as he came through the door but said nothing. Varkelins took a seat and crossed his legs.

"Well?"

"Well, what?" asked Albert.

"I think I deserve a thank you. My plan—"

"Our plan," Albert corrected.

"Our plan is coming along smoothly. The city is angry. The merchants are on your side. Now you can raise an army."

"Friedrich has raised an army. He will attack their fort in two day's time."

Albert laid the cassock on the back of his chair. "Friedrich and I are allies now."

"Albert, don't be a fool. It's a matter of time before he goes against you."

"Nonsense. He relies on my power. Did you see the crowd out there? I provided their desired retribution for our sufferings. This curse is claiming lives everywhere. The blame is now fixed—the Brotherhood and their heathen allies brought this curse. The city will now unite against the swine," Albert declared.

"Unless there is no city left to govern, then there is no gold or silver to collect. Albert, don't let Friedrich fool you."

Albert, in his white linen undershirt and breeches, stood resolute. "I will prevail," he declared. "Attaining this position was no simple task. If you believe some young, ambitious upstart can unseat me," he said, "then you take me for a fool."

Albert untied his stockings, placing them next to his cassock.

"You should be more worried about finding that gold. My reasons for keeping you around are dwindling," Albert warned.

"Our search efforts have not yielded anything," Varkelins admitted.

Albert walked over to a thick, dark cabinet, took a bottle from it, and poured some wine into a cup. He drank.

"I've been thinking, Varkelins. After today, my position with the people has been assured. Thanks to our loyal friends."

Varkelins ears perked at Albert's sudden condescending tone.

"The merchants of this great city who have been should be rewarded," Albert said, refilling his cup.

Varkelins nodded. "They have the shipyard now."

"That's Friedrich's. The others also need to wet their beaks. Entrench them into our plot, I say."

"Albert, we must be cautious. The Brotherhood hasn't been defeated. The siege hasn't even begun. You're getting ahead of yourself," cautioned Varkelins.

"The converts possess vast lands outside the city," Albert mused, his mind clearly working on a plan.

Varkelins sighed deeply, pressing his hands to his face.

"Levying rents from those lands could demonstrate our commitment to our allies," Albert continued.

Varkelins shook his head, troubled by the direction of Albert's thoughts.

"The danger of a revolt is too significant. Their numbers are vast. They will rebel against you and ally with the Brotherhood. Remember, the Brotherhood has fought alongside both freemen and tribes."

"Then we give them an option, stay and pay the levies, or leave."

"Albert, the land yields here are meager. For these people, their land is all that remains. They spend half the year hunting and fishing just to meet their tithes. If we strip this from them, they'll rise up against us," Varkelins declared.

Albert refilled his wine and looked down at a parchment spread out on the table in the corner. It was a drawing of St. Maurice: the halo around his head, the holy lance in his hands, his body bedecked in armor, and the heads of his Egyptian legion at his feet. Albert took a sip of his wine.

Varkelins stood next to him and gazed at the saint. "His men refused to worship Roman deities, and when the emperor Maximian ordered him to kill the local Christians, he refused," said Varkelins at last. "The emperor punished his legion by decimation. He still refused. The emperor killed more of his legion. In ultimate defiance, Maurice decided to kill his entire legion to save the Christians."

Albert looked at him in disgust. "Don't. I don't need your lessons. I'm the Archbishop of the Riga."

"We imposed our faith on them for their freedom, and they accepted. We've levied them heavily, and they've borne it. But there's a limit to everything. Seize their land, and you'll spark a war we cannot win. Even Friedrich won't prevail. Trade has stalled; no vessels have arrived in weeks. Your coffers are empty, Albert," Varkelins said.

Albert looked back at St. Maurice. "They can stay on the land, but we double the levies, and half will go to the new owners, the guilds who stand with us.".

"You won't succeed. An uprising by the freemen will distract Riga's citizens, shifting their focus away from the Brotherhood. Meanwhile, the Brotherhood will bide their time, watching the city descend into chaos. At its weakest, they'll strike, and they'll kill you. I refuse to be a casualty of your decisions."

Albert turned to Varkelins, placing his cup on the table near St. Maurice. Abruptly, he seized Varkelins by the hair, pulling his face close. "You think I don't know about you fucking the stable boy at night? Huh? Think you couldn't be the next one up on the scaffolds?"

Varkelins winced

"Be careful, Varkelins. I will not tolerate your disloyalty. I can feed you to the crowd as easily as I did with Ako. They're hungry for another sacrifice," Albert hissed harshly into Varkelins' ear before releasing his grip.

Varkelins clutched at his head, his fingers gingerly checking for blood. He fixed his gaze on Albert. After a tense silence, Varkelins forced a smile.

"I would never betray you, Albert."

"Good. We have a continued partnership. Don't ruin it," Albert took a piece of Varkelins' cheeks and pinched it.

Flinching, Varkelins pulled his head away and headed for the door.

"Varkelins," Albert said, extending his hand. Varkelins turned to look at him. "Don't ever forget your place again. You can address me as Your Excellency from now on."

Albert gestured to his finger, adorned with his clergy ring. Varkelins hesitated,

"Well, is this how you depart from Your Excellency?" Albert asked pointedly.

Varkelins stepped forward and kissed Albert's ring.

"Kneel." Albert motioned toward the floor with his chin.

"It's time people remembered who they are and where they belong."

Varkelins knelt with his right knee, put his forehead to the archbishop's hand, and then kissed it.

"Your Excellency," he murmured, standing up and slowly backing towards the door.

After closing the door behind him, Varkelins faced the thick, dark brown wood. His fists were trembling with restrained rage. He raised them, poised to pound on the door. Instead, he dug his nails deep into the wood, dragging them down. Splinters sliced beneath his nails, leaving behind faint traces of blood.

CHAPTER FORTY-TWO

The bitter cold gnawed at his flesh. His toes were black and frozen, and his lips cracked and bleeding. With every step, the sense of being hunted grew stronger.

The wound in his side no longer bled. A small comfort in the face of the bleak, unchanging forest that surrounded him. The snow fell softly, muffling all sound. He was unsure of which way he was headed. North, he thought. The sun was setting, and temperatures were dropping fast.

Amidst the dense pine forest, he came upon a towering rock formation. The jagged edges reached for the sky, weather-worn and colored in dull gray, brown, and black, like cathedral stone. He stumbled towards it, grabbing branches to stay upright. At its base, he saw a small, barely visible crevice through the underbrush. He halted and gazed at it.

The misty, snow-filled air was still and peaceful. He paused, straining his ears. Nothing but the rustling of a leaf or the distant call of a raven.

Anno crawled on his knees, clearing the underbrush, and forced himself into the cave mouth. It was dark and wet. Just large enough for him to crawl through. As protection from the elements and his pursuers, this damp hole was satisfactory.

He crawled back out and gathered dry twigs and wood, stripping the barren tree trunks until his fingernails bled. He carried the kindling to the small opening and arranged it into a neat pile. Rubbing two sticks together, he worked until his palms were calloused and bleeding. Finally, the fire lit.

He ripped a piece of his shirt and wrapped it around a thicker branch, creating a makeshift torch. The fire crackled. He held the branch to the fire, then scooped up the remaining kindling, carrying it carefully so as not to kill the torch.

He crawled through the mouth of the cave. The fire bounced off the black rocks. A gust of wind howled, causing the flames to flicker wildly.

Anno pushed his torch towards the walls. Finding another opening, he turned his head to the side to fit through, scraping against the stone. After twenty paces, he found himself in a large chamber. For the first time in days, he felt safe. He stood upright and placed the pile of sticks and branches in the middle of the cavern. Then he lit the pile with his torch. He warmed his hands and massaged his black, aching toes. He lay down with a sigh of relief.

He thought about God and his men, who were probably dead. God still wasn't talking to him, and he began to make peace with that. He no longer harbored anger towards God for forsaking him and his men. Thoughts of prayer crossed his mind, but he dismissed them.

A curious mixture of acceptance and resignation came over him as he lay on the cool dirt floor of the cave, with the fire licking at his toes. He examined God's absence and how it no longer shook him. He saw with a strange clarity that it had been his own decisions that led him to this fate. It was his own ambition that drove him to risk the lives of his men and take the lives of heathens and infidels.

He craved to justify the outcome of his fate: spreading the blood of Christ for the Holy Church and saving pagans from hell. For a moment, he considered the possibility that he was in the frozen reaches of hell. But reality crept in, and he realized where he really was: alone and Godless.

The epiphany came slowly at first, then all at once: he was no different than the pagans he had sought to convert. This realization made him laugh hysterically, an awful cackling that echoed throughout the cave. His laughter turned into tears, and the cave seemed to laugh back at him.

"I am not them!" he screamed into the emptiness of the cave. "You hear me? I am not them."

With anger, he sat up and took a branch from the fire, the end oozing with orange.

"Where is my redemption?"

He sucked his teeth and lay back on the ground, staring at the ceiling. Anno turned towards the fire and then, restless, pushed himself up hard with his hands to stand on his feet, but he struggled to get off all fours.

A flash, the slightest flicker in the corner of his eye, caught his attention. He glanced in its direction, looking carefully. Another flicker on the ground just ten arms' length away. He crawled toward the flash. He rubbed his hands in the dirt on the chamber floor, feeling for something.

There it was. He felt something underneath his palms, and his hands froze. He carefully raised his hand and gently blew away a cloud of dirt, uncovering a circular shape. Leaning down, he saw a coin embedded in the dirt, its edges marked with an insignia. He carefully lifted the coin from the ground, then spat on it, rubbing the coin against his skin. His fingers twirled the coin, examining it in the firelight. He could make out the face of Honorius III, head of the holy church who had ruled twenty years prior.

"God, I hear you." Anno laughed in disbelief.

He bit the coin and turned it over and over many times. He looked around the large chamber, wondering if this was a dream.

His pain suddenly eased. He turned his head from one corner of the cave to the other, taking inventory of the shadows where the fire could not reach.

From the pile of dried kindling, he took the thickest piece he could find, lighting it. Holding it far from his body, he began wandering around the cavern, exploring the shadows. Nothing worth noting. The small torch went out.

He breathed a sigh of disappointment and sat next to the fire.

He looked at the bark, the dry leaves, and the tinder he'd collected. He found a piece of birch wood, unwrapped the bark, and laid the piece flat on the ground. He placed dried pine needles, small twigs, and broken pieces of wood along the center. He folded the bark, carefully tying it with shaved wood fibers, creating a makeshift torch. The rigged torch caught fire almost instantly. He limped over to a yet unexplored area of the cave. A sudden draft blew the torch flame toward him. He smiled. Waving the torch, he found a narrow entrance, just wide enough for him to squeeze through.

He cried out in pain as he turned sideways and pushed through, the jagged rock scraping against the wound in his side. Finally, he emerged into a vast, open cavern.

Holding the torch high, he could make out the shapes of chests and barrels. He remembered the old rumors of the lost gold and silver. In the dim light, he could see the insignia of the church on the chests.

A large gust blew into the cavern and killed the flame. He dropped the burned-out torch. On the damp, cold ground, he felt with his hands and crawled until he felt the first chest.

He placed his fingers into the cleft and hauled open the lid, his heart pounding. He plunged his hands into thousands of coins. Taking two hands filled with coins, he stood upright and slowly walked backward, retracing his steps from memory. When he got lost, he would wait for the draft. When he reached the cavern wall, he felt around with his clenched, coin-filled fists. He found the opening. Turning sideways, he made his way back to where he had come from.

He stumbled back into the smaller cave and ran with a limp over to the fire and emptied his hands. The coins shone in the firelight. Anno collapsed to his knees and bent, laughing over the coins. He imagined the gold and silver hidden in the cavern, the solution to all his problems. When he stopped laughing, he looked up at the ceiling of the large chamber and sighed.

"Thank you," he whispered, clenching his fists together in prayer. He placed his new coins in his small clothes.

His breath smoked as he crawled out of the cave. Newfound hope made him forget his pain. He headed north, dragging one leg behind him in the snow. The sun slid down behind the trees.

CHAPTER FORTY-THREE

Varkelins rode from the Turaida Castle with Hans, Remko, and another of Albert's men down through the Guaja valley and toward the settlements of the freemen. The sun was high in the sky, and the snow was melting. The river gushed downstream with incredible force. They galloped along it for a while.

"What exactly are we doing?" Hans asked as they slowed their horses to a walk.

"We are telling the local converts that their land no longer belongs to them, and they must pay levies and tithes to continue using the land or else abandon it and find somewhere else to go," Varkelins replied without facing them.

Hans, riding a small brown *kleiner pferd*, drew up the reins and halted. The other two followed suit. Varkelins, realizing their defiance, turned to look at them.

"I'm not going any further. They will stone us on sight. I'm a monk, not a soldier," Hans said.

"Hans, let's just ride. Preferably in silence," Varkelins said, looking down at Hans' horse and motioning ahead.

"He's right. We're going to get killed. I'm with him," said the one riding the black Holsteiner.

Varkelins sighed and pinched his brow ridge together in pain. He gazed at them and forced a smile. "Nothing is going to happen. We will announce the news and then go. Shall we?"

"The only reason Albert sent me is because there are no other guards left. He wouldn't send armed men unless he expected retaliation," Hans reasoned. "I'm not intending to find out what happens."

Remko and the other guard nodded along in agreement.

"You don't expect me to go alone?" Varkelins asked.

Varkelins shot a quick glance at Hans.

"I'm serious," Varkelins said, motioning forward.

"As are we," Hans said, speaking for the group.

"I will discuss better compensation for you with Albert. More gold. More food. Better lodging within the castle."

"And a percentage of tax collected," Hans said in a calculated tone.

Varkelins clenched his teeth as he listened to the argument of these impudent, greedy men.

"I see you've heard the plans, Hans. Fine. I will discuss this with Albert on your behalf."

"Swear it."

"Yes," Varkelins said sharply. Varkelins made a dramatic motion in front of him, inviting them to lead the way. They shook their heads, allowing Varkelins to take the lead. They rode alongside the Guaja River with Varkelins in front and the three men riding behind. Whispers and snickers filtered through as he focused on the road ahead.

If the knights didn't show up in time like Markus had promised, he stood to lose everything. His fate would be exile or death. Another loud snicker interrupted his thoughts.

"What is so funny?" he asked without halting.

"I was just telling my fellas here that I may snatch myself a convert woman. I heard their pussies are worth their weight in gold."

The men laughed. Varkelins shook his head.

"Yeah, I may do that as well. Since we're taking their land, why not their women?" said the other.

"Fools," Varkelins murmured to himself.

"I've been with a herring eater once," Hans stated proudly.

"What was it like?" asked the taller one.

"Let's just say it lives up to the rumors," he smacked his lips and rolled his tongue at the others.

"I'm going to get me one of them herring eaters and just keep her for mounting."

"What about you, Varkelins? Would you take a convert?" asked Hans.

"I think Varkelins is more interested in the stable boy than any woman," said the man on the black horse. The other two men laughed loudly.

Varkelins stopped his horse, unsheathed his sword, and aimed it at the man's throat.

"Albert may have a need for you, but I don't. I can cut your throat right now, offer the other two a bag of gold, and your body will float down the river like you never lived. Are we in understanding?"

"Yes," said the guard, his voice squeaking at the point of the blade.

"My affairs are my own and no one else's, which means they are of no one's discussion but mine."

Varkelins lowered his sword, sheathed it, and continued riding.

"Besides, any traveled man knows that Portuguese women are worth double the weight of their behinds in gold," Varkelins added.

THE OUTSKIRTS of the settlement emerged next to a narrow river. The small wooden huts stood in neat rows, their thatched roofs casting shadows in the waning light. Approaching, Varkelins noted the smoke rising from chimneys and watched a group of women weaving hemp. A black dog with an enormous head and a dumb look on its face cautiously circled a pair of chickens.

Varkelins observed men at work by the river, efficiently scaling and gutting fish with practiced movements. Each fish, cleaned of its innards, was swiftly tossed into a barrel brimming with salt. A pack of dogs scuffled over the discarded, bloody entrails, eager to claim their share of the scraps.

The freemen stopped and stared at them as they approached. In the main square, a group of men had just returned from hunting, carrying foxes, ferrets, and pheasants with them.

In the middle of the square stood a church, the door ajar, hanging on broken hinges. Varkelins had the impression that no one had been inside for years. Children huddled in a large group on the other side of the main square, excitedly welcoming the returning hunters.

The hunters gave the pheasant to the children, who ran off to their mothers. Then, seeing the horsemen approaching, the hunters straightened, caressing their weapons. The other men of the town began to gather, surrounding Varkelins and his men.

Varkelins stopped his horse in front of the old church. Reaching for his satchel, he retrieved a parchment with Albert's seal. He tore it open and began to unroll it. His men unsheathed their weapons.

"Get off our land," a yell came from the crowd.

"Leave us alone. We're Christians," someone else said.

The leader of the huntsmen, with a chest the size of two men, approached Varkelins. The hunter's stony gaze met Varkelins' eyes, sending a shiver through him.

"*Turpini runāt.*"

Varkelins swallowed and stared at the parchment. He felt sick and turned to the side of his horse and vomited. The crowd and the huntsmen's leader laughed.

"Get yourself together," Hans whispered fiercely, "they smell your weakness."

Varkelins sat up straight and took a deep breath.

He cleared his throat and read. "By the order of Bishop Albert of Riga, sanctioned by the one and only true Holy Mother Church."

"*Pēc Rīgas bīskapa Alberta pavēles, vienīgās patiesās Svētās Mātes Baznīcas sankcionēts.*" The hunter translated for the village.

"You are hereby notified that the land which you occupy is no longer your possession or property but has been presented to the merchants of Riga. Should you wish to stay, you will be levied for renting this land. If you do not wish to stay, you are required to leave before spring arrives."

The hunter gazed at the three outsiders, unsheathed his sword, and let it hang from his hand by his side.

"*Zinājāt, ka zeme, ko ņemat, tagad ir Rīgas tirdzniecības uzņēmuma īpašums? Ja paliekat, nomājiet to, ja nē, tad aiziet pirms rīta.*"

The air became thick with the scent of anger. The murmur of the crowd began as a low hum, like the buzz of a hive of bees, growing in intensity with each passing moment. The villagers moved towards them, pressing them closer to the small stone church.

A frenzy took over the crowd. Thick mud hit Varkelins' face, followed by a shower of rocks slamming into his body and into his horse. The horse reared, and Varkelins pulled sharply on the reins, plunging into the crowd. Some tried to stop him and grab at him, but his horse trampled them.

The mob pulled Hans and Remko from their horses, laying into them with fists and stones. They smashed Remko's face into a bloody pulp. Varkelins spurred his horse as hard as he could. He turned to see if his men were behind him, but all he could see were three riderless horses.

He ran as far as he could until he and the horse were panting for air. He dismounted, allowing his horse to drink at a river tributary.

A sudden realization dawned on him: Albert never meant for him to return. A smile curved at the edge of his lips. He'd come through worse. He could see straight through the empty chest of the Archbishop. He remounted and drove his horse onward into the night.

CHAPTER FORTY-FOUR

Dzintara knelt over broken twigs and a depression in the bushes. Footprints in the mud were filled in with water from the melted snow. In the near distance, she saw jagged rocks extending to the sky, a dark weathered escarpment. Sniffing the air, she stood and walked towards the wilted and weathered formation. Branches torn off. Tree bark ripped from birch trunks. Visvaldis circled around a large oak tree deeper into the forest.

"He was here," she pointed to the torn branches.

"Could he still be here?" Austras asked.

"Maybe. He's wounded. And he knows he's prey. But he's not so foolish as to hide in the open," her eyes drawn toward the weathered sanctuary, "he would go somewhere hidden. Enclosed."

A low whistle, staccato, like a bird's call.

"I found something!" Austras yelled.

They followed the whistle to Austras, where they found him with his head stuck deep into the opening of the crevice. Dzintara looked at the opening, which was covered in moss and surrounded by broken twigs.

"Broken twigs and dry leaves rarely go looking for shelter on their own," Austras said. "The air smells like smoke, too."

Dzintara looked at him and then looked at the cave mouth. She unsheathed her khanjar.

"I doubt he's still in there unless he's a damn fool," Visvaldis said.

"Let's find out," Austras said, smiling at the possibility.

"We need a torch," Dzintara said.

Visvaldis found a long, sturdy branch and stripped it. Tearing a piece of cloth from his garments, he reached into his satchel and retrieved an item wrapped in cloth. He knelt on the ground and carefully unwrapped a cube of white fat and rubbed the torn cloth with it. Then he wrapped the dried branches and leaves into the cloth and tied it to the branch with a leather string.

"If he's in there, he's probably heard us by now. He's wounded and exhausted, but do not underestimate him. No matter how weak he is, he will kill us if he can," Dzintara warned both.

Visvaldis handed the torch to Dzintara and took iron and flint from his satchel, creating a spark. The torch-head went up in flames.

Dzintara motioned with her head and crawled through the opening with the khanjar in her teeth and the torch held before her. Eventually, she emerged into a larger cavern. Ready for a fight, she stood with her khanjar pointed. Visvaldis and Austras followed, spear points at the ready.

Feeling relieved that they wouldn't be ambushed, the three started exploring the cave.

"Here," Austras called out.

The logs were still warm to the touch. She looked at the two warriors and made a circling gesture with her finger. They split into the dark edges.

A bloody rag lay next to the dead fire — like the one at the previous campsite. She examined it and relit the fire in the pit with the remaining twigs and leaves. Light flooded the cavern, illuminating the rough stone walls and casting sharp shadows across the ground. Anno was nowhere.

"He can't be far. He's barefoot."

She threw the bloody cloth on the fire and watched it burn. A low howl of wind filled the cavern. She looked at the Austras.

"Do you hear that?" she called. "Listen."

"There is another opening," Austras said.

"You start on that side, Visvaldis in the middle, and I'll start on this side," she ordered, and they spread out, searching the dark pockets of the room.

Dzintara held the torch and ran her hands across the cool rock, searching for a crack or opening in the darkness. The low whistling persisted, coming and going.

"Anything?" she asked.

"No," the wolf-men responded.

"Keep looking."

Dzintara's fingers traced the cave's stone until she felt an area that was markedly colder. "What is it?" Visvaldis asked.

Dzintara held up the torch and answered: "Nothing. Keep looking."

"I think I found something," said Austras.

Dzintara went to him and lit up the dim corner with light. She saw a narrow opening in the wall. The torch flame flickered.

She gave the torch to one of them.

"Hold this and give it to me when I ask for it."

She turned sideways and put her leg into the opening, followed by her hips. Her stomach scraped against the stone, and her breasts flattened against the rocks, scraping with every step. She called for the torch.

The flicker of the torch cast an ominous shadow as she squeezed out of the narrow passageway and into the chamber. She walked forward with the torch, seeing what secrets the cave kept.

And there it was. The shadow of chests and barrels.

A dead torch lay on the ground, surrounded by footprints and scuff marks in the dirt.

The chests and barrels rested in the darkest part of the enormous cavern, piled on top of one another. Dzintara stopped, listening closely and sniffing the air. A cold, damp smell and the soft dripping of condensed water were coming from somewhere behind and to the left of the chests.

She went around a few paces, finding a dark, seemingly bottomless pool of water. It remained perfectly still and clear.

At the back of the pool, she saw a larger opening that led off somewhere, possibly to another entrance. The crystal-clear water reflected the torchlight like glass. As she approached, she looked up and saw the shimmering reflection on the ceiling.

"Dzintara?" Austras' voice bounced through the cave.

There were at least thirty or forty barrels and chests. One chest had a gold-plated lock engraved with two faces, each sporting a halo. One face had a beard and the other a mustache, with "SPA" above one and "SPE" above the other. She squinted hard at the engraving.

A memory flashed in her mind: she was nine years old, standing on ice and snow under a white-gray sky. Beneath her feet was the thick ice of the black Baltic. A dozen tribesmen waited with carriages as they crossed the frozen expanse to the shore, carrying chests and barrels bearing these same insignia.

"Dzintara? We're coming!" another faint yell interrupted the memory.

"I'm fine. Just stay there."

With a soft touch, she traced the lid of the chest. Placing the torch nearby, pried the lock open with her khanjar. Brilliant yellow light seared her eyes. She smiled, closing the chest.

A strong draft eddied through the larger opening behind the pool. It picked up, howling, calling to her to follow.

She followed.

"I need to look at something. Just wait there," she ordered her men.

Dzintara circled around the pool, staying close to the walls. She entered a vast cave tunnel with towering limestone walls, rising into darkness. Yellow-brown sandstone formations hung from the ceiling like udders, dripping water droplets that echoed softly as they landed.

After walking another hundred paces, a soft, glowing light pierced the tunnel. Cracks in the sandstone ceilings sent darts of sunlight to the cavern floor. She stopped and placed her hand in the shaft of sunlight, turning her palm upside down with a smile.

A short distance later, she reached a cave entrance, emerging behind a waterfall. Careful to keep the torch dry, she wedged it into a crack in the stone.

Dangerous moss-covered steps descended along the side of the gorge, just wide enough to sidestep to the bottom. It was slippery and narrow. Anno couldn't have climbed this—not in his condition, but she needed to make sure.

Cautiously, she shuffled along the path. Her foot slipped. Grabbing an uneven rock to keep her from falling to her death, she steadied herself. She collected herself and continued the shuffle.

In the forest, she searched for footprints in the mud, torn branches, and any sign that Anno had escaped this way. The riverbank was undisturbed. Looking at the sun, she guessed she was about a quarter-day walk from the other opening.

Ripping a bloody part of her breeches, she tied it to a blossoming pine branch, noting the marker's location.

She climbed back to the top of the gorge; she looked again at the sun's location. High and to the left on the horizon. She turned toward the mouth of the waterfall. The torch was where she left it, still burning. She took the note from her pocket and held it in the torch fire. It caught flame and turned to ash, carried away in the wind.

She made her way back the way she came, stopping to take two pieces of gold. When she limped through the narrow passageway, Austras and Visvaldis stood waiting anxiously.

"No, but I am sure he's alive." She looked at them gravely. "We have to find him and kill him. It's more important now than ever."

The two looked at her with a blank face.

"That's why we are here to help you—"

She raised her hand, halting Austras, "You don't understand. If we fail, it's the end of us."

CHAPTER FORTY-FIVE

Varkelins' horse foamed at the mouth, panting as it ran along the shore of the Gauja River towards Turaida. Vengeance boiled Varkelins' blood. Varkelins drove his heels into the horse's flanks, urging it forward. Eventually, the horse refused and slowed to a stop.

"C'mon, you God-forsaken beast."

In defeat, Varkelins dismounted and led the horse by the reins as the animal gasped for air.

"Fine, I'll walk, but if they find and kill us, it's your fault."

He came to a fork in the road. Left was Turaida. On the right was the Brotherhood's fortress. An old tree stump stuck out of the wide mat of pine needles at the center of the forking trail as if inviting one to stop before choosing the path.

Releasing the reins, Varkelins sat on the stump and considered which way to go. Watching as his horse stepped to the riverbank and drank deeply, he imagined gutting Albert and hanging him from the castle gate. Poisoning him. Pissing on his body.

Varkelins stared up at the sun, then looked down at his shaking left hand. Returning to Albert would be a risk. It seemed the Archbishop wanted him dead.

Seeking amnesty within Anno's fort would mark him as a

traitor to Albert. If the Order's army didn't arrive before Friedrich's assault, he would surely die anyway. He didn't know whether Anno had returned from his campaign. If he had, would he be willing to make an alliance?

He pinched his nose bridge and swore at the soil.

"Christ's blood!" he sighed.

He had so few cards left to play. Perhaps he should just ride west to Upper Saxony and start a new life as a simple merchant, trading from town to town.

The sound of a snapping twig made him turn. He reached into his tunic and felt the bone handle of his knife.

Another branch snapped by the riverbank, followed by a sudden splash. He bolted upright and held the knife out in front of him. The horse, returning from its drink, whinnied.

Varkelins rose to his feet, slowly approaching the embankment. Knife pointing ahead, he cleared the brush. He saw a man in the water, clutching a tree limb to keep the current from taking him.

Varkelins lowered his blade and slid down the ledge to the river, making his way downstream.

The man was wheezing and exhausted, trying to pull himself out of the river.

Varkelins noticed a terrible wound on his side, the exposed flesh turning dark purple. Then he noticed the man's long, dark hair and his frail frame. Varkelins rushed over. He grabbed the man's hand and pulled him onto shore.

"Anno?" Varkleins gasped.

"Yes. Thank you," he panted, patting Varkelins's arm.

Varkelins took his tunic and laid it over Anno's torso as he shook with cold on the ground.

"Everyone thinks you marched south into the lands of the Semigalians."

Anno swallowed hard, managing only a single word.

"Ambush."

"Where are the rest of your men?"

"Dead." Anno looked away.

Varkelins helped Anno sit up. He was shivering with his left fist clenched.

"Go. Get my men. All of them."

"Anno, are you mad? You're half dead. Don't be a fool!"

Anno laughed, coughing blood. "I found it. God gave me my redemption."

Varkelins looked towards his horse.

"Come on. We'll get you back to the fort."

Anno grabbed Varkelins by the collar with his right hand.

"You damned bastard. Listen to me. I am not mad. I found it."

Anno's hand opened like a blooming flower, revealing a gold coin minted by Honorius III.

"We will return with twenty hundred men. Rid them from these lands."

Varkelins' eyes widened. He took the coin from Anno's hand and held it up into the sun.

"It's mine. The order. We will amalgamate and..." Anno coughed again.

Varkelins placed the coin back into Anno's palms and closed his fingers around the coin.

"You need to get my men, and we need to get the rest. God has pressed this fate upon me to conquer these lands."

Varkelins stars across the river at thick brush and pine forest. "Where was it?"

Anno looked at Varkelins and raised an eyebrow. "Get my men, and you will have your share."

"You don't look good, friend. The fort is a half-day's ride, even more from here. What if you don't make it."

"I will. God is with me."

Varkelins helped Anno up. His toes were black from frostbite, his shins scraped raw and bloody.

"How did you end up in the river?"

"I couldn't walk anymore, so I floated," Anno said, shivering.

Varkelins looked upriver at the fast-flowing current.

"But the Semagalians are inland. The Gauja does not cross through their territory."

Anno snapped his head up. "Don't take me for a fool, Varkelins. I've outsmarted many enemies. Many with more wit than you. Get my men."

Varkelins helped Anno walk towards the horse. Then, he placed his foot slightly in front of Anno to trip him. Anno cried out in pain as he fell to his knees on the rocks and rolled over on his back.

Varkelins looked down at the struggling man, then placed the muddy sole of his boot gently on Anno's side.

"What are you doing? Help me up."

Varkelins pressed the heel of his boot into Anno's side. Anno screamed out loud, the power of the river drowning out the cries.

"You will take me there now. Unless you never want to see your God. I swear I will leave you here for the scavengers to find and tear your body apart and eat your flesh. No righteous man enters the kingdom of God without a proper burial. It's your choice."

"You will kill me once I take you there."

Varkelins took his foot off the wound.

"Anno, after our long friendship, is that what you think?" Varkelins knelt next to him, cradling his head.

"Brother, you have me so wrong. I am trying to help you. Look at you. You're dying. What if you don't survive to the fort? Your men all lost."

"What if I die on the way to the gold?"

"I will find it and ensure your men get what they deserve," Varkelins smiled. "Upon my honor."

Anno turned his head and looked up at the sky, searching for an answer.

"Time is running out," Varkelins said as he stood upright.

"I'll take you. But if any harm comes to me, my men will have revenge."

Varkelins grabbed Anno's arm. "Friendship is thicker than gold." He pulled Anno to his feet, and they limped together back to the horse. Varkelins mounted the horse, pulling Anno up to sit in front of him.

"South," said Anno.

Varkelins nodded and kicked the side, and the horse cantered north.

Albert snorted awake. His heavy frame shifted erect on the bed, feet swinging to the edge. He shuffled across the floor to the steel basin and plunged his face into the cold water.

Then, there was a knock at his door.

"Enter," he called out, and a messenger entered.

"Your Excellency," he bowed.

"Go on with it," Albert said.

"As you know, the nobles and merchants of Riga arranged for a surprise attack on the fort of the Brotherhood."

Albert took a cloth and dried his face. He sniffed twice and placed the cloth next to the basin. He turned and looked at the messenger.

"And?" Albert asked, annoyed.

"Well, your Excellency, the first day seemed to have gone well. They killed two of the Brotherhood's archers, but..."

"But what?" Albert barked.

"Once the element of surprise wore off, the Brotherhood assembled and drove the merchants back to the forest. "

Albert cursed.

"They need reinforcements. Weapons," the messenger continued. "They instructed me to come to you for these things and return with them."

Albert stared at the messenger. "Where am I supposed to get these things? I am a man of God, not war."

"I noticed you have some soldiers guarding the castle. I can take them with me, and we can visit your armory to see if there are any weapons that would be useful to our joint cause. Friedrich asked me to remind you of your pledged support ."

"No. I have eleven men guarding my estate. That already makes it easy for us rabbits to hunt. Do you understand? My castle needs thirty men for proper fortification—I have only eleven!"

The messenger stood his ground. "I understand. Perhaps we can take half and the weapons from the armory."

"Get out."

"Your Excellency, they asked me to relay the message that if you do not comply, the Guild will turn its attention on Turaida instead."

"Verdammter Friedrich!"

Albert turned to the basin and tried to lift it, but it was heavy with water. He struggled for a minute before spilling its contents and throwing the empty basin out the window, chasing its descent with a vomit of cursing.

Once Albert was done, he turned and walked past the messenger, calling after him, "Well, aren't you coming?"

The messenger followed.

They walked down the stairs, passing the hearth covered in ceramic-painted saints. "Any word from Varkelins or Hans?" Albert addressed one of his servants.

"No, Your Excellency."

Albert began to walk towards the stairs leading to the courtyard.

"Your Excellency, yarn is spinning about a disruption in the Freemen town."

Albert halted. "Disruption?"

"Yes, some Christians laid on spikes outside the town. A monk. Some of yours, perhaps?"

Perhaps he was finally rid of Varkelins. He regretted it came at Hans's expense. Albert continued down the stairs. He pushed the courtyard doors open and walked out into the nascent spring sun.

"Guards! Come!" Albert shouted. The eleven guards wobbled forward, coming to attention. He looked them up and down. Most were in no condition to fight. Overweight. Short. Stupid.

"You." He pointed to one. "Go with him."

The fat guard waddled over to the messenger. Albert turned away and walked towards his quarters.

"I'm afraid one won't be enough," the messenger called after him. Albert sighed and turned.

"Well, how many will be enough?"

"At least half your men. Are they well-trained?"

Albert laughed. "Well-trained. Don't mock me."

Albert chose five more men, telling them to go with the messenger. Next, they made their way to the armory. Albert took a large metal key and inserted it into the lock of an old, reinforced wooden door. The door opened, and the guard lit the room up with a torch.

"What in the name of our Jesus Christ?" Albert shouted as he looked around the near-empty room.

"Where the hell did our weaponry disappear to?" Albert asked in disbelief. He turned to the messenger, who had lost his smirk.

The fat guard was the first to speak.

"Your Excellency," he stammered, "we haven't received payment in many moons, so we sold some weapons to the merchants."

Albert turned to the overweight guard.

"You sold my weapons to merchants? Here? In Riga?"

"Yes, your Holiness."

Albert was turning red with rage. He spun to the messenger.

"Just take whatever's left and get these swine out of my sight. May they help the cause."

Albert turned and thumped out the door.

The messenger ordered the guards to pile up what weapons remained onto a cart and grab what they needed from their cots. They were leaving immediately.

After gathering the weapons, the messenger mounted his horse, and the five guards climbed into a carriage. They rode out of Turaida Castle, down the rust-colored mud road, towards the merchant camp uphill from the Brotherhood.

CHAPTER FORTY-SIX

Dzintara and Visvaldis lie low in the brush at the forest's edge. They had been waiting for hours. Occasionally, she caught Visvaldis glancing at her.

"You're looking at the scars, aren't you?" she asked without looking at him.

Embarrassed, Visvaldis responded, "No."

"Then why do you keep looking at me and looking away?" Dzintara asked, almost playfully.

"I heard stories about your grandfather and your father," Visvaldis paused for a moment and looked at the ground. "And your mother, when I was a child."

At that moment, she felt empty. She was alone in this world. Without a father, mother, or brother. The last of her blood.

"And?"

"I was trying to picture you as a chief," Visvaldis said. "I think you would have been good for our tribe."

Dzintara smiled at this. "Thank you."

There was a rustle in the trees behind them, and Austras appeared, joining them. "The Christian fort is under attack."

"By whom?" asked Dzintara.

"Hard to tell. Some wear plain clothes, but they wield weapons. Others look like soldiers."

"This is good," Dzintara said, more to herself than her than the wolf-men.

"It looks like they're losing. I saw them make several attempts, but none succeeded. Anyone who approaches is greeted by a shower of arrows."

"I have to get inside that fort," she said.

"But it's under attack," Visvaldis yelped.

"Surrounded?" she asked.

Austras shook his head. "No, the attacks come from the west. Across the valley."

"They'll be distracted. I will find a way in and kill Anno. These forts all have an escape tunnel."

She began to stand when Visvaldis grabbed her arm. "You can't go. I will."

"You don't know these men. I do. Besides, I promised Lamekins to get you home alive. Stay here for now."

She stood and made toward the fort. The battlefield was littered with bodies, speared and hoisted like flags. Hiding in the trees, she sat and scrutinized the tower walls. The sun was setting low on the horizon, and she saw swift movements in the narrow slivers of the archer windows. She guessed there were twenty to thirty men inside. The attackers outnumbered them, but the fort gave the Brothers the advantage. The drawbridge had burnt down, forcing the attackers to slog through the muddy moat.

Dzintara looked around and began to crawl along the tree line.

Two hours of hard scrambling later, she had circled around the back of the fort. It was plain to Dzintara that this entrance was much more vulnerable but harder to access, with no roads and hardly a path. Only one sliver window cast its view down from the bastion at each corner.

The full moon lit up the forest and elongated the shadows.

Rustling in the distance caught her ear. Dzintara steadied herself and unsheathed her khanjar.

Creeping silently in the mud, she soon found herself atop a rock formation. Below her was a grotto covered in moss around a small timber-framed entrance into the earth. Jagged boulders shielded the entrance from sight.

A soldier wearing light armor and plain clothes sat on a boulder. She waited. Eventually, the soldier's breathing slowed, and his sword dropped from his hands as he drooped to the side. She descended silently.

When she reached the bottom, a mere ten steps separated her from the sleeping soldier. The cave entrance yawned before her, shrouded in darkness.

She crept towards the opening, stepping invisibly past the guard.

The walls were cold and wet to the touch as she let the masonry guide her way. She groped along the walls until she came to a bend, spotting the glimmer of a torch ahead. She stopped to listen but heard nothing. A narrow hallway opened to her left, carved into what was already a natural hallway. The long passageway was now straight and lit by torches every fifty paces. Treading carefully down the long corridor, she wondered just what waited for her at the end of this interminable tunnel.

CHAPTER FORTY-SEVEN

On the saddle in front of Varkelins, Anno fell in and out of consciousness. Varkelins would nudge him or push against his wound, checking for life, waking him long enough to show them where they needed to go. The horse galloped hard, and dirt flew up behind as Varkelins held the reins tight and gripped Anno's slumping torso. The silver glow of the full moon lit the path before them.

Varkelins pressed his hand tight against Anno's wounded side.

Anno jumped awake, his swaying form steady in Varkelins' arms. He eyed a split in the trail.

"There," Anno struggled to speak.

Varkelins pulled the reins left, and the horse turned.

Sweat was beading off Anno's face, and his skin was turning a whitish blue. His eyes blinked only half open, the wound on his side roiling darker from infection. Varkelins reached into his pocket and looked at the coin as if for motivation to continue.

"Are you sure this is the way?"

Anno struggled to open his eyes and then looked around. He pointed. "I hid in those brushes for a night. So just beyond there, another half night's walk and we'll come across the cave. You'll need to clear it to get through."

Varkelins dismounted and unsheathed his sword. Anno fell forward, gripping the horse's mane. The blade shone in the moonlight as Varkelins swung it to warm his shoulders. He took a whack at the brush. A pair of pheasants flew into the air, wingbeats thunderous and fearsome. Varkelins jumped back and swung his sword blindly. Embarrassed, he looked around with a smirk on his face, but Anno was slumped across the horse's neck, looking the other way.

He continued to hack through the damp thicket. With his free hand, he pulled as hard as he could on the stalks to rip them from their roots.

After a hard half-hour's work, he had carved an entryway into the forest. He took the horse by the reins and led it under the arbor of chopped branches and torn brushes. Thorns scratched at his face and grabbed at his tunic. The horse neighed nervously, head slung low, and Anno occasionally grunted as they moved deeper.

The moon was traveling lower on the horizon by now. Varkelins, breathing with effort, wiped the sweat from his forehead.

Anno moaned from the back of the horse. Varkelins turned, shaking his head in disgust.

"As if you were lying at the House of the Blackheads or one of the fine Inns of Riga," he spat and continued forward as he hacked at the brushes, pushing them deeper through the undergrowth.

"It's there," Anno's weak voice broke the hacking. The brush was so thick Varkelins could see nothing.

"Where?"

"Just past this bush," Anno pointed.

The sound of a blade striking wood filled the silent night. The vegetation thinned, giving way to a towering rock formation jutting into the sky, its rough edges and sharp angles silhouetted by the moonlit night sky.

"That?"

Anno sat up on the horse's back and squinted.

"Yes."

Varkelins reached up to him, pulling him from the horse, careful to not inflict more damage to the wound.

"What are you doing?"

"You're coming with me."

"I can't. I'm too weak."

"I'm not leaving you here. Do I strike you as a fool?"

"Varkelins, I'm a dead man. Why would I lie? There is a small opening at the base."

Varkelins looked into Anno's half-open eyes. Anno lifted his shirt. His wound was black.

"I got maybe 'til morning."

Varkelins nodded in agreement and, with a swift motion, pulled him off the horse. Anno cried out loudly.

"Will you keep it down? We don't know who else could be nearby."

Varkelins tied the horse to the trunk of a fir tree.

Anno treated every breath like his last and bit his lips raw. He put one arm across Varkelins's shoulders and leaned on him as they made their way through the brush. They walked for some time, Varkelins breaking the trail for the two of them.

"This reminds me of my childhood when my father would take me on hunting trips for days," Varkelins said nostalgically, a soft smile across his face.

Anno looked up at him.

"That's what you're thinking about at a time like this? Fucking hunting?"

"Just a memory."

Anno continued to drag his feet through the muddy forest floor, clinging to Varkelins, the dry brush on the ground snapping and breaking as they made their way toward the cave entrance.

"What did you kill?" asked Anno after a long quiet.

"A rabbit once. It was wounded in a field. I came upon it and drove my dagger through its heart. My father had been on me about not being able to kill anything."

"You did him a favor. He would probably have been eaten by something else," said Anno.

"That's what I told myself."

"Was your father proud?"

Varkelins let out a short laugh.

The trees suddenly cleared, and the rocks towered into the sky. Near the base, an entrance just large enough to crawl through.

Anno pointed, "There. You have to make a torch. Pitch black inside," he said.

Varkelins dropped Anno's arm and sat him on the ground. He reached inside his tunic for some cloth, oil, and flint. He found a branch about as thick as a forearm.

He collected dried twigs and leaves that he then bundled into a cloth.

"I've been having similar thoughts as of late myself," Anno whispered quietly, almost to himself.

"What?" Varkelins asked.

"About rabbits."

Anno touched his fingers to his beard, and they came away wet. His forehead felt clammy. "I keep having dreams about them. About the heathens. It's always different."

"The heathens?"

"Maybe we're no different."

Varkelins said nothing, tying the cloth bundle together and beginning to fix it to the end of the stick.

"I'll not live to see the sunrise again," Anno said simply. "I keep dreaming I'm in a battle. Fighting uphill. At the top of the hill, there is the most beautiful sunrise I've ever seen. My father is there. Younger than me, but he's in the battalion I command. These savages just keep coming out of the earth. We're not advancing, you see, just losing ground. In the middle of battle, my father drops his sword and kneels to pray..."

Varkelins turned, looking at Anno.

"...one of the savages cuts his head off and then turns to me, and it's my father now. He charges at me." Anno stopped, trying to catch his breath.

"Did you kill him?" asked Varkelins.

Anno shook his head. "No, I wake up. Every time."

Varkelins wrapped the oil-soaked cloth around the top of the branch and then lifted it, pleased with his work. He walked over to Anno and knelt down, helping Anno rise. They shuffled towards the entrance, Anno struggling to keep up with Varkelins.

"Seeing as I'm one foot in the grave, I can't help but wonder whether God is with me or if it's just plain dumb luck."

"Same thing. Men need things to believe in."

At the opening, Anno's fingers pointed directly into the small dark entryway.

"Get on your knees," wheezed Anno. "Just crawl through."

Varkelins squeezed himself through the small opening. He lit the torch, and the wet stone of the cave lit up.

"Well, come on!" Varkelins yelled to Anno. He stared back through the dark opening. "Anno?"

After a moment, Varkelins heard a rustling at the cave's entrance. He turned and watched Anno clawing his way through.

Anno looked around the chamber. "Someone's been here."

"What?"

"Footprints. Not mine. Three men, maybe four."

"Where is the gold?" Varkelins asked.

Anno pointed to a dark corner. Varkelins helped Anno to the wall and looked at the narrow passage, just large enough for a man to squeeze through.

"Maybe the footprints were here before. You just missed it."

"They weren't—" Anno shook his head. "Nobody's been in here for years."

"Are they in there?" Varkelins asked, pointing.

Anno shrugged, gave the torch back to Varkelins, and pointed to his sword. "You'll need that if they are."

"You're coming with me," Varkelins said, taking a knife from his boot and handing it to Anno.

Varkelins extinguished the torch lest they give themselves away. He turned sideways as he squeezed himself into the crevice. Anno followed close behind.

Varkelins fell on his face in the pitch black and moaned loudly. They'd made it.

He sat up in the dark, reaching into his purse and taking out the flint and steel. A few strikes later, the torch caught.

Anno turned towards the belly of the cave and watched as the flame lit the chamber.

"It's all here," Anno said with relief.

Varkelins stood up, dropping his sword. He forced open a chest.

"Albert..." he shook his head and laughed. He turned right and saw Anno opening a barrel and digging through yet more gold and silver.

"This will seal the deal with the Order," Anno said, relieved.

Varkelins looked behind him and saw his sword flickering in the torchlight. He stood slowly, walking to his blade. Fingers wrapped around the haft, he walked towards Anno's turned back.

The old monk, drinking his fill of gold, began to cough. Blood spurted from his mouth, and the coins dropped from his hand, rolling onto the cavern floor.

Varkelins stopped within striking distance from him.

"I'm sorry, friend, but this is the end of your journey."

Anno turned to face Varkelins, blood staining his lips.

"Then do it," Anno whispered.

Varkelins stared at the sword in his hand.

"Never killed a buck," Anno said and laughed at this.

Varkelins raised the sword above his head, taking two steps forward. Anno leapt at him, knocking him to the ground. Varkelins held onto the sword, but his hands were pinned above his head. Anno straddled his torso, pressing one knee into Varkelins' sword arm. He took the knife from his belt and spat blood in Varkelins' face.

"I may be wounded. But no fucking rabbit, am I."

He grabbed Varkelins's face with his other hand, squeezing his cheeks.

"At my blade, 356 men, women, and children have met their end. I ordered the executions of at least five times that. I'm a fucking lion."

He aimed the tip of the knife at Varkelins' eye.

Varkelins struggled under Anno, but the man's legs clamped tight. Anno lowered the tip to Varkelins's left eye and pressed it into the skin beside the bridge of his nose. He made a quick incision and repeated the same action on the outside of the eye.

Anno ran his blade along the top of the eye, and then, with a flick of the wrist, Varkelins's eyelid was hanging on the tip of the knife. Anno tossed it over his shoulder and grimaced.

"Allow me to do you a favor." It's easier this way," said Anno. With this, he pressed his blade behind the eyeball and, with a scooping motion, popped it forward.

Anno grabbed Varkelins's eyeball in between his thumb and index finger.

"Don't! You fucking bastard! Don't!" screamed Varkelins.

With the knife, Anno severed the tissue tendon, and the eyeball fell to the ground.

"One more," smiled Anno.

He pointed the tip of the blade towards the second eye. Varkelins' free hand found a loose rock and grabbed it, hitting Anno in the head. Anno froze as the shock hit him, and blood dripped from his temple. Varkelins' pulled his other arm free, swinging his sword blindly. The blade crashed into Anno's collarbone. The monk screamed and fell to the side.

Varkelins stood, stepping on Anno's chest and yanking the sword from the bone.

He aimed his sword at Anno's face.

"You can kill me, but I'll be with you for the rest of your life," Anno laughed.

Varkelins stood over him, shoved his blade in Anno's throat, and pushed straight to the ground until the sword pierced the dirt.

He pounded his boot into Anno's face until there was no face left. Spent, he stopped and looked around. He stood upright and adjusted his tunic. He walked to the open chest.

He quickly filled his tunic with fistfuls of the treasure. Then, he stripped Anno of his clothes and made sacks from the cloth. When the sacks were as heavy as he could carry, he stopped and rested.

The sound of a drop hitting water caught his attention. Standing and holding his torch in the air, he followed the sound, finding the clear green pool.

He caught his own reflection in the water. Crouching down, he filled his palms with the crystalline water and splashed it against his face. The cool water flooded him with relief. Once the blood had cleared, he ripped a piece of cloth from his undertunic and wrapped it around his head.

He held his torch high and gazed into the pool. Looking closely, he noticed a cenote, an opening in the pool's wall leading to another underwater cave.

Anno's body made a splash as it hit the water. Varkelins undressed and followed him, entering the cold pool and pushing Anno's body forward. The gaunt crusader's body floated towards the cenote. With a deep breath, he dipped under, bringing Anno with him. He fed Anno's body into the hole, sending him into the abyss.

As the torch's light dimmed, Varkelins surfaced. Emerging from the pool, he stood, water cascading off him, while he caught his breath and dressed.

He tied the makeshift sacks to his belt and began to retrace their path through the cave. Then, a subtle change in the air caught his attention—a cool breeze hinted at another way out. He turned, moving back to the pool. He felt the gust of air and saw the path ahead.

Working his way around the pool, he came to a tunnel. Eventually, he heard the unmistakable sound of roaring water and could see the light at the end of the tunnel.

Finally, he stood at the mouth of the cave, behind a waterfall. He was covered in dirt and blood, a blood-caked cloth wrapped around his head. Sacks of gold hung from his belt.

As he climbed down the waterfall, he slipped, miscalculating how close the next step was. One sack fell from his belt, raining gold into the whitewater.

When his feet touched the ground, he heaved a sigh of relief. He looked about, trying to decipher his location.

Something caught his good eye, fluttering in the wind. He turned. There it was. A ragged white cloth, blood-stained, tied purposefully to a flowering pine.

CHAPTER FORTY-EIGHT

Dzintara pushed against the platform door, but it wouldn't budge. With a soft grunt, she shoved harder, and the trapdoor finally gave way. She climbed out and quietly closed it behind her. She was in a small, closed vestibule that seemed like a dead end—there was no obvious way out.

The indistinct chatter of men outside reached her ears.

"They won't mount an attack tonight. They exhausted themselves in last night's skirmish, so let our men sleep," one voice said.

Another man laughed, mocking the merchant army's wasted efforts. Their voices faded as they moved away.

Dzintara found herself trapped in a hot, pitch-black room. She tapped the stone at her side, feeling along the walls for an exit —it was warm to the touch. The wall behind the trapdoor was colder. Her fingers found wood, and she felt along the surface, searching for a lever or latch. She traced the wall until she found a slight indent. Holding her breath, she pressed down. A hidden door groaned softly as it creaked open.

She slipped into the inglenook, hidden within the grand hearth of the castle's great hall. She crouched behind the fireplace, listening intently, her breathing shallow. The snores of men echoed through the hall, but none stirred. She moved carefully, creeping out and staying low as her eyes adjusted to the moonlight spilling through the grand arched windows.

A dozen men lay sprawled among the rushes on the floor, in front of the banked fire. She thanked her gods for the thick layer of grass muffling her steps. One false move, one sound, and she knew she would be dead.

Dzintara crouched low and peered through the arched windows into the courtyard. Her eyes darted across the scene— several men slept bundled up outside, likely exhausted from the day's battle, too confident to bother with their guard duties.

Off to the right, there was a small chapel marked by a wooden cross. And next to it, the castle keep—where, no doubt, Anno lay sleeping.

She pressed her body close to the walls, navigating around the sleeping men and slipping out.

UNDER THE MOON'S CLOAK, she moved toward Anno's keep, her heart pounding in her chest. She tread carefully, stepping around the sleeping guards, their breath heavy in the still night.

She counted about twenty-three men in the courtyard and hall.

Close to the keep, the quiet was punctuated by faint voices. She froze, hearing footsteps echoing off the wooden walkways above. She waited, heart racing, until the sound faded.

With the path clear, she proceeded cautiously towards the door of the keep. It was completely dark—no betraying candle-light shone from within.

Dzintara reached for the iron ring on the door and eased it open, the hinges whispering softly. Quietly slipping inside, she closed the door. Moonlight spilled through a window, illuminating a bed. A figure lay upon it, outlined in silver light, its chest rising and falling in rhythmic breaths. Across from the bed stood the silhouette of an altar.

The sharp smell of piss hit her, and she stepped around the chamber pot on the floor. Her eyes adjusted, making out scattered parchments, a drinking vessel, a pitcher, and a garment draped over a chair.

Gripping her khanjar, she slowed her breath. The sleeping figure shifted and grunted. She froze, watching as the man rolled onto his back. After a tense moment, his snoring resumed. She remained still, waiting in the darkness.

She stepped closer, approaching the edge of the bed. A silver beam of moonlight revealed the face of her prey.

"You're not Anno," she said in surprise.

The man's eyes snapped open, widening at the sight of her. In one swift movement, she grabbed the garment from the chair and shoved it over his head, jumping on top of him. She pressed her weight down as he struggled, trying to scream. He froze when he felt her khanjar at his throat.

"Where's Anno?" she asked, pressing the blade deeper. Blood trickled from a pinprick on his neck. The man shook his head frantically. Her blade sliced across his forehead, tearing the garment and releasing a gush of blood.

"The next cut will kill you."

She peeled back the garment, revealing his desperate, wide, pleading eyes. A loud gong rang out, followed by shouts. The bell was ringing, calling the brothers to action. She glanced outside and saw men jumping to their feet, rubbing the sleep from their eyes. The door behind her burst open.

"Master, we're under attack—"

In one swift motion, she plunged her khanjar into the intruder's stomach and sliced upwards. She grabbed him by the collar, yanking him inside and slamming the door shut behind them.

She hurried to the window and saw men rushing toward the gate, carrying buckets from the courtyard well. Overhead, she heard the pounding of feet as archers rushed to the arrow slits. The man she had gutted was slumped on the floor, clutching his belly, trying to scream.

Dzintara yanked the cloth from her first victim's head and shoved it into the dying man's mouth, muffling his groans. She pulled off his bascinet and struggled to strip the white robe from his body. He resisted, clinging to the garment in desperation.

With a forceful stomp to his wound, she compelled him to let go. With a muffled cry, he collapsed. Dzintara swiftly donned the robe and helmet, then delivered the final blow, silencing him.

DZINTARA LOOKED OUTSIDE, surveying the chaos. Crossbowmen aimed through the narrow slits while others rushed to douse the flames engulfing the gate. If she tried to return to the hall now, she'd be noticed.

She spotted an abandoned bucket near the well and made her decision. She threw the door open and dashed forward, blending into the frenzy.

A battle-scarred crusader paced the courtyard, shouting orders to the archers. "Attend to the fire! Archers, take down as many of these bastards as you can!"

Dzintara grabbed the bucket and filled it at the well. The heavyset man from earlier stomped toward her.

"You! Where's the meister?"

She pointed to the keep.

"Go get him!" he barked, stopping a few paces away.

She ignored him, tightening her grip on the bucket, and ran toward the fire.

"Hey! Hey! Go get the meister!" he yelled after her, but when she glanced back, he was already heading toward the keep. Her breath quickened as she neared the blazing portcullis, hoping to blend in with the men.

In a coordinated effort, the men hoisted buckets of water through the murder holes in the gatehouse, trying to douse the flames. On the ground, a dozen more fought the inferno, hurling water into the fire in a desperate attempt to stop it from spreading.

A toothless, towering crusader stepped in front of her.

"Take that bucket over there and prepare it for hoisting," he ordered, gesturing to the group at the gate.

Orange flames illuminated the night.

She brought the bucket to the group, and one of the men took it and secured it to a rope. Almost immediately, an empty bucket dropped, which he handed to her for a refill.

With the path clear, she headed back toward the well and the great hall. The toothless crusader had his back to her, barking orders to the men above. She ran past him and continued across the courtyard, her gaze fixed on the keep.

Suddenly, the door to the keep swung open. The battle-scarred crusader bellowed, "Enemies in the fort! We're infiltrated!"

Dzintara glanced back briefly, then sprinted towards the great hall and the hidden bolt hole by the hearth. She wrenched open the trapdoor, clambered down, and slammed it shut behind her.

Her feet hit the ground, and she sprinted down the underground hallway, her heart racing. After a few paces, she stopped near a lit torch and realized the Crusader robe could still hide her identity. She threw the torch to the ground and stomped it out, extinguishing the light. She ran on in the pitch-black, using the second torch to guide her, snuffing out each flame as she went.

She continued to run in the pitch-black darkness. As she glanced back, she only saw empty darkness. Then she heard the slamming of the trapdoor behind her, echoing through the corridor.

"I will skin you alive, you filthy animal!" A man's enraged voice resounded from the ladder into the oppressive blackness. She pressed on.

The smooth-carved walls gave way to jagged rocks, and the passage narrowed. She tightened her grip on the knife. She slowed her steps. Ahead, faint moonlight filtered through the cave's entrance. She paused, listening to the distant echoes of curses and threats behind her. Outside the cave mouth, she found the guard lying on the rocks, still asleep.

Without hesitation, she lunged. In a fleeting moment, her khanjar found its mark, piercing the guard's heart.

With catlike grace, she leapt from rock to rock until she reached the forest's edge. After delving a hundred paces into the dense woods, she came to a halt behind the massive trunk of an ancient oak, completely engulfed by its shadow. Eyes closed, she focused on steadying her breath and calming her racing heart. The forest floor was damp beneath her feet, the air still.

Leaving the cave and its curses behind her, she stood tall once more, ready to retrace her steps.

CHAPTER FORTY-NINE

Dzintara crept along the edge of the forest as the orange light of dawn chased the blood-filled night from the valley. She stopped to rest for a moment on high ground. From her vantage point on the hill, she could see the carnage below.

The attackers had laid a makeshift bridge across the moat and sent wagons of fire crashing into the wooden gate. The gate stood charred but unbroken, with the ashes of burnt wagons heaped around the base of the fort. Most of the cross timbers on the makeshift bridge had also burned to ash.

She steadied her shaking hands. The memory of the previous hours lingered: the men shouting, the fire sizzling as water splashed and extinguished the flames. Once again, she'd come close to dying but found herself, somehow, walking away unscathed. Her mother's fire, without her mother's fate. Maybe.

It wasn't fear that shook her, but anger, she realized. She wanted retribution, to watch Anno's terrified animal eyes dim beneath her Khanjar's blade.

In the rising sun, a forsaken hay wagon stood stranded in the valley, its load glistening with spilled oil. Along the moat's edge, a dozen lifeless bodies lay contorted and rigid, bristling with arrows.

The attackers seem to have retreated but could very well be hiding nearby. Her men may have been captured, or worse — they could be among the corpses in the field below.

She retraced her steps as the sun rose over the horizon. A flock of geese flew across a clear blue sky, honking in the bright morning light.

She squatted low in the foliage and mimicked a bird call: a low, melodic whistle followed by a high-pitched one. She waited. No response from Austras or Visvaldis. She repeated the call several times and waited. Cautiously, she crawled toward the site where she had left them.

When she reached the small clearing, she found the branches, leaves, and mud trampled and darkened with blood. She unsheathed her khanjar and scouted the area but found no bodies and no source for the blood. Taking a deep breath, she touched the blood-stained forest floor and examined her hand. Dark, clotted blood mixed with dirt coated her fingers. She wiped the thick residue from her fingers and looked around, considering her options.

She needed to stop Anno. If he'd returned to the fort and left again, he would have warriors with him. If they reached the gold before her, they would use it to replenish their men, weapons, and power. It would be the end of her people. She had to find her men, and she needed Lamekins and the wolf warriors.

To her right, she spotted a trail of blood moving towards Riga. The opposite direction from the gold. If they'd killed Visvaldis and Austras, they would have left them in the mud and not taken the trouble of dragging them to her camp.

She was decided. With her khanjar gripped tightly in her hand, she followed the trail of blood.

Varkelins circled back to where he had left his horse, waiting patiently in the underbrush. Weighed down with his sacks of gold and off-kilter with the phantom throbbing of his missing eye, he untethered the reins and led the horse back through the thick brush. The sun was just beginning to peek on the horizon, and he turned his face towards the warmth of the rising sun streaming through the thick forest ceiling. Once he'd cleared the underbrush, the woodland opened up. He mounted the horse and rode north with his gold coins jingling.

The morning mist clung to the ground as the Riga army camp came to life. Dzintara watched from her position, prone in the grasses along the tree line. Realizing she was still wearing the robe of the enemy, she quickly tore it off and shoved the white robe under a brush.

Men groaned and stretched, rubbing the sleep from their eyes. The sound of clanging armor and men's voices filled the air as they went about their morning routines, readying themselves for another day of siege.

In the middle of the camp, she saw Austras and Visvaldis stripped of their furs and masks. To the right of the camp, those injured in last night's battle sat or lay prone while others tended to their wounds, pulling out arrows and searing flesh with hot iron.

Dzintara observed the scattered hide tents, looking for the command pavilion. One tent stood larger than the rest, with a banner flying above it. A man emerged, young but exuding authority. A younger man, barely a boy, ran towards him, carrying a bucket. "Friedrich, your water.'"

Friedrich drank deeply, splashed his face, and then strode to the forest's edge, where Dzintara was hiding, to take a piss. She considered dismembering him, but she needed to rescue her men first.

When the sun peaked at midday, a group of makeshift merchant soldiers mounted their horses or took up the reins from wagon seats. Friedrich handed a parchment to a mounted man, who swiftly departed. The other wagons and horses lurched forward, following the messenger towards Riga.

Dzintara waited in the forest, watching and weighing her options. She needed to save her men, but the camp was a constant ebb and flow of soldiers, making it difficult to see a way through. Then, emerging from a tent, she saw Wulfric. He was clothed in fine linen and wore a hammered breastplate, utterly unlike the flea-ragged drabs he'd worn on the cog.

Would he remember her...or rather him?

She stood and walked forward through the tree line and directly into the camp, her left hand raised in surrender, her right clutching her khanjar. And in that exact moment, Wulfric mounted a horse and rode off. Her stomach dropped. It was too late.

"Stop right there!"

Dzintara stopped, and the soldier approached with his sword drawn. She laid the khanjar on the ground. Other soldiers took notice, and soon, four of them surrounded her. Her own men watched from the center of camp. "I want to speak to your leader. I know how you can take the fort."

The men let out hearty laughter and mocked her.

"What should we do with her?"

"It's been a while since we had any women come to the camp," said another, followed by more laughter. The commotion began to draw in other soldiers.

With hands raised, she surveyed the men gathered around her. "I know how you can win this war."

"She knows nothing. This could be a trap," said one man.

"I say we take her in the woods and have a good time."

"There will be none of that," Friedrich interrupted.

The men parted, clearing a path. Friedrich, wearing gold-plated armor with a long sword at his side, approached. The soldiers lowered their swords as he stopped in front of Dzintara.

He looked down at the khanjar, its blade marked with dried blood. Bending down, he picked it up and examined it, noting the congealed blood in the fuller, near the hilt.

"Who does this belong to?" he asked with curiosity.

"It's mine."

"I mean the blood."

"To someone important enough to be sleeping in Anno's bed. Friedrich stared at her and twirled the khanjar by the handle, admiring it. "Magnificent piece of metal. This isn't from these lands."

He bent down and wiped the blade on the grass, then held it up to the remaining sunlight. The handle's yellow gold glinted, and the iron blade shone, decorated with writing he did not understand.

"Far east?" he asked.

"No," she replied.

"I see."

"There are only twenty—"

Friedrich swiftly raised his hand, interrupting her. "Magnificent," he said, admiring the blade.

He lowered the khanjar and gazed at her dirty face and ragged, bloodstained clothes.

"Go inspect the perimeter and see if any of ours are dead."

A man moved to follow his instructions.

"If any of my men are dead, it will not go well for you," he said, pointing the tip of the khanjar at her face.

"You lost a lot of men last night attempting to burn the gate down."

Friedrich stepped closer, his eyes locked on hers, tapping the end of the khanjar against his palm with a deliberate, threatening rhythm.

"You have to take the fort now before Anno returns—"

"Who does the blood belong to?"

"I was in the fort last night and killed two of them."

Friedrich halted and cocked his head at her.

"Liar."

He placed the khanjar in his belt and held out his hand. A lanky soldier next to him walked off, took an iron rod from the fire, and handed it to Friedrich.

"Whose blood is on your blade?"

Dzintara locked her eyes on the blazing red tip of the rod.

"I swear to you I was in the fort last night."

"Wrong answer," Friedrich said, aiming the iron bar at her face.

"Wait! I can prove it. Over there, in those bushes, you'll find a helmet and a robe."

The soldier pivoted and walked to where Dzintara indicated.

"This is not going to end well for you if you're lying."

The tip of the iron rod was cooling. Friedrich handed it back to a soldier, who returned it to the flames. They all waited in silence.

Then, from the tree line, the soldier held up a bascinet and a bloodied Brotherhood robe. He carried them back and dropped the evidence in front of Friedrich.

"I was inside when the first wagon hit the gate. I killed two and disguised myself to escape."

"Impeccable," Friedrich said, staring at the evidence.

"I can get you and your men inside."

"Krists?" Wulfric's voice rang out in excitement.

Friedrich turned as Wulfric dismounted his horse and sprinted towards them. Wulfric ran to her and hugged her hard. Then he grabbed her by the shoulder, looking in her face, and grinned.

"You're alive! I spent all winter trying to find you. I was told you were dead. I swore my vengeance on that coward," he spat, "Varkelins."

Friedrich looked confused. "Wulfric?" he asked, rod in hand.

"You can't kill him. This is the man I told you about, the cog captain. A just and disciplined man. He will be of great use to us."

"Wulfric, this is a woman. A heathen woman."

Wulfric looked at Dzintara's face and then scanned up and down. "Krists?" he asked softly.

Dzintara nodded. "Yes. But my name is Dzintara. It was the only way to make the journey."

"But...You killed Gorm," he blurted. "He was a giant. Ruthless."

"You misremember. Vlad killed Gorm. He saved my life. But yes, it's me. The same person that got us to Riga."

"You. I thought Varkelins killed you."

"No, I snuck away," she said.

"I saw your head scarf floating in the river," Wulfric said in disbelief.

"I had to get rid of it to blend in."

"Marble Jaw," he blurted, "He and the crew absconded with the ship."

Steadying himself, he looked at Friedrich. "She fights with us. Not as a prisoner, but a freeman."

"Very well. Get her some food and water. Make up the table in my tent. We have much to discuss," Friedrich ordered.

"Wait. My men." She motioned with her eyes at Austras and Visvaldis.

"They're with you?"

She nodded.

"Damn strange morning," Friedrich said

He whistled. "Get them clothed and fed." His soldiers rushed to obey.

"What's news with Anno?" Wulfric asked.

"You're looking for Anno, but so far as I know, he's still off in the south, waging the Holy War. We've laid siege for four nights now. No one in, no one out. Well, until you, of course. So perhaps Anno has returned?" Friedrich asked.

"I was there to kill him. He wasn't there," she said.

Austras and Visvaldis stepped into their leather footwear and pulled their furs back over their shoulders, drawing the sides in for warmth. She stepped towards the men and greeted them one by one, arms clasped in respect, forehead pressed to forehead.

"*Diekou*," they whispered to each other.

"Your heathens put up a fight. We thought they were working with Anno," Friedrich said as she returned to his side.

"These heathens are my people. The same people who are going to help you get inside the fort."

"Very well. So, how do we get inside?" Friedrich asked.

"I discovered the sally-port. It's concealed but was lightly guarded. However, following last night's events, they're likely to seal it off."

"Not your first battle?" Friedrich asked.

"No."

"Sir, sir, sir!" came a distant yell.

They turned. A leather-clad figure approached with a bow and quiver, holding a freshly killed pigeon in hand.

"We intercepted a message,"

He gave Friedrich a small parchment the length of a finger. A moment passed as he read silently.

"Send word to the merchant families that we need reinforcements. We press forward now. Wulfric, go to Riga and get more men. Double the wages," he said in an urgent tone.

"I stay with you and with my Captain."

"Wulfric, that's an order," Friedrich said.

Wulfric shook his head. "If it wasn't for this man—captain, you and I would have never been acquainted. My good fortune is because of... her. I fight with you and the Captain."

Friedrich nodded, then motioned to another soldier. "You, go to Riga and get more men. Double the price."

"Yes, sir."

"Prepare for battle!" Friedrich yelled out across the camp. "Now. Halt everything else and prepare."

"What's going on?" Dzintara demanded.

"Where is this passage? We must go now," Friedrich said.

"I am not your servant. Tell me, what was in the message?"

Friedrich handed the message to her. Her eyes scanned the words: *TUT NICHTS. WIR SCHICKEN EINE ARMEE. -BM.* The parchment bore the Teutonic Order insignia.

"The message says, 'Do nothing. We are sending an army,'" Friedrich said.

"How is this possible?" Dzintara asked, baffled.

Friedrich shook his head. "I don't know. A traitor, perhaps.

These men," he said, scanning his makeshift army, "their loyalty lies with gold."

He stormed into his tent, followed by Dzintara and Wulfric. A squire appeared, tightening his chest plate and placing a bascinet on his head.

"But who?" Friedrich asked. "Only the nobles knew about the surprise attack. No pigeons have come or gone since we laid siege."

"One of the families or the guilds," Wulfric suggested.

"Wulfric, don't be naive. They have no incentive to swap one group of mercenaries for another. The Brotherhood has long aspired to align with the Teutonic Order, but it remains just that —an aspiration. Anno headed south, and there's talk that Markus was seen there, too, recently. This could mean he's found a significant ally, someone willing to betray both Anno and the city. A player with enough influence to access crucial information."

Wulfric locked eyes with Friedrich. "Varkelins."

"That swine? Hardly. He lacks the cunning to forge an alliance with the Knights."

"Think about it, Friedrich." Wulfric looked at him and then at Dzintara. "Who wanted power more than anyone else? Who would have the most to gain to see you and the guilds fail?"

Friedrich's face froze as if he had seen the light of God.

"Albert said he would take care of him. He's probably dead."

"And if he isn't. If he is guiding the Knights through the woods?" Wulfric asked.

"Upon victory, I will chop him to pieces in the square."

Friedrich lifted his sword. "Prepare your men. The time to take the fort is now," Friedrich commanded, his voice carrying an unsettling calm. "The Teutonic Knights could arrive within two days, possibly even by today. They show no mercy. If we're to have any hope of survival, we must secure the fort and hold our ground."

He stopped for a moment, pulled the khanjar from his belt, and handed it to her.

"This is yours."

Dzintara nodded, taking the khanjar.

"Now tell me, where is this sally-port?"

"It's about a half a day's walk from here. We'll have to circle the fort."

Friedrich adjusted the last straps of his armor, exhaling deeply. Dzintara broke the silence, "Inside the fort, there are thirty-three men. I've taken out two. The sally-port won't support all our men for entry. We need a diversion to open the main gate."

Friedrich nodded, his strategy clear. "We'll deploy thirty men for the inside assault. Our camp has a hundred warriors. Thirty will advance behind blazing carts for the initial breach. Twenty more will hit the flanks to distract the archers while we build an additional bridge across the moat. The carts will hit their gates again. The rest of our force will stay here, ready to face the Teutonic Order if they arrive before we do."

"And you?" Dzintara asked.

Friedrich looked at her with a blaze of fire in his dark brown eyes.

"I will be the first in the tower ripping their flag in victory."

CHAPTER FIFTY

The waning gibbous moon lit the night, casting a pale glow over the forest. Thirty men moved silently, making their way to the sally port. Friedrich raised his hand. They halted.

"How much farther? We've been marching for the better part of the night," He asked quietly.

Dzintara waved her hand forward, and Friedrich continued ahead.

Wulfric moved next to Dzintara.

"I don't know if we're going to make it out, but thank you."

Dzintara nodded in acknowledgment. "We'll make it out. The forest watches over us."

"I feel foolish. I should have realized...sooner, maybe on the cog."

"Realized what?" she asked as they leaped over a thick fallen pine trunk. It was snapped in half, its bark scaly and covered in moss.

"That you were a woman."

"Why? Does it make a difference?"

"Well, no, but yes...maybe."

"Wulfric—"

"I should have done more to protect you," he blurted out

"Wulfric, all my life, I've been surrounded by men convinced they had all the power," she said, her voice tinged with a mix of bitterness and amusement. "But in the end, they were the ones who needed protection."

Wulfric smiled, and for a while, they walked along in comfortable silence.

"You seem to have done well for yourself," she said, glancing at him. "How did you come to serve Friedrich?"

"I saved his life," Wulfric replied, a hint of pride in his voice. "He brought me into his inner circle. I manage his affairs, so to speak, and in exchange, he ensures my well-being."

"I had my silver on you stealing the cog and becoming your own merchant," she said with a playful grin.

Wulfric's smile faded, and he went silent for a moment. "After you disappeared, I was lost. For weeks, I wandered the streets until one fateful night when I met Friedrich."

Dzintara's expression softened. "The Goddess Laima determines men's fate. This is yours. Trust it," she answered, her voice steady and reassuring.

"Truth is, I was running when you met me with Gorm's crew," Wulfric confessed. "I had drifted from crew to crew, trying to get as far away from home as possible. I did terrible things, and one day, it all caught up to me. I had two choices: death or run. So, I ran."

Dzintara stopped and turned to face him. She placed a hand on his shoulder. "Whatever you did belongs to the past. You are here now, fighting against evil. You are a good man, Wulfric."

Wulfric looked into her eyes. For the first time in a long while, he felt a glimmer of hope.

A low whistle broke their conversation. Friedrich was motioning for Dzintara to join him.

"I'm sending a scout," Friedrich said.

"Up ahead about two hundred steps should be a ridge line. From there, the scout should see the entrance," she said.

Friedrich clicked his tongue and motioned to one of his men to push forward. The scout disappeared into the darkness as the others sat and waited.

Friedrich stared off into the forest, then sat down next to Dzintara.

"Who are you?" he asked.

An owl hooted in the distance. The trees swayed in the spring wind.

"Just someone returning home," she replied.

"For revenge."

When she smiled, her teeth flashed in the moonlight. "I came for revenge. Now, I am here for our survival."

"So you came back for revenge," Friedrich reiterated.

Dzintara shifted her weight and dug at the ground with a twig, creating a shallow hole. "That, and I was looking for my brother," she said.

He looked at her khanjar, clenched in her fist. Her hands were covered in dirt. Battle calluses and cuts marred the skin, but her fingers were still slender and graceful.

"You are after Anno?" he asked. She nodded.

"Why?"

"He took someone from me. Then I watched him and his men skin and burn my people alive. I've watched them slaughter children and women for enjoyment."

"Heathens."

She shot him a look. "People. My people."

Friedrich glanced at the shallow hole she'd dug with the twig. "An unfortunate sacrifice to the changing order of things."

"We didn't ask for this change," she said.

"Change needs no permission. It just comes. Wherever there are men, change will always come. One group conquers the other, and then the conquered conquer the conquerors. It's a cycle. I just want to be at the top of the order when the change happens," Friedrich said.

Friedrich's words hung in the air, a cold justification. Dzintara's eyes narrowed, and she squeezed the twig until it snapped in her hand.

They heard rustling in the bushes nearby. They all looked over, alert, as the scout slipped back into their circle.

"Well?" Friedrich whispered.

"There are two guards piling rocks into the opening. They've set their swords aside," the scout said, panting.

"Five of us will go and secure the entrance. We'll take them by surprise. Once I whistle, the rest of you come," Friedrich said.

Friedrich signaled to Dzintara, her fighters, and two archers to follow him into the silent, dark forest. With swords ready, they reached a ridge line where two crusaders, torches swinging wildly, searching for stones below. Their swords rested nearby.

Friedrich gestured. An archer drew his bow, releasing an arrow that struck one crusader in the chest. The archer quickly notched another arrow, ending the other crusader with a precise shot to the chest.

Friedrich gave a low whistle, and the rest of the group emerged from the forest and descended to the tunnel. They worked quickly, clearing enough rocks and stones for a man to squeeze through.

"Where does the tunnel lead?" Friedrich asked.

"A trap door in the great hall of the fort. It's behind the hearth, in the inglenook. There's a hidden latch midway on the north wall," she replied, gesturing to the height of the latch.

He breathed deeply, summoned his resolve, and then turned to the men.

"Listen, I will take the lead and face whatever is waiting for us. Once we are in the fort, we take no prisoners."

Grabbing the torch next to the dead guard, he ventured into the passageway's dark abyss. Dzintara was right on his heels, with the rest of the men filing in one by one behind her.

After a damp journey, they finally reached the ladder. Friedrich's gaze fixed on the trapdoor above them.

As Friedrich placed his foot on the first rung, his hands gripping tightly to the side rails. Upon reaching the trapdoor, he paused, listening, then gently pushed the trapdoor open and climbed into the darkened alcove. Following Dzintara's instructions, he felt for the latch.

Finding it, he motioned to his soldier below and then opened the panel, slipping into the concealed inglenook aside from the grand fireplace.

A man was speaking in the hall, apparently warming himself near the hearth. "It's about time the two of you finished up at the entrance. What took so long?"

Friedrich slunk back into the shadows, a bead of sweat tricking down his temple. Dzintara came up behind him, her khanjar drawn, motioning that the others were following. With a deep, calculated breath, he steeled himself and vaulted out into the main hall, finding himself face to face with the toothless crusader standing in front of the hearth, sword drawn.

The crusader launched himself at Friedrich, who countered around the refectory table. Dzintara, accompanied by her men and two merchant warriors, emerged from behind the hearth. A towering crusader swung around and lunged for them in a desperate bid to seal the entrance. Dzintara and her men descended on him like a pack of ravenous wolves, blades taking him down with deadly precision.

The other two mercenaries killed one gormless crusader, who just stood, mouth agape, as Friedrich handily slashed his toothless attacker across the throat.

Three Crusaders down. Another thirty to go.

The rest of the men filed in through the trapdoor and into the hall, several taking a position at the hall's large wooden door, leaning their weight against it.

Dzintara peeked from the hall window, checking if anyone noticed the commotion. Looking into the courtyard, she saw men working tirelessly, fortifying the gatehouse and reinforcing the half-burnt portcullis with wagons and large stones. Craning her neck, she spotted the helmets of at least a dozen archers relaxing between the crenellations.

Friedrich joined her, looking out into the courtyard. Their eyes met, silently acknowledging the gravity of their situation.

"My men should be outside, attacking their gates by now. Where the hell are they?"

Dzintara shook her head. "We might be on our own. There are only thirty men out there. Anno didn't leave his best, and besides, I don't think we've time to wait. We have the element of surprise on our side."

Friedrich considered this. "You and some of these men need to take out the archers. I'll take the rest and hit the courtyard. Those men aren't even wearing their steel."

Dzintara nodded. "Fifteen of you, come with me—and move fast. The rest can take out the swine in the courtyard." She gestured towards her wolf-men, then selected twelve more from the merchant army, Wulfric among them. They formed a line at the hall's entrance, Dzintara at the front.

In the courtyard, a fat old monk was yelling at his soldiers, "Keep the barricades coming. The gate won't repair itself."

Dzintara dashed up the stairs with her men, taking the parapet. Her men's footfalls on the staircase caught the attention of the courtyard master, and he turned. The first archer turned twenty paces away. Dzintara sprinted towards him.

The archer dropped his bow and reached for his knife, but Dzintara leapt and cut his throat with her khanjar before he could draw.

"We're under attack!" The courtyard master shouted. Bewilderment struck the Crusaders at the gate. Confused, archers searched for an attacking army beyond the gates.

"Inside, you idiots."

With a battle cry, Friedrich and his group charged, their blades gleaming under the moonlight. Friedrich attacked the courtyard master, taking him down in one deadly blow.

The crusaders by the gate scattered, desperately seeking their weapons. The archers turned toward the keep, drawing their bows to stave off the attack, but in the chaos, they couldn't get a shot without killing their own men.

Dzintara and her men advanced down the narrow walkway, slashing and cutting down the archers. Meanwhile, a few archers tried to target Friedrich's fighters but took out two of their own instead.

One crusader, who had been quick enough to recover his weapon, was engaged in a heated battle with Friedrich, who was countering him blow for blow. Friedrich missed a slash, and the crusader overpowered him, knocking him to the ground. With his sword high, ready to deliver a fatal blow, Friedrich rolled away, and the sword sliced into the earth. From below, Friedrich struck, his blade slicing through the crusader's neck.

Friedrich leapt to his feet, rejoining his comrades in the slaughter.

As Dzintara and her warriors pressed the attack, the remaining archers began to falter and retreat. Only five held their ground, shooting wildly at the courtyard below and the advancing warriors on the walkway. They clumsily loosed another volley toward Friedrich.

Now covered in blood, Dzintara pushed forward like a demon, slashing and stabbing with her khanjar. A thud behind her made her turn—Austras lay on the walkway, an arrow buried in his heart. Her eyes snapped to the source; the archer was already notching another arrow, aiming at her. She sprinted toward him. Before he could release, she was on him, driving her blade into his throat. Fueled by anger and grief, she threw him over the railing, sending him crashing into the courtyard below.

As her men advanced, the few remaining archers broke, attempting to free. As the soldiers panicked, they lost their footing and fell from the heights, and the remaining enemies were quickly cut down.

The battle was over. It had been a massacre, the blood of the

Crusaders soaking the ground. Out of all Friedrich's warriors, only Austras had died.

There would be time enough for sorrow later.

Friedrich's men let out a cheer. The fort was theirs.

Friedrich climbed the tower above the gatehouse and tore down the banner bearing the hated Red Cross. With a torch in hand, he set it ablaze, drawing more cheers from the men below.

IN THE HOURS after the battle, Friedrich's men had thrown the bodies over the walls, raided the kitchens for sustenance, and taken up their guard posts in the towers.

Friedrich paced the courtyard below, joined by Dzintara and Wulfric.

"Where is the rest of my army? They had their orders. And the reinforcements. Even with delays, they should have arrived by now."

Dzintara and Wulfric exchanged uneasy glances. The silence between them spoke volumes. The possibilities were deeply unsettling.

From the west tower came a shout and a piercing whistle. Friedrich, Dzintara, and Wulfric all turned sharply. The tower guard was waving a black flag.

"It's them! Black Crosses! In the forest! Hundreds of them. I see their banners!"

The Teutonic knights had arrived.

Friedrich and Dzintara ran to the ramparts and looked out across the corpse-littered battlefield.

"They're here," Friedrich said.

A thick, swirling murder of crows took flight as dawn's orange light crept over the forest. The pine trees trembled as if the earth itself was shaking. Then, a black swarm of arrows shot up from the forest into the sky.

Knights in white robes bearing large black crosses emerged from the edge of the forest. Dzintara guessed at least a hundred, likely more. Their archers aimed for the sky and sent forth another dark cloud of arrows, which rained down into the courtyard.

The men on the ramparts took cover behind the crenellations while Dzintara grabbed Friedrich, pulling him down the ladder to the relative safety below.

A volley of flaming arrows rained down. Taking cover beneath the ramparts, the men swiftly stomped out flames and called for water.

"Master Friedrich! Come, quickly!" a soldier cried from above.

Friedrich raced up to the battlements. At the edge of the field, knights feverishly constructed siege engines with disciplined precision.

The arrows stopped. Friedrich's men went silent. The air was thick with the sounds of hammers striking iron and men barking orders.

As the sun dipped lower in the sky, the knights worked with relentless efficiency, their siege engines steadily rising.

Every passing minute felt like an eternity. The fort's defenders stood on edge, eyes locked on the enemy's progress, hands gripping their weapons.

Suddenly, the ground shook as the first boulder crashed just outside the walls. Friedrich's heart sank as a second regiment of foot soldiers emerged from the treeline, their armor glinting in the fading light. They carried tall ladders, ready to scale the fortress walls.

Friedrich's stomach twisted. He watched, frozen, as the enemy force swelled, their numbers growing by the minute. Their supposed advantage had just slipped away.

He climbed back down, his face pale.

"We've lost," Friedrich said calmly. "We need to retreat."

Dzintara grabbed Friedrich's arm. "We stay and fight!"

"We can't keep the fort, Dzintara. We'll die here." Wulfric appeared at Dzintara's side.

"How many men do we have left?" she asked Wulfric desperately.

"We're mostly intact. We've lost but a few, Dzintara. But he's right. We cannot fight them. We must retreat."

"We need to hold the fort!" Dzintara was in tears.

At that moment, a stone the size of a man's head crashed into the middle of the courtyard.

"They're calibrating the mangonels. It's only a matter of time," Friedrich said.

Two more stones slammed into the courtyard, one crushing a defender's head. Men shouted and scrambled for cover.

"One up and working," one of Friedrich's men yelled from behind the tower's crenelations. "Seven more being built."

"We must fight," Dzintara said, fury in her voice.

"Dzintara, it's over," Friedrich yelled, gripping her shoulders, his voice raw with agony. "We've lost."

Dzintara stood silently, fire in her eyes, staring at Friedrich. She could feel her mother's fierce spirit coursing through her veins.

A barrage of stones pounded the earth, creating a deafening staccato. Rocks clattered against the fortress walls, chipping away and breaking through. Visvaldis emerged from the dust unscathed while Dzintara and Friedrich lay on the ground, coughing violently. Suddenly, another loud bang echoed through the air. Stones, torn from the fort's walls, tumbled into the courtyard in a relentless cascade of rock and dust.

Dzintara and Friedrich coughed as Visvaldis pulled them to their feet. Before the dust had settled, another volley of arrows rained down, pinning several men to the ground. Two towers had collapsed, burying a dozen of Friedrich's men beneath the rubble.

"Retreat!" Friedrich ordered.

Dzintara halted, her eyes frantically searching the devastation. "Wulfric!"

"Dzintara, we have to go!" Visvaldis shouted, grabbing her arm as another volley of arrows struck nearby.

The cool spring wind began to lift the cloud of dust, and Friedrich looked past Dzintara. As she turned, her eyes locked onto the breach in the gate wall, wide enough for a cart. Dzintara sprinted after Visvaldis, with Friedrich and the remaining survivors close behind.

They burst into the great hall and headed straight for the fireplace. Friedrich broke through the hidden panel and wrenched open the trapdoor, and the group, with Dzintara in the middle, plunged into the inky darkness. No one spoke. They raced through the tunnel, eyes straining against the blackness. Suddenly, torchlight flickered on the walls, casting their shadows long and merging them into one, like collapsing columns as they passed.

"Stop!" Dzintara suddenly yelled.

They halted in line as she sniffed the air, her nostrils flaring at the pungent, noxious odor that scraped at her throat. The stench grew thicker, and one by one, they all began testing the air.

They could barely make out the scattered objects—shrubs, branches, and wood—littering the passage. A man with a torch stepped into the tunnel, silhouetted against a sliver of sunlight.

The flared torch somersaulted through the entrance. Instantly, flames and smoke roared to life, hitting the constriction of stone and dirt before funneling forward, roaring towards them, hungry for more air. In an instant, the men in front were swallowed. Dzintara turned to flee back toward the trapdoor, but the smoke was faster. It filled her lungs. Her skin began to peel, and she glimpsed Friedrich, the last down the hole, outrunning the flames. Everything went black.

CHAPTER FIFTY-ONE

Varkelins entered the Guaja Valley that afternoon, the gold jingling with every step his horse took. With the partially destroyed stone fort in his sights, he rode through a sprawling encampment of rough-spun canvas and crude wooden poles. The Teutonic Knights, their white robes emblazoned with black crosses, moved purposefully among the tents, their pennants fluttering in the breeze.

Soldiers slumbered in the shade, oblivious to his presence. Beyond them, horses nuzzled the spring grass, their flanks twitching and tails swishing as they grazed. Varkelins watched as a man in the distance stumbled and cursed, flailing his arms in a futile attempt to catch a flock of clucking chickens.

The scent of wood smoke and cooked meat mingled with the low murmur of voices and the shuffle of feet as soldiers went about their daily routines. Men in white robes inspected massive siege engines, checking the ropes, readying them to launch a barrage of rocks at any who stood in their way. As Varkelins passed, they halted, their gazes fixed on him—his eye covered by a bloodied rag, his clothing stained with dirt and blood. Yet he rode with his head held high, calmly crossing the field.

The south-facing wall and gate had been battered by cata-

s. Varkelins crossed a makeshift drawbridge and approached the crumbled gate, where two men motioned for him to stop.

"State your business."

"Tell Brother Markus Varkelins is here."

The men sized him up, and then one walked inside the fort and disappeared.

"What happened here?" Varkelins asked the other guard.

"A group of merchant soldiers breached the fort."

"How?"

"Secret passageway. We burned the fuckers alive."

Varkelins glanced into the courtyard and saw men gathering the dead, some with skin melted away, revealing raw flesh beneath.

"Did anyone survive?"

"All dead, except for one."

Varkelins nodded, retrieved a gold coin from his belt pouch, and flipped it to the guard, who stared at it in astonishment before quickly pocketing it. The other guard returned and motioned for him to enter.

Varkelins rode through the rubble, the bloodied corpses being prepared for the pyre. Arrows speared the soil, and wooden planks were soaked in blood. The guard directed him toward the keep where Anno had once ruled. Varkelins dismounted and pushed open the wooden door.

Inside, a small, clean-shaven man with a receding hairline sat at what had once been Anno's desk, reading through papers.

"Where is Markus?" Varkelins demanded.

"Varkelins, come in," the man said, motioning him forward. The fire crackled in the hearth, casting flickering shadows across the room.

The man regarded Varkelins with disdain. "What happened to your eye?"

"The road to victory requires certain sacrifices."

"That it does."

"Who are you?" Varkelins asked.

"Konrad," the man replied with a forced smile.

"I'm—"

"I know who you are. Where's Anno?" Konrad interrupted.

"Where is Markus?" Varkelins repeated. "My business is with him."

Konrad dropped the parchments and leaned back in his chair. "Markus couldn't make it. But I'm here, and I'm aware of your agreements."

Varkelins noticed the jug and wooden cup on the table. He poured himself a cup of wine, drinking it as Konrad watched.

"So, back to Anno. Shall we wait for him?"

"I'm afraid that road is no longer available," Varkelins replied.

"And these local sources told you they were ambushed? All of them?" Konrad asked, peering into Varkelins's one good eye.

"You should have our physician look at that before it turns sour," Konrad added, his tone dripping with false concern. "And what's that?" he pointed at the satchels on Varkelins' belt.

Varkelins unbound the satchels and dumped them on the desk. Gold coins spilled across the table and onto the floor.

"This is my payment for the fort and forty knights to be stationed here."

Konrad's grin stretched across his face like a scar, revealing teeth yellowed by rot. His eyes, though, remained cold. The scoff that escaped his lips was brittle and mirthless.

"You want to be Anno."

"That was my agreement with Markus. If Anno failed, I am next in line."

Konrad shook his head. "Unfortunate as it is, I understand the position of the Order. Seeing as the Livonian Brotherhood has been wiped out, the position is yours, but you'll have to join the Teutonic Knights."

Varkelins nodded.

"Then you must also be aware of what joining means." Konrad held out his hand.

Varkelins threw another belt sack onto the table. "I'll have to count it."

"Is that all?" Varkelins asked.

Konrad nodded.

"Then we're done here," Varkelins said, turning for the door.

"Just one more thing," Konrad called out.

Varkelins halted. Konrad leaned back in his chair. "The horse you rode in on...it's the same one you rode when you met Markus in the woods."

Varkelins slowly turned to face him. "How would you know?"

"I was there."

"I see," Varkelins said, his voice tight.

"How did you get it back from the bandits with only one eye?" Konrad asked, leaning forward.

Varkelins met Konrad's gaze. "Sometimes even the best warriors make bad calculations."

He walked out and shut the door behind him. In the courtyard, the weapons of the dead had been collected. One item caught his eye. He walked over to a group of soldiers passing an elegant small sword back and forth.

"I'll give you three gold coins for the khanjar," Varkelins offered.

"What?"

"That," Varkelins said, pointing at the khanjar.

The soldier shrugged and handed it to Varkelins in exchange for three gold coins.

Varkelins looked at the burnt corpses lined up in the courtyard. "Did you find a woman?"

"What?" the soldier asked, removing his face covering.

"Did you find a woman among the dead?" Varkelins repeated.

The soldier scoffed. "Fool."

Varkelins strode across the courtyard, where a group of soldiers were torturing a badly burned man who was somehow still alive.

Friedrich looked up into his eyes.

"What an interesting turn of events, wouldn't you say?" Varkelins said, kneeling beside Friedrich.

"And who the fuck are you?" asked one of the men.

"You can address me as Hofmeister," Varkelins said coldly.

Friedrich, his trousers burnt away, his legs charred and blistered, spit at Varkelins in disgust.

Varkelins leaned in close to Friedrich's ear. "I sent for them."

"Traitor! You'll die for this!" Friedrich screamed with what strength he had left.

Varkelins looked around at the remnants of the once-great fortress. "Maybe someday. But not for this."

Varkelins looked down at Friedrich and smiled. "Keep him alive."

CHAPTER FIFTY-TWO

The knights stood in the valley across from Turaida Castle, their armor gleaming dully in the dim morning light. Varkelins sat tall on his horse, commanding the force. His white robe was adorned with the black cross of his order, and his bascinet was a masterpiece of gold and jewels. A purple velvet patch covered his eye, a symbol of his hardened resolve. The wind howled through the columns of warriors, the only sound breaking the silence. The heavy gray sky cast a gloomy pall over the valley as his forces waited in stillness.

By afternoon, a rider approached, waving a white flag. He reined in his horse a short distance from Varkelins.

"Albert seeks a truce."

Varkelins nodded and followed the rider to Turaida Castle. He dismounted and entered Albert's dining hall, his boots heavy on the wooden floorboards. Albert sat at the head of the table, his white beard blending with his ashen skin. Varkelins pulled out a chair and sat at the opposite end of the table.

Albert's mocking laughter echoed through the hall. "Have you come to negotiate the terms of my surrender?"

"There is no negotiation."

"You've come to kill me, then?"

"I wouldn't do that to an old friend."

"Well, you might as well. You've starved this entire castle for two weeks now."

"I know you have a taste for indulgence. Food is one of them. Starving you seemed preferable to destroying this beautiful estate."

"I built this city," Albert began, his voice trembling with a mixture of pride and despair. His once-commanding presence had crumbled under the weight of his own greed and indulgence.

"Which you will now leave," Varkelins interrupted coldly. "There is a boat waiting for you. It departs for Lower Saxony."

"The Teutonic Knights," Albert spat, venom twisting his words. "Do you know what you are? A band of thieves, no better than the Templars."

"Aren't we all?" Varkelins replied, his tone indifferent. "We just wear different colors. Thieves for the same God."

Albert struggled to his feet, the effort clear in his labored breath and the way his hand gripped the edge of the table for support. "I will never leave this place," he growled, his voice thick with defiance.

"Very well," Varkelins said with a casual shrug that belied the threat in his words. "We attack at dawn. And once we attack, no one will be spared."

Albert's eyes burned with anger as he leveled his gaze at Varkelins. "The coins you paid the order—they were a unique minting," he said, his tone laced with accusation. "You found it, didn't you? The Honorius cache."

Varkelins remained silent, his expression giving nothing away.

Albert's voice rose, fueled by desperation. "I'll take you down! I'll tell the church you're a thief and a liar! Once they find out, they'll come for you—"

"With what army?" Varkelins cut in, his voice dripping with condescension. "May I remind you that we are the pope's army?"

Albert surveyed his lavish dining hall for the last time, his gaze lingering on the hearth tiles, each meticulously molded from clay and glazed in rich shades of red and brown. Vibrantly painted, the tiles depicted the lives and trials of saints, meticulously arranged to weave a tapestry that bridged heaven and earth.

"They're watching you," Albert murmured, more to himself than to Varkelins.

"As they watched you all these years," Varkelins replied, his voice devoid of sympathy.

Tears welled up in Albert's eyes, spilling down his cheeks as he was overcome with grief. "I gave my life to this city. You think you've won, but in time, there will be another Anno, another Friedrich, another Varkelins—each one eager to take you down for their own gain. You're a fool in lion's clothing."

Varkelins stood up from the table, his expression unreadable. He walked toward the door but paused, his gaze drifting past Albert to the tiles on the hearth, the saints staring back at him in silent judgment.

Without a word, Varkelins pulled on his purple suede gloves and left.

CHAPTER FIFTY-THREE

Under the gentle embrace of spring, Varkelins stood on the gallows, his lips sealed in dignified silence. Dressed in the vestments of his office and with the khanjar at his side, he watched Friedrich's lifeless body sway back and forth.

"Do not cut him down until the gulls pick him raw."

Stepping off the wooden platform, Varkelins descended, followed by Wilhelm, his fellow guild members, and a contingent of guards. As they approached his awaiting horse, the crowd parted in silent acknowledgment of his authority.

A guard approached, out of breath. "Hochmeister, word is that a two-mast cog has gone missing from the shipyard."

"I thought they were all burned in last year's fire."

"A few, but half a dozen have been restored."

"Curonians?" Varkelins asked.

"We're not sure. Shall we send out a search party?"

Suddenly, a crooked old woman stumbled out of the crowd, her face hidden beneath a tattered hood. She fell into Varkelins' arms. Snarling, he shoved her violently to the ground.

Varkelins brushed off his clothes, rage twisting his features. "You filthy hag! Know your place!"

The old woman scrambled to her knees, keeping her face down as she bowed and groveled. "Forgive me, Your Excellency."

Varkelins mounted his horse, still seething. Seizing the moment, the old woman vanished into the crowd.

"Forward!" Varkelins spurred his horse, galloping off toward Turaida, his men following closely behind.

VARKELINS and his entourage gathered for a lavish feast within the halls of Turaida Castle, their table set beside the revered tiles bearing images of saints. Wilhelm, now a fawning admirer of Varkelins, entertained the group with sycophantic jokes. Though Varkelins found Wilhelm's obsequiousness revolting, he secretly savored the power he now held over his former adversary.

After the lavish dinner, they gazed up at the star-studded sky, welcoming the onset of a clear spring evening. As the night wore on and the effects of wine and ale took hold, some ventured to the castle's underground baths, seeking solace in the warm waters, while others retired to the privacy of their chambers. The saints depicted in the hallowed tiles seemed to watch silently, their presence a solemn reminder of the eternal amid the fleeting moments of the night.

A YOUNG BLONDE STABLEBOY, savoring the scent of the linen covers, lay in the bed where Albert, the former Archbishop, had once rested. Nearby, Varkelins attempted to pour himself a cup of aqua-vitae but missed, spilling some on the table.

"Damn it," he muttered.

With a glint of mischief in his eyes, the stableboy smirked. "I can't believe you almost died today."

"What are you talking about?" Varkelins asked.

"Don't think I didn't hear about your encounter with that old woman."

"I'm still getting used to seeing out of one eye. I didn't see her —she was just an old fool," Varkelins said, latching his sword to his girdle.

"You are Riga now. People will make attempts on your life."

"I know, but a crippled old woman is no—"

Suddenly, Varkelins froze as if lightning had struck. His eyes widened with realization.

"Varkelins?"

Ignoring the stableboy, Varkelins frantically patted his girdle, lifted the chair, and rifled through his desk drawers before tearing the linens off the bed in a panic.

"What's gotten into you?"

"Where is the khanjar?" Varkelins asked, his voice trembling.

"The what?"

"The curved dagger I wear at my waist."

The stableboy shrugged. "I don't remember you returning with it."

Varkelins slammed his fist on the table with a force that rattled the cups and bottles. "Get my horse ready. Now."

"Seriously?"

Varkelins stood straight, his face a mask of cold fury. "Now."

The stableboy dressed quickly and raced down the stairs. As soon as he was out of earshot, Varkelins collapsed onto the bed and let out a guttural scream, the sound reverberating off the stone walls. In his mind, the old woman's face flashed—shiny, burnt—and suddenly, he recognized it. It was Dzintara. She was alive. And she was a threat to everything.

CHAPTER FIFTY-FOUR

Varkelins rode through the night, his horse foaming at the mouth from the hard pace. Though he knew the route by heart, he still glanced at the stars above to guide him. As dawn broke, he descended into the gorge, the growing light helping to show the way. At the cave's entrance, he found the torch he'd hidden earlier and lit it. He clambered quickly into the cave, driven by a deep sense of dread.

LAMEKINS STOOD AT THE SHORE, gazing out at the two-mast cog bobbing in the distance as the last dinghy prepared for its voyage. Laden with chests and barrels, the small craft floated low in the water, its sides gently caressed by the sea. The tranquil spring dawn bathed everything in a soft, golden light.

A gathering of tribesmen and women assembled to bid farewell behind Lamekins. Wagons were loaded and ready, their burdens of barrels and chests awaiting the start of their journey. Two figures, cloaked in dark robes and hoods, emerged from the dinghy and sloshed through the shallow water toward the shore, the pine-covered sandy beach stretching out before them.

"Is that all of it?" Lamekins asked.

"Just about," Dzintara replied, lowering her hood.

Her face shone in the new daylight, fresh scars marking where the old ones once were.

Lamekins wiped at his eyes, his voice trembling. "Damn, seawater always gets to me."

Dzintara smiled and placed her burnt hands on his shoulders.

"You're taking the Christian with you?" Lamekins asked, nodding toward the robed figure.

"Wulfric saved my life. Because of him, I live to fight another day."

Wulfric pulled back his hood and nodded. "I fight for her now. We fight them together."

"Stay," Lamekins pleaded, his voice breaking as the words came out, though he knew it was futile.

She cupped his face, her hands swallowed by his beard.

"This is a new beginning for us," she said, glancing at the waiting wagons. "Fight them with all your might."

Lamekins couldn't hold back any longer. He broke down in sobs, embracing Dzintara as he lifted her off the ground, his face buried in her robe.

VARKELINS REACHED the cave's deepest chamber and halted beside the pool that had become Anno's grave. He stared uneasily at the still blue waters, half-expecting Anno's vengeful spirit to emerge from the depths, hungry for retribution.

Shadows flickered across the walls of the empty chamber, dancing in the torchlight.

"No!" Varkelins screamed.

He scanned the chamber with his one good eye, praying that his gold, his power, and his future would somehow reappear. But all he found was a note.

Varkelins,

I spared your life. Do not go south or north. Let the tribes live in peace, or else we will return.

In darkness, we come, so in light, we may prevail.

Varkelins tore the parchment to shreds and let out a feral growl of fury.

DZINTARA WATCHED as the shoreline receded into the distance, the sea's spray lapping against the hull and casting a fine mist across the deck. The Curonians toiled diligently on the massive cog, their movements steady and purposeful. She stood at the helm, Wulfric at her side, her khanjar snugly secured in her belt, ready to be drawn at a moment's notice.

THE END

ABOUT THE AUTHOR

 Z.S. Winters immigrated to Canada at a young age from Hungary, because getting into America was just too freaking hard. Not speaking the language and being the friendless weirdo in suburbia, Z.S. Winters found friendship and refuge in books. By age 10, he had read the entire Anne Rice Vampire series, "Catcher in the Rye," and the Bible. He wrote his first story around that age, as well as created several volumes of homemade comic books. His fascination turned to history and read stories like *King Arthur and the Knights of the Round Table*, *Achilles*, and *Ivanhoe*.

As time passed on, Z.S.'s passion for history, knights, and nobility only deepened, yet he grew increasingly aware of the stark contrast between the romanticized tales of western authors and the gritty, often grim reality of history. This awakening, recognizing the historical figures often depicted as heroes were more complex, sometimes dark characters driven by ambition and violence, inspired him to pen "The Khanjar's Crusade." This revisionist take on the Northern Crusades marks his venture into shedding light on the authentic, unvarnished side of history.

He lives in New York City with his family and a historical map-cluttered desk, Z.S. Winters balances life as a dad, husband, and the family's designated poop-picker-upper for their dog.

When he's not engaging in these day-to-day adventures, he's time-traveling at his desk, through his writing, Z.S. offers a lens to view history not as it's often romantically portrayed but with a raw, unfiltered gaze, inviting readers to explore the depths of human nature and the complexities of our past.

Made in the USA
Monee, IL
06 November 2024

69167577R00204